Frank Davis Cooks
Naturally N'Awlins

Also by Frank Davis

The Frank Davis Seafood Notebook
The Frank Davis Fishing Guide to
Lake Pontchartrain and Lake Borgne

Frank Davis Cooks Naturally N'Awlins

by Frank Davis

Illustrations by
Shelby Wilson

Pelican Publishing Company
Gretna 1990

Library of Congress Cataloging-in-Publication Data

Davis, Frank, 1942-
    Frank Davis cooks naturally N'Awlins / by Frank Davis
        p.   cm.
    ISBN 0-88289-772-1
    1. Cookery, American—Louisiana style.   2. Cookery—
Louisiana—New Orleans.   I. Title.
TX715.2.L68D38   1990
641.59763'35—dc20   89-28333
                                        CIP

Cover and illustrations by Shelby Wilson

"Naturally N'Awlins" trademark used with permission of WWL
Broadcasting

Manufactured in the United States of America
Published by Pelican Publishing Company, Inc.
1101 Monroe Street, Gretna, Louisiana 70053

*To my wife, Mary Clare,
and my daughter, Amanda,
who are undoubtedly my best food critics.*

*And who have given me the inspiration to
continue creating new recipes from old ones.*

*And who have patiently endured the hardships of
having me turn their cozy little home
into a commercial test kitchen.*

I love you both very much!

Contents

Acknowledgments

It has taken countless hours of keyboarding to put this cookbook into print. But prior to that, it took mountains of chopped onions, diced celery, crushed garlic, and minced parsley—to say nothing of the dishpan hands and vats of chicken stock—to test the recipes typeset on these pages.

So simmering, stewing, sautéing, stir-frying, poaching, baking, basting, broiling, barbecuing, roasting, braising, smoking, and steaming notwithstanding . . .

I thank my wife, Mary Clare, for always being there each time I kitchen-tested a new dish. And I thank her for being brave enough to taste every one of my creations, yet still having supporting things to say about the results.

I thank Ruth Tannehill, Charlotte Howard, Pat Armand, Glenn Randall, and all my other kitchen assistants for being so patient every time I changed my mind about mixing and whipping and blending and chopping, which caused them to scrub a whole lot more pots, pans, and dishes than any staff should ever have to wash.

I thank my daughter, Amanda, for all the times she made do with a slice of Weight-Watchers pizza because Daddy was once again making a mess in the kitchen.

I thank Dean Shapiro for taking time to meticulously edit nearly a thousand pages of hunger-provoking food type, while usually having only a pack of peanut butter crackers to keep up his energy.

I thank my illustrator, Shelby Wilson, who undoubtedly has one of the finest conceptual minds and two of the most talented hands that God ever fashioned, and who can create artistry within the framework of last-minute deadlines faster than anyone I've ever met!

I also genuinely thank a very special cadre of food professionals that I've had the good fortune and opportunity to meet and work with over the years—Paul Prudhomme, John Levy, Louis Evans, Frank Sclafani, Alex Patout, Goffredo Fraccaro, Chris Kerageorgiou, and Justin Wilson. I thank each of them for helping me to refine my culinary techniques.

But most of all, I thank Mike Early and WWL-TV, Channel 4, for making me . . . *"Naturally N'Awlins."*

Introduction

Okay, y'all—here it is! This is what you've been asking me about for the past year! The new cookbook!

So, if I can be so cliche . . . *welcome to my kitchen—again!*

In *The Frank Davis Seafood Notebook,** I concentrated exclusively on fish, crabs, crawfish, oysters, shrimp, and all the other delicacies of the sea. But from this point on, we're going to go in-depth—you and me—on just about *everything* that can be cooked.

The chapters in this book cover a host of secrets to great New Orleans cooking, including tricks you can use in *your own kitchen* to make everything you cook easier and better-tasting. You're gonna find old authentic recipes from all the ethnic origins . . . new recipes that I've created for my long-running television shows on WWL . . . dishes I've served to folks all over the country on my national cooking tours . . . and some extra-special recipes that I'll give you from some of New Orleans' greatest chefs.

You'll notice right away that unlike other so-called standard cookbooks done in "standard cookbook form," this one varies from the chapter and verse format and allows you to combine and prepare dishes—and even full meals—the way most people feel like eating them. In other words, you could start at Page 1 and go all the way through the end and provide your family with a superbly versatile selection of a variety of foods of which they will never tire.

Further, I was determined to make my second cookbook so easy to use you would want to use it every day to find out how to prepare both the simple as well as the complicated New Orleans dishes your family favors—whether you're a veteran in the kitchen or a novice at the stove.

More importantly, I wanted to be sure it *informed* you—so I again wrote it in the same "cooking school" style as my *Seafood Notebook,** which means that if you follow my recipes and instructions *you* will be able to cook for your family every bit as well and as confidently as *I* could cook for your family if I were standing beside you in your kitchen. That's a guarantee!

But *most* importantly, I wanted every single page to be entertaining . . . and   fun . . . and   tantalizing . . . and   tempting . . . and mouth-watering! If I could have done it "scratch-and-sniff," that's what you would be doing right now.

So, let's get started! I want you to promise me right now that from this day forward you won't ever again just throw something together for dinner—cuz, y'all, that's not necessary! I want you to promise me that you'll never again cook with water when you can use a stock instead—cuz those stocks add 80 percent of the flavor to the dish. You also have to promise me that you'll use as many fresh ingredients as possible in whatever it is you're going to cook—cuz there's no substitute for freshness. And you have to promise that you will never again be afraid to try something new or different on your own—cuz that's how great chefs are born.

And finally—and probably most important of all—you also have to promise me that you're going to change your attitude that cooking is hard, cooking is too much trouble, cooking is drudgery, and that you can't cook! Cuz I'm here to tell you that you *can* cook—*Naturally N'Awlins!*

Ya' ready? Let's do it!

---

*The Frank Davis Seafood Notebook is the first Frank Davis cookbook, published by Pelican. It is a best-selling reference work on seafood cookery, done in a Southern style. Presently he is working on sequel editions to *Naturally N'Awlins,* to be released one per year.

Frank Davis Cooks
Naturally N'Awlins

CHAPTER 1

Appetizers

Frank's Shrimp-Stuffed Avocado Boats

This is probably the best dish you'll ever taste combining shrimp and avocados. Serve 'em as appetizer or main course.

4 large avocados, halved lengthwise
1 lb. peeled shrimp (raw)
1 stick real butter
4 tbsp. finely chopped shallots
½ cup coarsely chopped onions
½ cup coarsely chopped celery
juice of one lemon
¼ tsp. lemon zest (yellow rind), grated

1 tbsp. Worcestershire sauce
2 tsp. salt
2 tsp. black pepper
dash Tabasco sauce
1 tbsp. paprika
8 tbsp. grated Romano cheese
16 strips mozzarella cheese (1″ × 3″)

Start off by melting the butter in a skillet over high heat until it almost *browns*. Then toss in the shrimp and the chopped shallots and cook for about 4 minutes until pink and tender, watching that the butter does not burn. Now remove the shrimp from the skillet and cut them into both thin slivers and medium-size chunks. Then take the skillet off the fire and set it aside to cool slightly.

Next, scrape out into the skillet the pulp from the avocados (but watch that you don't poke holes in the shells—you're going to restuff them). Mash about ¾ of the avocado pulp into a paste and leave the remaining ¼ in chunks (for presentation). Be sure to work in the butter and shallots from the skillet, too.

Then add all the remaining ingredients to the avocados, but be careful when you blend them together so you don't mash the "chunky pieces." Be sure to taste the mixture at this point and adjust your salt and pepper.

When everything is mixed well, gently fold in the shrimp slivers and pieces so that they are evenly distributed into the paste. Then, using a tablespoon, restuff the mixture into the avocado shells (heap it up in rounded portions), liberally sprinkle a tablespoon of grated Romano cheese over the top of each avocado half, and top off each avocado with 2 strips of mozzarella.

When you're ready to eat, place the stuffed "boats" under the broiler briefly (just enough to melt the cheese) and serve on a bed of chilled lettuce with garlic bread sticks. Y'all . . . this is a must for avocado lovers!

Frank's Real New Orleans Potato Salad
(Jus' like yo' Momma usta make!)

Here's a potato salad I guarantee you're gonna love . . . whether you love potato salad or not! And it goes great with my "Stuffed Crab" recipe. I want you to try this one the next time you serve seafood, chicken, or barbecue!

10 small red (Irish) potatoes, boiled and peeled
6 hard-boiled eggs, whites and yolks separated
½ medium-size finely chopped white onion
¼ cup finely sliced green onions
½ cup finely chopped celery
3 tbsp. finely chopped parsley
1 large finely diced dill pickle
1 cup real mayonnaise
1 tbsp. Creole mustard
2 tbsp. yellow prepared mustard
salt, black, and red pepper to taste
2 tsp. paprika

Start off by chopping your potatoes until they are in chunks about an inch or so square—*they shouldn't look like mashed potatoes, y'all!*

Next, mix into the potatoes—*one ingredient at a time*—the onions, the green onions, the celery, and the parsley. And when everything is thoroughly blended, coarsely chop the egg whites and stir them in, and toss in the diced pickle and gently fold it in—*evenly!*

Now, in a separate bowl, cream together the mayonnaise, the egg yolks, the Creole mustard, and the yellow mustard. And I mean *cream it* until you end up with nothing but a yellowish paste that is smooth and silky. *This is the secret step to making a good-tasting potato salad!*

At this point, you want to gently fold the egg yolk and mayonnaise paste into the potatoes—being careful not to mash too many of the potato chunks. Then stir in half of the paprika and season the salad to taste with the salt and pepper. But be careful not to over-salt or you'll lose the delicate enhancement of the individual ingredients.

Finally, sprinkle on the remaining paprika to garnish and color the top. Then cover the potato salad with plastic wrap and chill it in the refrigerator for at least an hour before you serve it.

This is good stuff! And it goes good with almost anything from barbecued chicken to pot-roasted pork to boiled crawfish!

Note: Use small Irish potatoes in this dish, not "B" size creamer potatoes.

Variation: To make Cajun-Style Potato Salad, try adding about a half-cup of finely chopped smoked sausage to the recipe.

Frank's N'Awlins Coleslaw

There's good coleslaw and there's bad coleslaw. But what makes coleslaw good or bad is the dressing you put on it. I want you to try this one . . . I'm sure you'll love it!

1 small head green cabbage, shredded	**2 tsp. tarragon vinegar**
1 small head red cabbage, shredded	**2 tbsp. confectioners sugar**
4 carrots, peeled and coarse-chopped	**¼ cup applesauce**
1½ cups real mayonnaise	**¾ cup finely minced onions**
	1 cup crushed pineapple, with juices
	salt and pepper to taste

First, take a clean kitchen towel and completely remove (wring out) all the excess water from the cabbages and the carrots. Then put the chopped vegetables into a large salad bowl and place it in the refrigerator to chill for about 2 hours.

Meanwhile, in a mixing bowl, thoroughly blend together the mayonnaise, vinegar, sugar, and applesauce. Then fold in the onions and the crushed pineapple, making sure they are evenly distributed throughout the mayo base, and season to taste with salt and pepper.

At this point, cover the bowl with plastic wrap and put it, too, into the refrigerator for about 2 hours.

Finally, pour the dressing over the coleslaw and toss everything together well, making sure all of the cabbage and the carrots are coated. Then refrigerate again until fully chilled—*remember, the colder the slaw the better the slaw.*

Frank's Bronzed Mushrooms in Cognac

Most times, when you eat mushrooms, they are either boiled down to a brownish, yuckky mess or rendered tough by overcooking. But not these, m'frien! I've discovered that with just a little bit of margarine heated to almost the burning point . . . you have taste treats fit for royalty!

Try 'em and let me know what you think.

½ cup melted margarine
1 lb. small button mushrooms
   (fresh)
½ cup finely chopped shallots
½ cup finely grated Romano
   cheese

salt and pepper to taste
4 tbsp. real butter
3 tbsp. cognac

Start off by preheating a 12-inch Teflon or Silverstone skillet over high heat until a drop of water sizzles away immediately when dropped into the pan. At this point, pour in about 3 tablespoons of good margarine and swoosh it around in the skillet until the surface is coated well and the margarine *just starts to smoke slightly.*

Now toss in your mushrooms . . . but just enough of them so you can continually jostle them around in the skillet. Keep flipping them over and over like flapjacks (use wrist action—not a spoon!) until they absorb most of the margarine and start to "toast" to a golden color.

Then spoon in another tablespoon or two of margarine, toss in a few tablespoons of chopped shallots, season gently with salt and pepper, and sprinkle lightly with Romano. Keep flipping them all the while . . . *and keep the fire on high!*

Finally, when they have turned a pretty bronze (which should take no more than about 4 or 5 minutes if your fire is hot enough), add a tablespoon of real butter to the pan, swoosh them around once more, and turn them out onto your serving dish. Then de-glaze the hot pan with the Cognac, pour it over the mushrooms, sprinkle on a little more Romano, and eat them hot! (You can use additional butter for the mushrooms as needed.)

This is how mushrooms should be served!

Hint: Mushrooms prepared this way are an excellent complement to Salisbury steaks, broiled hamburgers, barbecue beef, roasted pork, baked ham, and grilled seafood.

CHAPTER 2

Soups and Salads

Frank's Instant Homemade Split Pea Soup

As anybody from the Crescent City will tell you, nothing beats a steaming bowl of split-pea soup on a cold, rainy New Orleans winter night. But it takes a long time to make good split-pea soup . . . right? Right! Unless, that is, you have my "instant" version. And I guarantee you it tastes almost as good as the slow-cook method.

4 cups chicken stock (or chicken broth)
¼ cup finely chopped onion
1 cup coarse-chopped country-smoked sausage
¼ cup finely chopped ham
½ cup crumbled bacon
2 cans petit pois green peas (303 size)
2 tbsp. real butter
4 tbsp. heavy cream
salt and pepper to taste

Start off by bringing the stock to a boil in a 4-quart Dutch oven and adding the onions, smoked sausage, the ham and the bacon to it. Then when the mixture comes back to a boil, reduce the heat to medium, cover the pot, and cook for about 30 minutes to form a delicately seasoned stock.

While the meats are cooking, empty the 2 cans of peas into your food processor (or blender) and puree them until they turn very smooth (you don't want any of the pea hulls remaining). Now set the "pea paste" aside for a moment.

When the stock is ready, gradually stir in the pea paste and (using a whisk) dissolve it into the liquid. Then—very slowly—stir in the butter and heavy cream, and season the soup with salt and pepper to your taste. Now . . . turn the fire down to low and let everything "simmer" for about 15 minutes longer so that the individual flavors will blend.

And that, y'all, is Frank's Instant Split Pea Soup!

Hint: If you want a thicker soup, just simmer the mixture uncovered until some of the liquids reduce. For a thinner soup, add a little bit of whole milk to the mix and cook it into the blend for about 5 minutes. Oh—for a variation, try adding shrimp sautéed in butter to the green pea soup about 15 minutes before you serve it.

Frank's New Orleans Corn 'n Shrimp Soup

Want a great way to warm up on a cold winter's night! You whip up a pot of this . . . serve it with a stack of buttered saltine crackers . . . top it off with a fine bottle of white wine . . . and throw another log on the fire! Dat's N'Awlins!

2 lb. fresh shrimp (31-35 count)	1 cup whole milk
1 stick real butter	2 cans cream-style corn
1 cup finely chopped yellow	(303 size)
onions	½ lb. lean bacon (fried and
½ cup finely sliced green onions	crumbled)
½ cup finely chopped celery	1 tsp. sweet basil
¼ cup finely chopped bell	2 tsp. salt
pepper	½ tsp. garlic powder
1 cup reduced shrimp stock	1 tsp. white pepper
1 pint whipping cream	3 tbsp. finely chopped parsley

Start off by peeling the shrimp, washing them well under cool running water, and gently boiling the heads and shells for about 30 minutes in a quart of water to make a good rich stock. Continue to cook (reduce) the stock until you end up with about 2 cups. Then strain the liquid into a bowl and discard the shells and the heads.

Next, in a 5-quart heavy aluminum Dutch oven, melt the butter over medium heat and quickly sauté the onions, green onions, celery, and bell pepper until they turn soft. But be gentle and don't burn the butter! When the vegetables are tender, toss in the shrimp and simmer them *over low heat*—stirring constantly—until they turn pink (it should take no more than about 4 minutes). *Remember—you don't want to overcook them!*

At this point, separate the shrimp and vegetable mixture into 2 portions. Set one portion aside . . . and run the other portion through the food processor until it becomes finely shredded . . . *but not pasty!*

Now put into the Dutch oven the shrimp stock you made earlier, the portion of shrimp you shredded, the whipping cream, and the whole milk. Then mix everything together well and turn up the heat to medium-high. When a "gentle boil" begins, stir the mixture uncovered for about 3 minutes and add the creamed corn and the crumbled bacon. Now stir again for another 3 minutes, making sure that all of the ingredients are thoroughly and evenly blended.

As the mixture simmers, season it with the basil, garlic powder, salt, and white pepper. Then add the other half of the shrimp (the unshredded portion), stir once more, cover the pot, and cook over low heat for about 20 minutes.

Then, when you're ready to eat, ladle out a big helping of the shrimp-corn soup in bowls that you've preheated in your oven . . . garnish with the parsley . . . and serve piping hot with plenty of crispy French bread!

Frank's Oyster Artichoke Bisque

If you like oysters, if you like artichokes, if you like to eat . . . you're gonna love this recipe! Especially on one of those cold, damp, Louisiana winter nights!

½ stick real butter	2 cups oyster liquor
1 cup chopped onion	1 cup artichoke stock
½ cup chopped celery	2 tsp. sweet basil
¼ cup chopped bell pepper	2 pints heavy cream
10 strips cooked, crumbled bacon	salt and pepper to taste (black and cayenne)
¼ cup bacon drippings	parsley for garnish
3 doz. fresh oysters, chopped	
6 small artichokes (scraped pulp/chopped hearts)	

Start off by melting the butter in a 5-quart heavy aluminum Dutch oven and sautéing the chopped onions, celery, and bell pepper until they soften. Then toss in the crumbled bacon, the drippings, and the chopped oysters and simmer gently over low heat—stirring constantly—until the oysters curl and a rich gray-colored base forms (this is the oyster concentrate). Then drop in the chopped artichoke hearts and pulp and blend them well into the mixture.

Next, stir in the oyster liquor and the artichoke stock (this is the water you poached the artichokes in and then reduced to half its original volume). Now bring it to a boil . . . *but be sure you keep stirring!* Otherwise, the oyster liquor will scorch and stick to the bottom of the pot.

At this point, boil the mixture for about 4 minutes. Then stir in the basil, reduce the heat to simmer, and let the bisque cook slowly for another 5 minutes.

Finally, go ahead and stir in the heavy cream (a half-pint at a time) and turn the fire back up to high! When the mixture comes back to a boil, reduce the heat again so that the bisque just barely "bubbles" and add the salt and pepper.

One suggestion: taste the sauce before you add salt—the oysters and bacon may provide enough salt for you.

After 10 minutes of slow cooking (stirring occasionally) remove the bisque from the burner and allow it to "set up" for 15 minutes so that the flavors blend and the sauce becomes smooth. Then when you're ready to eat, reheat it gently, ladle it piping hot into soup bowls, garnish with parsley, and serve with saltine crackers and a glass of white wine.

Frank's N'Awlins She-Crab Soup
(Crabmeat Bisque)

A rich creamy bisque, loaded with lump crabmeat, sweetened with butter, and spiced with a unique blend of herbs and fresh vegetables . . . that's N'Awlins She-Crab Soup! And nothing is more perfect for those chilly December evenings!

The Roux:

½ cup real butter
½ cup all-purpose flour
1½ cups finely chopped onions
1 cup finely chopped celery
¼ cup finely chopped bell pepper
½ cup finely sliced green onions

The Stock:

1 gallon water
12 fresh cleaned crabs
1 cup coarsely chopped onions
1 cup coarsely chopped celery
½ cup fresh diced carrots
10 whole peppercorns
3 bay leaves

The Bisque:

½ gallon crab stock (reduced)
3 bay leaves
2 cups fresh diced carrots
1 tbsp. minced garlic
1 tbsp. sweet basil
3 tsp. dill
1 tsp. cayenne pepper
4 cups heavy cream
1 stick softened butter
salt to taste
1 lb. white crabmeat
1 cup thinly sliced green onions
½ cup finely chopped parsley
croutons

First, take a 12-inch skillet, combine the butter and the flour together, and make a light roux (cook over medium heat only until smooth but not browned). Then toss in all of the seasoning vegetables, cook them until they wilt slightly, and set the mixture aside.

Next, add the gallon of water to a 10-quart stock pot and bring it to a boil. Then drop in the fresh crabs, along with the onions, celery, carrots, peppercorns, and bay leaves. When the water comes back to a "slow boil," cover the pot and cook everything gently for about an hour.

When it's done, remove the crabs, strain out all of the seasoning vegetables, and reduce the stock to one-half of its volume *(in other words, boil the gallon of stock until only a half-gallon remains)*. This concentrates the crab flavor!

While the stock is reducing, pour the heavy cream into a 3½-quart saucepan and heat it to *"just bubbling."*

Meanwhile, spoon the roux into the hot stock and stir it until it dissolves and thoroughly blends in. Then—*one at a time*—add the remaining bisque ingredients: the bay leaves, carrots, garlic, basil, dill, cayenne, *and the heated heavy cream.* At this point, mix everything together until creamy and smooth, cover the pot, and simmer the bisque on *low heat* for about 20 minutes.

After the allotted cooking time, begin dropping in small chunks of the softened butter and stir them into the cream base. This is also when you add your salt to taste. Then when the mixture is velvety smooth . . . *very gently drop in the crabmeat and fold it into the base.* Do not stir briskly or you will break up the crabmeat! Cover the pot again and cook the soup over low heat for 10 minutes more.

When you're ready to eat, gently stir in the parsley, ladle the bisque into heated bowls, and top with a sprinkling of sliced green onions and a handful of croutons. Serve with buttered saltine crackers and a crisp salad!

Note: Authentic "she-crab" soup is made with female *blue crabs because the fat and orange egg paste is used to flavor the base. But when female crabs are not available, regular crabmeat is used and diced carrots are added in place of the fat and egg paste.*

Hint: If the bisque turns out too thick *to your liking, a little bit of milk can be added to thin out the consistency. If, on the other hand, the soup turns out* too thin *for your tastes, simply uncover the pot and simmer the soup base 15 minutes or so longer (before adding the crabmeat!).*

Frank's Old New Orleans Onion Soup

Really good onion soup is probably one of the most exacting recipes ever created when it comes to subtleties of flavor. Prepared wrong, it tastes like "oniony water." But done just right, it'll make you lick your chops! Try this one. . . . I don't think you'll find one easier or better!

1 lb. lean bacon
8 large onions (white or yellow), sliced thin
1 cup finely chopped celery
4 tbsp. all-purpose flour
8 cups fresh beef stock
2 cups fresh chicken stock
2 whole bay leaves
1 tsp. basil
pinch thyme

1 cup Chablis Blanc white wine
1 loaf French bread, toasted and cubed
2 cups shredded Parmesan cheese
2 cups shredded Swiss cheese
1 cup shredded sharp cheddar
salt and pepper to taste
parsley to garnish

First, start off by sautéing the bacon in a 12-inch skillet until each strip turns brown and crisp. When cooked, place the bacon on several thicknesses of paper towels so that they drain. Then crumble them into coarse pieces and set them aside for a while.

Next sauté your onions and celery in the bacon drippings until they turn a "caramel color." *This is probably the most important part of the recipe,* because it converts the acids in the onions to "natural sugars" and makes them sweet. When they are browned, gently sprinkle in the flour and mix it into the onions well (but do not let the flour cook into a roux!). All you want is the flour to absorb the onion juices so that it can act as a thickener. (Don't be afraid to add a "tad" more flour if you want to.)

At this point, transfer the sautéed mixture to a 6-quart Dutch oven and pour in your stocks (both the beef and the chicken). Bring the mixture to a boil . . . but as soon as it boils, reduce the heat to the point of it "just bubbling." Then stir in the remaining seasonings—bay leaves, basil, thyme, salt, and pepper. Go ahead and mix everything together well. Then turn the fire to *low* and simmer the soup base for about 45 minutes . . . *covered.*

Now, put in the wine, turn up the fire to medium, and cook off the alcohol (it will take about 15 minutes, so the pot should be uncovered). This is also when you make your final adjustments with salt and pepper.

When the soup is done, fill soup crocks with toasted French bread and ladle in enough liquid to fill the crock about an inch from the top. Then, in a bowl, mix the three cheeses and the crumbled bacon together, generously sprinkle the mix over the soup, garnish lightly with parsley, and put it under the broiler until the cheese melts and the soup is hot and bubbly.

It's a perfect answer to a cold winter's night!

Spiced Carrot and Raisin Salad

Nothing goes better with ham than a good spiced carrot and raisin salad. And here's how you make one that the whole family will love!

2 cups finely julienned carrots	**2 tsp. confectioners sugar**
1 cup raisins	**¼ tsp. allspice**
½ cup mayonnaise	**dash cinnamon**

First, wash and peel the carrots. Then cut them into extremely fine (julienne) strips and place them into a bowl.

Next, gently fold in the raisins until the carrots and raisins are uniformly mixed. When they are combined, put the bowl in the refrigerator to chill.

Meanwhile, take a large measuring cup and, with a wire whip, beat together the mayonnaise, the sugar, the allspice, and the cinnamon. Feel free to adjust the amounts of spice you add according to your tastes. Then stir the dressing into the carrots and raisins until everything is uniformly coated.

All that's left is to chill the salad once more. And I recommend you serve it cold as a side-dish.

Note: The finer the strips of carrots, the better this salad will taste. And for a little variation, you can also add any combination of chopped walnuts, coconut, drained pineapple chunks, or anything else your heart desires. Incidentally, carrot-raisin salad is an excellent dish to serve with any ham or pork entree.

Frank's Chef's Special Salad
With Caesar Dressing

I give you fair warning! If you make this salad once . . . you'll make it over and over again! And the next thing you know, it'll end up being your favorite of all time!

The Salad Fixings:

¼ head iceberg lettuce
¼ head romaine lettuce
1 cup finely shredded red
   cabbage
1 large tomato, wedged
1 rib celery, bias-cut
¼ cucumber, sliced

½ cup mushrooms, sliced
½ zucchini, sliced
½ yellow squash, sliced
1 cup shredded cheddar cheese
2 hard-boiled eggs, sliced
⅔ cup Italian olive mix

Simply take all the ingredients, wash them well, dry them thoroughly, and prepare them for the salad, Then place them either in a large bowl or on a large serving tray, cover with plastic wrap, and chill in the refrigerator for at least 3 hours.

The Caesar Dressing:

2 whole eggs
1 tbsp. Worcestershire sauce
juice of one lemon
6 tbsp. red wine vinegar
2 tsp. chopped garlic

2 small cans flat anchovy fillets
1 tbsp. Dijon mustard
1½ cups extra virgin olive oil
4 tbsp. Romano cheese
salt and black pepper to taste

First, in a food processor, whip the eggs to a froth. Then add the Worcestershire, lemon juice, vinegar, and chopped garlic and blend these ingredients into the eggs.

Next, with the processor running, add the anchovies and the oil they come packed in. You want to whip them into the dressing mix until the mix is smooth and none of the anchovy pieces can be seen.

At this point, add the Dijon mustard and blend it into the mixture.

Now, again with the processor running, start adding the olive oil in a thin stream . . . and continue processing the dressing until all of the oil is used and the mixture turns thick and creamy.

Finally, stir in the Romano cheese, adjust for salt and pepper, and serve chilled.

CHAPTER 3

Fish and Seafood

Frank's Cajun Fish 'n Onions

Don't think all you can do is *fry* fish! There's a whole world of flavor you can awaken just by changing a few ingredients and a few basic cooking techniques. I want you to try this . . . and see if you don't agree!

6 fish fillets (any kind of fish)	**3 large onions, sliced thin**
1 tsp. seafood seasoning	**4 tbsp. butter**
** (optional)**	**4 tbsp. Crisco oil**
1 cup Italian seasoned bread	**1 tbsp. cognac**
** crumbs**	**salt and pepper to taste**

Start off by sprinkling the fish fillets with seafood seasoning (or salt and pepper), lightly coating them with the seasoned bread crumbs, and setting them aside.

Then in a 12-inch skillet, melt the butter and the Crisco oil over medium heat "just till it bubbles." Then toss in the onions and stir them constantly until all of the butter/oil mixture is absorbed by the onion rings and the onions *caramelize* (this is what happens when the acids in the onions turn to natural sugars and the onions turn a dark brown color).

Next, remove half of the smothered onions from the pan and spread the remaining rings out evenly. Then place the fish fillets on top of the onions you left in the pan, and cover them with the other half of the onions you removed from the pan.

At this point, put the lid on the skillet, turn the fire to low, and let the fish and onions steep until the fish fillets begin to flake (this should take about 8 minutes or so). Then pour in the cognac, flambé it quickly to burn off the alcohol, and serve the fish and onions piping hot alongside hash-brown potatoes, creamed fresh spinach, and garlic bread.

Hint: To make a great sauce to go with this dish, de-glaze whatever sticks to the bottom of the skillet with a cup of chicken stock. Then, over high heat, toss in about a quarter-cup of sliced green onions, along with a mixture made with 2 tablespoons of cornstarch dissolved in 4 table-spoons of cold water. Then stir everything together, immediately remove from the fire, and pour the sauce over the catfish and onions. Uuuuummmmmmm!

Frank's N'Awlins Mock Crabmeat
(From Poached Sheepshead)

Compare real lump crabmeat (which sells for about $8.00 a pound) with mock crabmeat from sheepshead (which you can make for about 69 cents a pound) . . . and you're gonna love this recipe, Babe! And here's how you do it!

FIRST . . . YOU CATCH A SHEEPSHEAD!

Now don't turn up your nose and say, "Oh, I don't keep them things! They're hard to catch, hard to clean, and they don't taste good!" Because I'm here to tell you that they're easy to catch, simple to clean, and they taste like gourmet fare if you know how to fix them.

So how do you catch 'em?

First you find their habitat—submerged stumps, pilings, rocky break-waters, and anyplace else that is encrusted with barnacles ('cuz they feed on those barnacles).

Then you fish smack up against those structures, jigging the bait up and down in the water. Start off fishing bottom, but keep varying the depth until you find the feeding level.

Next, use baby crabs as your primary bait. Oh, sure—live shrimp and market bait will also catch some fish . . . but if you want to increase your catch considerably, tempt them with crabs!

And finally, *fish those crabs on a 12-inch shock leader and a heavy short-shank hook.* Remember, sheepshead have strong teeth (which also means that under no circumstances should you put your fingers in their mouths) . . . but they also have rather small mouths. So a heavy short-shank hook will hook them every time.

Clean the sheepshead with a *carpet knife* by cutting just behind the head down to the rib cage. Then pull the point of the knife parallel to the lateral line of the fish, around the ribs, and down to the anal fin. Next, following the back bone as a guide, cut from the anal fin to the caudal fin (tail) of the fish.

Now spin the fish around so that the head is facing away from you and begin cutting (again using the backbone as a guide) from the initial incision behind the head directly down the dorsal fin to the tip of the tail.

At this point, put the carpet knife down and pick up the filleting knife. And using just the tip of the knife, begin stripping the flesh away from the backbone—lifting the fillet with your fingers as you cut. If you do it properly, the entire fillet should come right off the backbone. Turn the fish over and remove the fillet from the other side the same way.

Note: There is no need to scale, gut, or de-head the sheepshead, and you should never have to break open the belly cavity. This technique also works well for bull croakers, drum, redfish, and any other heavy-bodied fish.

But remember, to clean fish this way, you need both a filleting knife and a carpet knife. No substitutes!

To Make Mock Crabmeat

While you're filleting the sheepshead, take a stockpot and fill it with about a gallon of water. Then for every 2 pounds of sheepshead you plan to cook, add to the water 1 lemon cut into slices, 1 large onion, 1 cup of diced celery, ½ cup of sliced green onions, ½ cup diced bell pepper, ½ cup milk, 2 tablespoons of liquid crab boil, two cloves of garlic, 1 teaspoon of salt, and ½ teaspoon of black pepper . . . and bring everything to a rolling boil. At this point, boil the mixture for about *10 minutes* to release all the flavors of the seasonings.

Now wash the fish thoroughly (being sure to remove any trace of the bloodline), wrap the fillets in cheesecloth, and drop them into the boiling seasoned stock. *As soon as the water comes back to a boil remove the pot from the fire and let the fish "soak" in the stock for exactly 10 minutes.*

Finally, remove the poached fish from the stock, cut the cheesecloth and place the pieces into a shallow bowl to cool. Then flake the meat with a fork and mix about a tablespoon of lemon juice into the flakes.

Now you're ready to use it in any dish calling for *crab meat!* And if you don't tell it's really sheepshead . . . !

Frank's Crawfish Pomadora

Full of flavor and just spicy enough to make it New Orleans, *Crawfish Pomadora* is light on the diet and extremely simple to prepare. In fact, the entire dish can be done in just a bit over *5 minutes!* If you like New Orleans foods but you don't have time to do a lot of cooking . . . this is you!

4 tbsp. butter + 2 tbsp. butter	2 cans Rotel tomatoes with
4 tbsp. Crisco oil	chilies
½ cup finely chopped celery	2 lb. peeled crawfish tails
¼ cup diced bell pepper	(with fat)
½ cup finely chopped onions	2 tsp. basil
1 bunch green onions, thinly	½ cup minced parsley
sliced	salt to taste

In a 12-inch skillet, melt together the 4 tablespoons of butter and the Crisco oil and heat it on "high" just until it begins to foam. Then immediately toss in the celery, bell pepper, onions, and green onions and stir-fry them until they soften. At this point, coarsely chop the Rotel tomatoes and add them (plus the liquid in which they were packed) to the skillet.

Now, still using high heat, *stir constantly* until the tomatoes wilt considerably and the tomato liquid reduces to at least one-half of its original volume—this should take only about 2 or 3 minutes.

Next, add the crawfish tails. And (again over high heat) continuously stir them until they begin to curl tighter—just about 4 minutes should do it. At this point, drop in the basil and the parsley and salt the dish to your taste. Then cover the skillet and let the tails simmer for another 3 minutes!

Note that when you take the lid off the pot again, the natural juices from the crawfish and the crawfish fat will have formed a light but robust sauce.

Finally, stir in the remaining 2 tablespoons of butter and serve immediately over steamed rice with a salad, a fresh green vegetable, and French bread sticks.

Hint: You can also do this dish with shrimp or scallops if you can't find crawfish tails available.

Frank's N'Awlins Fried Shrimp
(In a Beer Marinade)

Do you have trouble consistently frying juicy, crispy fried shrimp? Well, don't feel bad! Lots of folks do! That's why this recipe is included in this cookbook. Next time you fry shrimp . . . try doing them this way. You'll be surprised how good they turn out!

The Shrimp:

First, wash, peel, butterfly, and de-vein the shrimp. Then place them in a deep plastic container. And for each pound of shrimp, cover them with a 12-ounce can of beer—not light beer . . . the real stuff!

The Cornmeal Mix:

Make a coating mixture by blending the following:

2 cups yellow cornmeal	**½ tsp. garlic powder**
1 cup cornflour (fish-fry)	**salt, black pepper, and cayenne**
½ cup cornstarch	**to taste**
2 tsp. onion powder	

For traditional N'Awlins fried shrimp, the coating is light. So all you have to do is take the shrimp directly from the beer marinade, roll them in the cornmeal mixture, let them sit on the countertop for about 5 minutes to "cure," then drop them into 400-degree Crisco oil or peanut oil (either in a deep-fryer or a skillet) and quick-fry them until they turn a golden brown *(which should take no more than a minute or two!).*

Note: Cook only *until golden brown and tender. If you overcook, the shrimp will turn tough and chewy!*

For crispier N'Awlins shrimp, take the shrimp out of the beer marinade, dip them in an eggwash made with 3 eggs and a cup of milk, roll them in the cornmeal mixture, and cook as you would above.

For heavy-battered shrimp, take the shrimp out of the beer marinade, dip them in seasoned self-rising flour, dip them into the eggwash then back in the seasoned flour, set on the countertop for 2 minutes to cure, then cook as above.

Hint: You can either deep-fry or pan-fry your shrimp . . . but re-member to keep the oil at least 375-400 degrees so that the shrimp come out light and crispy. Below 375 degrees, the shrimp absorb oil, become greasy, and will be soggy instead of crispy.

And if you're cooking in a deep-fryer, place the basket in the oil as the oil heats . . . then drop the shrimp one at a time into the basket. Never overload the basket—give them room to fry. But even more important, never load the basket with shrimp then place the whole basketload in the frying oil. If you do this, the oil drops below frying temperature and your shrimp turn oily and soggy.

Frank's Shrimp Boiled in Butter

Easier to prepare than boiling, lighter and more succulent than barbecu-ing, all the flavor and goodness of "scampi," and finger-licking good hot or cold . . . this shrimp dish will get you rave reviews. You're gonna love this! Especially the part about sopping up the sauce with hot, fresh, French bread! Ooooooh . . . I can taste it now!

1 lb. real butter	2 tbsp. salt
2 cups coarsely chopped shallots	2 tbsp. black pepper
½ cup coarsely chopped bell peppers	1 tbsp. cayenne
1 cup coarsely chopped celery	3 tbsp. sweet basil
2 cups coarsely chopped onions	4 tbsp. paprika
¾ cup finely chopped parsley	1 cup white Chablis wine
6 cloves finely chopped garlic	juice of one lemon
5 lb. headless shrimp (21-25 count)	

Start by preheating an 8-quart, heavy aluminum or cast-iron, Dutch oven over medium-high heat. Then toss in the butter and melt it down until it starts bubbling and foaming—*but do not let it burn!*

Next, turn up the heat to high, add all the chopped vegetable seasonings and stir them rapidly—*and continually*—into the melted butter for about 4 minutes. You will notice that as the ingredients cook, the yellow tint of the butter will turn to a pale green color. *That's the vegetable butter base.* It's what makes this dish so savory!

Now drop in the raw shrimp, along with the salt, black pepper, cayenne, sweet basil, paprika, wine, and lemon juice. And immediately stir everything together into the vegetable-butter mix so that every single shrimp is thoroughly coated. *I suggest you stir for at least 3 minutes.* Then once the shrimp are coated, cover the Dutch oven and cook—*still on high heat—* for about 3 or 4 minutes.

The next time you uncover the pot, you will notice a sauce beginning to form. This is natural shrimp juice mixing with the vegetable butter. Stir again . . . and when you have everything mixed, taste the sauce for seasoning and make whatever adjustments you want. Now, cover the pot once more and cook for another 3 minutes or so, or until you begin to see the shrimp breaking away from the shells. (*Hint:* A slight air-space will form along the dorsal or upper part of the shrimp. That's your best indicator that they're done.) *Don't overcook or the shells will stick and the shrimp will be hard to peel!*

Finally, remove the pot from the heat, put the cover back on, and let the shrimp "steep" for about 10 minutes in the sauce to pick up the full flavor of the seasonings before you serve them.

Hint: I suggest you serve the shrimp open-face over a 6-inch piece of French bread (which, of course, you ladle well with the sauce) alongside an authentic Italian salad made with extra virgin olive oil, tarragon vinegar, imported anchovies, and grated Romano cheese.

Variation: This dish may be prepared with heads-on as well as headless shrimp . . . but it should not be done with peeled shrimp. *Peeled shrimp tend to become tough and rubbery when cooked this way.*

To serve this dish as an elegant dinner party entree, remove the shrimp from the sauce, peel them, and set them aside. Then strain the sauce, reheat it in a skillet to a gentle boil, and cream it with extra butter until it shines and glazes.

When you're ready to eat, drop the peeled shrimp back into the hot sauce and serve them over creamed potatoes, rice, or pasta.

New Orleans Shrimp Paté Supreme

The next time you throw a party (or you're invited to one), make this dish and serve it as the primary appetizer. But let me warn you . . . you'd better make a lot of it! This stuff is so good it practically disappears!

1 stick real butter
  (not margarine)
½ cup finely chopped shallots
½ cup finely chopped celery
¼ cup finely chopped bell
  pepper
1 lb. peeled shrimp
  (40-50 count)
1 tsp. sweet basil
½ tsp. Italian seasoning
2 tsp. paprika

½ cup shrimp stock
  (reduced from heads/shells)
1 large pkg. Philadelphia cream
  cheese
1 large carton small-curd
  cottage cheese
1 tsp. salt
½ tsp. black pepper
¼ tsp. cayenne pepper
¼ cup finely chopped parsley

First, take a 12-inch skillet, melt the butter to bubbling, and stir-fry the chopped shallots, celery, and bell pepper until tender. Then toss in the shrimp and sauté them over medium heat until they turn pink and some of the shrimp juices begin to render out (this is going to take about 4 minutes).

Just before the shrimp are cooked, add the basil, Italian seasoning, and paprika, and stir it into the mixture well. Also pour in the ½ cup of shrimp stock and gently simmer until everything is blended.

Next, using a food processor with the cutting blade, run the shrimp mixture through on "pulse touch" until the shrimp are "just shredded." Do not overchop! And be sure to keep 6 or 8 large shrimp for decoration on top of the paté.

At this point, add the shredded mixture to a bowl and fold it into the large package of Philadelphia cream cheese. Then put the cottage cheese into the food processor and blend it until it turns creamy (about a minute or two).

Now add the creamed cottage cheese, the salt, and the pepper to the shrimp mix and stir until all the ingredients are consistent. Then sprinkle the top lightly with the finely chopped parsley and place the whole shrimp you saved on top to garnish.

Finally, chill the paté in the refrigerator for at least 4 hours to allow it to "set up." Then serve it cold with crackers, chips, or fresh vegetable sticks.

Suggestion: To serve hot as a fondue, add 1 half-pint of heavy cream (whipping cream) to the mix and heat till bubbly in a chafing dish. Serve with nacho chips or croutons.

THE BEST CALAMARI YOU EVER ATE!

Ain't no doubt about it . . . I love my seafood! Fish, shrimp, crabs, crawfish, oysters, you name it. But if you told me I could have only one seafood dish the rest of my life, it wouldn't be something I cooked for myself. It would be *Goffredo Fraccaro's Fried Calamari.* Cuz nobody makes calamari better! I'd even go so far as to say it's the closest you're gonna get to heaven without dying. Here's how he does it!

You need 3 pounds of squid, enough peanut oil to fill a pan an inch deep, a cup of unseasoned all-purpose flour placed in a large baking pan, salt, and lemon wedges. Simple, huh? And, y'all . . . that's the secret to this recipe—simplicity.

What you do is clean the squid by pulling the head and tentacles away from the body. Then remove the quill bone, cut the head and eyes away from the tentacles, peel the outer covering away from the body (it comes off easy under running water), and cut the body into rings about the size of a man's wedding band.

The rest is simply a matter of heating the oil to very hot (almost the point of smoking), dipping the squid in the flour, shaking off the excess, and slipping it gently into the pan. But listen . . . make sure you don't crowd them—give the rings room to fry! And watch your oil! Calamari is just like softshell crabs—sometimes they pop while they fry, and popping oil can cause a nasty burn.

Then when the rings reach a crispy-crunchy honey brown color (it takes about 4 minutes or so), scoop them out of the pan, strain them on several thicknesses of paper towels, sprinkle them with salt (you never salt them before you fry them because they get tough!), squeeze the fresh lemon over them as garnish, and serve them piping hot!

All I can say is . . . grazie, Goffredo, paisano!

Frank's N'Awlins Shrimp a la Creole

Make a roux . . . *then* add the vegetables and tomatoes and you have "Shrimp Stew." But cook the flour into the sautéed shrimp and vegetables *then* add your tomatoes . . . and you have a "Creole" . . . the classic New Orleans shrimp and tomato dish!

3 lb. fresh peeled shrimp (36-40 count)	4 cloves minced garlic
½ stick butter	½ tsp. thyme
¼ cup vegetable oil	2 tsp. sweet basil
2 strips of lean bacon, shredded	3 bay leaves
¾ cup minced carrots	1 tsp. cayenne pepper
2 cups finely diced onions	1 tsp. black pepper
1 cup finely diced celery	2 tsp. salt
½ cup finely diced bell pepper	2 tsp. sugar
¼ cup all-purpose flour	3 thin lemon slices
1 large can tomato puree (1½ lb. can)	¼ cup minced parsley
3 cups shrimp stock (heads/ shells)	½ cup sliced green onions

First, take a 5-quart cast-iron Dutch oven and melt the butter and the oil together over high heat. Then—about a half-pound at a time—quickly sauté the shrimp . . . *only until they begin to turn pink* (which should take about 3 minutes for each batch).

Now, remove the shrimp from the pot, toss in the carrots, onions, celery, bell pepper, and bacon, and sauté the vegetables until they soften. Then, stir in the flour, work it thoroughly into the vegetable-butter mixture, and cook it gently over low heat for about 6 minutes (or until it turns smooth).

Next, pour in the tomato puree and the shrimp stock, mix them until completely blended, and increase the heat to high. Then stir in the garlic, thyme, basil, bay leaves, cayenne pepper, black pepper, salt, sugar, and lemon. And when the mixture comes to a *slow boil,* reduce the heat to simmer, cover the pot, and cook for about an hour, stirring occasionally so that the flour doesn't stick to the bottom.

At this point, sample the sauce for salt and pepper and readjust the seasonings to your taste. Remember—you still have to put in the shrimp; and they are going to absorb some of the seasoning. So you should season the sauce so that it is slightly salty and a little bit on the piquante side.

Then, when you're ready to eat, drop in the shrimp, the green onions, and the parsley, stir them together, and simmer everything once more for 15 minutes.

When it's done, ladle a generous helping of the shrimp and the sauce over steamed rice and serve it alongside a crisp lettuce, tomato, and cucumber salad, accompanied by a cold beer in a frosted glass.

Note: Do not put the shrimp into the pot until 15 minutes before you are ready to eat—you don't want to overcook them!

Louisiana Shrimp Puffs

Make this dish and you'll be surprised at how something so quick, so easy, and so simple can taste so rich and fantastic. I'm willing to bet you that this ends up being one of your all-time favorite party foods!

3 lb. raw shrimp, peeled	1 large Philadelphia cream
1 cup white wine	cheese
2 sticks real butter	4 large boiled eggs, finely
1 cup finely chopped shallots	chopped
1 cup finely chopped celery	1 cup finely chopped black olives
½ cup finely chopped bell	salt and pepper to taste
pepper	Romano and parsley as garnish
1 pint heavy cream	24 small pastry shells

First, take a heavy aluminum 12-inch skillet and poach the shrimp in the white wine until they turn pink and tender (this should take about 4 minutes over medium-high heat). Then scoop the shrimp from the poaching wine (but save the wine!), separate them into 2 portions, and place each portion in a bowl to cool. At this point, leave half of the shrimp whole and shred the other half into small slivers using the cutting blade of your food processor.

Next, in the same skillet you used to poach the shrimp, melt the butter and gently sauté the shallots, celery, and bell pepper until they soften. Then pour in the heavy cream and the poaching wine and stir everything together until well-blended. Now over high heat, reduce the cream-wine sauce to one-half of its original volume—*stirring constantly.*

Next, drop the shrimp that you shredded into the skillet and simmer it gently into the sauce for about a minute or two. Then, little by little, start adding (and stirring in!) the cream cheese. And when it's all well-blended, season the mixture with the salt and pepper and remove the skillet from the heat.

At this point, toss in the chopped eggs and the black olives and fold them into the mix thoroughly. Then, taste for salt and pepper once more, stuff the mixture into the pastry shells, top each one with a whole shrimp, sprinkle with parsley and Romano, and bake in a 375-degree oven until bubbly!

Hint: Of course, the puffs can be served by themselves as appetizers. But, if you prepare a little buttered shoe-peg corn, a crisp fresh spinach salad, and a bottle of chilled white wine to go with them, you have everything you need for both a family meal as well as an elegant main course for a dinner party.

Topless spinach and burpless beans

Did you know that if you leave the lid off the pot when you cook fresh spinach the leaves will stay bright and green?

And did you also know that if you cook dried beans (like red beans, blackeye peas, great northerns, lentils, pintos) and you *cook them uncovered,* they won't give you gas? Which means you won't burp and so forth!

Oysters Cangelosi

Using as much seafood as I do for my television show, it's important to have a good seafood supplier—someone who can guarantee top quality regardless of the season. Well, Vincent Cangelosi does that *for me*. So I created this recipe *for him!*

2 doz. fresh raw oysters (unwashed)	¼ cup heavy cream
1 stick unsalted butter, melted	1 tsp. black pepper
2 tins of flat anchovies	1 cup crumbled bread sticks
2 tsp. sweet basil	1 cup finely chopped parsley
2 heads baked garlic	1 cup grated Romano cheese

First, pick through the oysters to make sure all the shells have been removed. Then lay out 12 aluminum ramekins and place 2 oysters into each of them. Place the ramekins on a baking sheet and set them aside momentarily.

Next, in a food processor, blend together thoroughly the melted butter, anchovies, basil, baked garlic, cream, and black pepper, along with half each of the parsley and Romano cheese. This should take about a minute or two at the high-speed setting and give you a mixture that is smooth and creamy.

Now, spoon a couple of tablespoons of the mix over the oysters in the ramekins, sprinkle on a little more Romano and parsley, and top it off with a handful of the crumbled bread sticks.

Then bake the oysters in a preheated 400-degree oven for 10 to 15 minutes (or until the oyster edges curl and the sauce is hot and bubbly).

Note: You can serve this dish as an appetizer or an entree, alongside buttered angel-hair pasta, creamed potatoes, or Cajun dirty rice. But whichever you use as an accompaniment, I suggest you serve it with a chilled blush wine *and lots of* garlic bread!

To Bake Garlic:

Lay the heads of garlic on their sides. Then cut off the tops (as you would trim an artichoke). All you want to do is expose the pods slightly. Now, place the pods in a shallow baking pan and pour a couple tablespoons of *olive oil* over each head. Then cover the pan with aluminum foil and bake the garlic for 45 minutes in a 400-degree oven.

Frank's Louisiana Seafood Fritters

Even though I make this dish most of the time with Louisiana oysters, I've also substituted shrimp or crabmeat (and sometimes a combination of both!). And what you come up with is a batch of "seafood fritters" that's guaranteed to make your bulldog break his chain.

3 doz. oysters, cut in pieces	½ cup finely chopped onions
6 strips bacon, cut in pieces	⅓ cup shallots
3 cups all-purpose flour	⅓ cup chopped bell pepper
2 tbsp. baking powder	⅓ cup celery
2 tsp. salt	4 tbsp. finely chopped parsley
1 tsp. white pepper	1 lb. fresh shrimp, peeled and
2 eggs, slightly beaten	diced
2½ cups oyster liquor	1 cup Crisco oil for frying
1 tsp. Tabasco sauce	

First, drain the oysters, save the liquor, and fry the bacon until it is super crisp. Then crumble the bacon onto several thicknesses of paper towels . . . *but save the drippings*.

Then, in a large bowl, thoroughly mix together the flour, baking powder, salt, and white pepper. When everything is blended well, toss in the eggs and the oyster liquor and *whip* until you get a smooth fritter base.

Next, add the Tabasco, the crumbled bacon, and all of the chopped vegetables. You want to take your time with this step—it's going to take some elbow grease to get all these ingredients mixed thoroughly. But when it's done, you can stir in the oysters and shrimp . . . but stir 'em in *evenly!*

When you're ready to cook, pour the bacon drippings you saved (along with some of the Crisco oil) into a cast-iron or heavy aluminum skillet (remember, you want the oil just deep enough to *almost cover* the fritters) and heat it to about 375 degrees. Then drop teaspoon-size servings of the batter into the oil mix and fry on each side until golden brown.

All that's left is to drain the fritters on paper towels and serve them piping hot! You're gonna love 'em!

Hint: I suggest that whenever possible you use fresh-shucked oysters. And by the way, this recipe should make about 40 fritters.

Frank's Catfish Frascati

If you've got a hankerin' for some fresh catfish, but you're tired of eating it grilled, broiled, and deep-fried . . . try this recipe. The wine brings out a unique flavor in the fish—yet you really never *taste* the wine. Do this one for your next party! I promise it'll get you rave reviews!

8 catfish fillets, cut in cubes	1 tsp. paprika
1 cup seasoned all-purpose flour	2 tsp. Italian seasoning
1 stick real butter	2 tsp. sweet basil
1 cup finely chopped onion	¼ cup heavy cream
½ cup finely chopped celery	2 cups Frascati wine
¼ cup finely chopped bell pepper	salt and black pepper to taste
1 cup coarsely cut fresh mushrooms	

Start off by dusting the catfish cubes lightly in the flour. Then, in a 12-inch skillet, melt the butter over high heat just to the point of bubbling, and quickly sauté the catfish cubes to seal in their juices. Now remove them from the pan and set them aside on paper towels to cool.

Meanwhile, using the same skillet, reduce the heat to medium-low and sauté the onions, celery, bell peppers, and mushrooms until they soften. You should *continually stir* the vegetable mixture as it cooks to ensure an even blend. Then stir in the paprika, Italian seasoning, sweet basil, and heavy cream. Turn the heat up to high and cook the mixture for about 5 minutes or until the cream begins to thicken.

At this point, pour in the Frascati wine and stir it well into the sauce. And with the heat still on high, cook the mixture for about 10 minutes more so as to drive off the alcohol and retain only the essence of the grapes. This is also when you should add your salt and pepper to the sauce.

Then, when everything is blended right, drop in the catfish cubes and reduce the heat to low. Now cook the fish uncovered for about 5 minutes or until the fillets turn opaque and tend to want to flake. When this happens, remove the pan from the fire and let the dish "set" for another 5 minutes to pick up the wine stock flavors.

And it's ready!

Hint: I suggest you serve Catfish Frascati with a creamed vegetable, brabant potatoes, and a tossed green salad. And, of course, another bottle of chilled Frascati to sip between bites!

Frank's Crawfish Quiche

Most folks will tell you that quiche is nothing more than a glorified egg pie. Well, maybe it is in some parts of the country! But in New Orleans, when you fix quiche and you load it up with succulent little crawfish . . . pod'nah you're chowing down on real Cajun gourmet!

Quiche Crust:

2 cups all-purpose flour
2 tsp. baking powder
pinch salt

2 tbsp. Crisco shortening
½ cup vegetable oil
¼ cup milk

First, take a large bowl and mix together the flour and the baking powder. Then, with your fingers, work in the salt and the shortening until the mix turns grainy (similar to cornmeal).

Next, whip together the vegetable oil and the milk and pour it over the flour. Then, with a rubber spatula, mix everything together well. When thoroughly blended, roll the dough into a ball, divide it in half, wrap both pieces in plastic film, and chill for about 30 minutes.

When you're ready to cook, take your rolling pin and thinly roll out the dough between two pieces of waxed paper. Then place the crusts into two 9-inch Pyrex pie pans, lay a sheet of waxed paper over the crust in each pan, pour about 2 cups of dry red beans over the paper, and bake at 400 degrees for 12-15 minutes in the lower middle oven. Then carefully remove the beans and set the crusts aside to cool.

Quiche Ingredients:

2 tbsp. margarine
1 medium onion, diced fine
3 green onions, sliced
2 tbsp. minced parsley
1 cup sliced mushrooms
1 tbsp. flour
3 tbsp. white wine

4 eggs, beaten
1 cup half-and-half
½ cup heavy cream
1 tbsp. paprika
1 lb. crawfish tails
1 cup Monterey Jack cheese
salt and cayenne pepper to taste

First, take a heavy 10-inch skillet and heat the margarine to sizzling. Then toss in and sauté until tender the onions, green onions, parsley, and mushrooms . . . *but do not brown them!* Remember, they still have to bake in the quiche and you don't want them overcooked.

When the vegetables are soft, add the flour and the wine, stir everything well, and cook over medium heat for about 3 minutes. Then set the skillet aside to cool.

Next, in a large mixing bowl, whip the eggs until they turn frothy. Then add the half-and-half, the heavy cream, and the paprika . . . *but do not beat them into the eggs!* Just stir the ingredients thoroughly. This is also when you add your salt and pepper to taste.

At this point, add the crawfish and the cheese to the cooled vegetable mixture and blend everything evenly. Then spoon the mix into the pie pan (about three-quarters full).

Finally, pour the egg custard mixture over the crawfish filling, place it into the oven uncovered, and bake it at 375 degrees for 30-40 minutes (or until a knife blade inserted into the center comes out clean). *But do not overcook or the quiche will turn rubbery!*

I suggest you allow the quiche to cool for about 10-15 minutes before slicing. I also suggest you serve it with a good white wine and a crisp mixed salad.

Quiche Tips:

1—Always pre-cook your pastry shell. This will keep the crust from becoming soggy on the bottom.

2—Always remove unnecessary moisture from the seasoning vegetables by cooking them before pouring on the egg mixture.

3—Always have your eggs at room temperature. They will froth and fluff much more easily.

4—To make other quiches—asparagus, broccoli and Swiss, crabmeat and cheddar, bacon and spinach, shrimp and broccoli, artichoke hearts, Italian sausage, anchovies and black olives—just eliminate the crawfish and the Monterey Jack cheese and use the same recipe. They will all turn out great!

Note: You can use the red beans over and over again for baking other pie crusts. I suggest you put them in a Ziploc bag and store them in your refrigerator.

How to Cook Seafood Sausage

Pete Giovenco's shrimp sausage in the Meats chapter, made primarily with shrimp, pork, fresh vegetables, and specially blended herbs and spices, can be prepared a variety of ways. But these are the methods I like best.

GRILLING

Take the sausage links and place them on an outdoor grill set on "high." While they cook, gently roll them back and forth across the grill surface *using a pair of tongs* so that the links cook evenly on all sides. Avoid using a fork or any other cooking utensil that will break the casing and cause the natural juices to run out of the sausages. The links are cooked when the casings are golden brown and crispy all over. Approximate cooking time—15 to 20 minutes.

BROILING

Place the links about an inch or two apart on a broiler rack (one that has a pan underneath to catch the drippings). Then pre-set the oven to "broil" (500 degrees). When the thermostat indicates the proper temperature, put the links into the oven and let them cook about 3 minutes. Slide the rack out of the oven and give the links a "quarter-turn." Put them back under the broiler and cook another 3 minutes. Turn the links another quarter-turn, cook another 3 minutes then turn again, cooking an additional 3 minutes. In other words, in about 12 minutes or so, the link sausage should be fully cooked and succulently juicy. (Note: you may have to adjust the cooking time slightly depending upon your broiler element. Just don't overcook them!)

OVEN BAKING

Place the links into a shallow baking pan so that they are separated by about an inch—you don't want to crowd them into the pan and you don't want them to touch. Add just enough water to cover the links about one-quarter way (about a half-inch deep). Then slice a handful of onions and bell pepper and sprinkle the vegetables over the sausage. Next, cover the pan tightly with aluminum foil, making sure you seal all the edges. Place them in a preheated oven set to 375 degrees and allow them to bake for about 45 minutes. Just before you serve them, remove the foil and pour the juices, along with the smothered onions and bell peppers, out into a skillet. Bring the juices to a boil, reduce the liquids slightly, and stir in a little bit of cornstarch mixed with water to thicken the liquids into a smooth, creamy sauce. While the sauce is cooking, place the sausage back into the dry pan—this time "uncovered"—and return it to the oven to brown. I suggest you occasionally turn the links over so that all the sides will brown (approximate cooking time in the dry oven = 5 minutes). Then serve them piping hot, covered with the seafood sauce.

PAN FRYING

Using a heavy aluminum 12-inch skillet (or one with a non-stick coating), heat about 3 tablespoons of Crisco oil to "medium high." Then one at a time, place the links into the oil (being careful not to crowd them together) and begin agitating the pan. *Do not use a fork or pierce the casing!* You want to coat each link thoroughly, and sauté them until they turn a slight crispy brown. Approximate cooking time is 12 to 15 minutes.

IN ITALIAN GRAVY

Make your favorite Italian gravy and let it simmer about 20 minutes. Then drop in the seafood sausage, reduce the heat to "low," and allow the links to cook slowly until tender (about 45 minutes to an hour). This is one method of cooking when it *is* desirable to pierce the casings so that the juices can "seep." What you end up with is a rich, shrimpy-tasting, and full-flavored sauce that enhances any kind of pasta. I recommend you serve it with Romano cheese.

SMOKING

Because seafood sausage contains a small amount of fat, it can be cooked on a smoker. But usually the method results in a rather "dry-tasting" sausage. So for the best flavor and texture, I don't recommend you smoke the links.

MICROWAVING

Seafood sausage can be cooked in the microwave, but it should be noted that microwaving causes the sausage to lose some of its texture. Furthermore, the casings won't crisp up in the microwave, so the links tend to come out tough. If you want to cook the sausage in your microwave, I suggest you place them in a Pyrex or Rubbermaid dish, add a small amount of water to the bottom, cover the dish with a lid, and "steam" them until tender—about 8 to 10 minutes on high power. Keep in mind, though, that the casings will still be tough.

Hints: I recommend that to get the richest, most succulent flavor from these delicate gourmet links you prepare seafood sausage either by oven baking, grilling, or frying—and preferably in that order.

Remember, natural casings (not synthetic ones) are used to make seafood sausage. So you want to cook the links until the casings reach a "gentle crispness." But do not overcook them. The links should be tender and juicy . . . not tough and dry.

Because seafood sausage is highly perishable, I suggest you always keep it well refrigerated. But do not try to cook the links while they are frozen. And once you defrost them, do not refreeze them uncooked. Cooked sausage may be frozen and reheated without a considerable loss of texture.

Frank's Old N'Awlins Corn-Shrimp Stew

Ever since I was a little boy, this has been one of my favorite dishes. It's good in summer, winter, spring, and fall! It's good for a pot-luck church supper or an elegant dinner party! In other words, it's good anytime. And it's good for you! But if that weren't enough . . . look how easy it is to make!

½ lb. lean, meaty bacon
1 cup finely chopped yellow
  onions
1 cup finely sliced green onions
½ cup finely chopped celery
1 cup julienned bell pepper
2 lb. fresh shrimp (31-35 count)
2 cans Rotel tomatoes with
  chilies

3 cans shoe-peg corn (303 size)
1 cup shrimp or chicken stock
1 tbsp. finely minced garlic
1 stick real butter
½ tsp. savory
1 tsp. marjoram
2 tsp. salt
½ tsp. white pepper
3 tbsp. finely chopped parsley

Start off by peeling the shrimp, washing them well under cool running water, and gently boiling the heads and shells for about 30 minutes in a quart of water to make a good rich stock. Continue to cook (reduce) the stock until you end up with about 2 cups. Then strain the liquid into a bowl and discard the shells and the heads.

Next, in a 12-inch skillet, fry down the bacon until it turns crisp. Then remove it from the pan and crumble it onto paper towels to drain. Now take the pan of bacon drippings and quickly sauté the onions, green onions, celery, and bell pepper. When the vegetables are soft, remove them from the skillet with a strainer spoon and toss them into a 6-quart stew pot. Then turn the heat under the skillet back up to high, drop in the shrimp, and fry them until they turn pink (it should take no more than about 3 minutes). *Do not overcook!* Now, take the shrimp from the skillet and set them aside on a platter for a while.

At this point, turn up the heat under the stew pot to medium-high and stir the Rotel tomatoes into the seasoning vegetables. With a spoon, break up the tomatoes slightly. And when the liquid begins to bubble, add the crumbled bacon, the garlic, the corn, and the shrimp stock you made earlier. Mix all these ingredients together well.

Now continue to cook the corn mixture over medium heat *just until it comes to a gentle boil.* At that point, reduce the heat to medium-low, cover the pot, and simmer the stew for 30 minutes. After the allotted cooking time, sprinkle in the savory, marjoram, salt, and white pepper and stir the seasonings in well. Cover the pot again and cook for another 15 minutes.

Finally, increase the heat to high. And when the stew comes to a boil, turn the fire off, toss in the butter and shrimp, and stir them into the corn. Once more, adjust the salt and pepper to your taste and let the pot "set" for 5 minutes before serving.

Meanwhile, preheat your serving bowls in the oven. And when you're ready to eat, spoon some steamed, buttered rice into the bowls, ladle on a hearty helping of the corn-shrimp stew, and lightly top with fresh parsley to garnish.

Serve with plenty of crispy French bread and . . . enjoy!

The aromatics of onions

You know how difficult it is to get the smell of onions off your hands after you've finished chopping a bunch of 'em? Well, here's what you do!

Just squeeze a little fresh lemon juice into your palms, swoosh it around on your hands and fingers, and . . . presto! The odor will disappear instantly!

N'Awlins Sweet and Sour Crawfish

Loaded with fresh onions, celery, bell pepper, broccoli, carrots, mushrooms, bok choy, and shallots, this dish blends together rich natural flavors of vegetables with the delicate richness of crawfish . . . all bound together in an Oriental-style sweet and sour sauce. You gotta make this one!

4 tbsp. Crisco oil	**½ medium bell pepper**
1 cup yellow onions	**2 lb. peeled crawfish tails**
1 cup bias-cut celery	**(with fat)**
⅔ cup bias-cut carrots	**4 tbsp. soy sauce**
½ cup sliced broccoli florets	**¼ tsp. white pepper**
½ cup thick-sliced mushrooms	**½ cup Tiger Sauce***
½ cup shallots	**1 cup chicken stock**
½ cup bok choy	**2 tbsp. cornstarch**

You're going to need a Chinese wok or heavy aluminum skillet for this dish. And the first thing you want to do is place it on the stove on high heat—*empty*—and get it hot. Remember the old Chinese proverb—"Hot Pan . . . Cold Oil . . . Food Not Stick!"

Then, when the pan is hot, pour in the vegetable oil and swoosh it around to coat the metal. And at the point when the oil *just begins to smoke,* toss in all the vegetables and quickly stir-fry them for about 3 or 4 minutes until they cook "tender crisp"—*tender, but still crunchy.* One important note: you're going to have to constantly stir and toss the veggies once you drop them into the wok or they'll burn!

Next—still over high heat—toss in the crawfish tails, and mix them well into the cooking vegetables. Then cover the wok and let the mixture cook for about 2 minutes. No, don't worry . . . it won't burn!

At this point, remove the wok lid and stir in the soy sauce, the Tiger Sauce, and the white pepper. Cover the pot again and cook once more for about 2 minutes.

Then dissolve the cornstarch into the chicken stock in a small bowl and stir it into the crawfish/vegetable mixture. Almost instantly, a rich

---

*If you can't find Tiger Sauce in your grocery store, you can substitute the recipe for Frank's Sweet and Sour Sauce. Just add it to taste.

reddish-pink sweet and sour sauce will bind all the ingredients together. You should serve it immediately over steamed rice.

Hints

1—I want you to know that this is a peppery dish! So to reduce the spiciness, just cut back on or eliminate the white pepper.

2—For a thick sauce, let the finished mixture cook a little longer; for a thinner sauce, add a little extra chicken stock.

3—Most importantly, don't overcook the dish. You want to keep the vegetables crispy and the crawfish firm.

Frank's N'Awlins Shrimp Trinity

This is one of my first gourmet creations! It was done originally to be served over pasta as an entree. But since it can be transformed into at least three other recipes—a dip, a sauce, and a fondue—hence the name "trinity." Regardless of how you serve it . . . it's magnificent!

¼ cup extra virgin olive oil
2 lb. peeled and butterflied
   medium shrimp
4 tbsp. finely chopped green
   onions
4 cloves finely minced garlic
1 pint heavy cream
¼ tsp. thyme
2 tsp. Italian seasoning

½ tsp. sweet basil
⅛ tsp. oregano
1½ tsp. salt
1 tsp. cayenne pepper
2 tsp. paprika
½ cup grated Romano cheese
black olives to garnish
1 lb. pre-cooked spaghetti
   (al-dente)

First, take a heavy aluminum 12-inch skillet, pour in the olive oil, and heat it almost to the point of smoking.

Now pay close attention to this step! Drop in the shrimp *(and you want to make sure they are drained well!)* and stir-fry them quickly until they start to bronze. Then immediately reduce the heat to medium and gently sauté the shrimp until the natural juices begin to render out (about 3 minutes or so). *But do not overcook!*

Next, add the green onions and the garlic and sauté them until the onions wilt slightly and the garlic just starts to brown *(do not let it burn or it will become bitter!)*.

At this point, remove the shrimp from the skillet with a strainer spoon, leaving as much liquid as possible in the pan, and set them aside in a bowl.

Now increase the heat to "high" again, pour in the heavy cream—along with all the dry seasonings—and cook it at a quick bubble until it thickens. *Make sure you watch the pan and continue to stir as it cooks, though, because the cream has a tendency to boil over easily.*

When you're ready to eat, drop the shrimp and the Romano cheese into the pan and mix everything together well. Then drop in the pasta, thoroughly coat each strand with the sauce and serve piping hot with black olives for garnish.

Oh—and make sure you have a loaf of either fresh French or Italian bread for sopping!

Hints: If you mix this dish with Philadelphia brand cream cheese and whip it in the food processor . . . you've got a great shrimp dip. If you thin out this dish with half-and-half and melt 8 ounces of Velveeta cheese into it you've got a great fondue. In fact, your variations are endless! Shrimp Trinity can also be served as an entree with steamed rice or brabant potatoes, or as a topping (sauce) for fried or broiled fish, fried oysters, and broiled softshell crabs, as well as broccoli and cauliflower.

Toothbrushes in the kitchen?

You know those old toothbrushes you're forever throwing away? Well, stop tossing them out and start putting them in your kitchen gadget drawer! They're great for cleaning rotary beaters, graters, food choppers, processor blades, and other utensils. And nothing is better than a toothbrush for scrubbing away those little traces of blood from along the backbone of small panfish you clean.

Frank's N'Awlins Barbecue Shrimp Deluxe

If you want all the flavor of traditional New Orleans barbecue shrimp done in the oven, without having to use the oven, without having to wait 40 minutes or more, and without taking the chance of having the shells set on the top layer, then you're gonna love this recipe! I want you to try it tonight!

½ lb. real butter
½ cup Crisco oil
1 cup finely diced yellow onions
½ cup finely chopped green onions
½ cup finely chopped celery
¼ cup finely chopped bell peppers
2 heads garlic (cut in half crosswise)
1 tbsp. whole cloves
1 tsp. cayenne pepper
2 tbsp. black pepper
1 tbsp. McCormick's barbecue spice
1 tbsp. Worcestershire sauce
1 tbsp. rosemary leaves
2 sliced lemons
2 bay leaves
1 can of warm beer
salt to taste
5 lb. jumbo shrimp (heads-on)

First, drop the butter and the Crisco oil into a 6-quart Dutch oven and melt them together over medium-high heat (just make sure the mixture doesn't burn). Then toss in the onions, green onions, celery, bell peppers, and garlic and gently sauté them for about 5 minutes until they soften and release their juices. Now add the remainder of the seasonings and spices and stir everything into the vegetable oil-butter base really well, and cook for another 6 minutes until all of the flavors "marry." This is also when you salt the sauce to your taste, but I recommend you overseason slightly because the shrimp will absorb a lot of it.

At this point, take the sauce off the burner and allow it to cool slightly. Then add the beer and stir it into the mix until the foam disappears.

Now put the pot back onto the fire over *high heat*. And when it comes back to a boil, drop in the shrimp and stir them thoroughly into the sauce. You want to cook them for about 5 minutes or until they've all turned pink. Then cover the Dutch oven, remove it from the burner, and set it aside to "cure." *But about every 5 minutes or so, stir the mixture so that the shrimp soak up the sauce.* This is an important step—it's what makes all the shrimp cook evenly.

Then, when you see a slight air space appear along the back of the shrimp (actually, the shell pulls away from the meat) . . . *they're ready to eat!* Of course, you can let them soak in the sauce longer, but very few folks I know do! They smell too good!

Suggestion: Don't overcook' em! The shells will set and the shrimp will be hard to peel. I recommend you serve barbecue shrimp with creamed potatoes, a broccoli-cheese casserole, and a crisp Italian salad. But most of all . . . you got to have a good supply of French bread to sop up the juices!

Oysters Broiled in Heaven

If your mouth waters over Oysters Rockefeller, Oysters Bienville, Oysters Casino, and Southern Deep-Fried Oysters, wait till you sink your teeth into this creation! I guarantee . . . you'll eat a lot more than your share!

3 heads fresh garlic
3 tbsp. extra virgin olive oil
2 sticks real butter
1 cup sauterne wine
1 cup oyster liquor
3 tbsp. Dijon mustard
¾ cup finely chopped parsley
½ cup finely chopped green onions
1 lb. cooked and crumbled bacon
½ gallon oysters, shucked and unwashed
2 tsp. marjoram
2 tbsp. seafood seasonings
juice of one lemon
2 tsp. Louisiana Hot Sauce
2 cups crushed Ritz crackers
salt to taste

First, cut the tops off the garlic heads and place them into a shallow baking pan with the cut sides up. Then pour the olive oil over the garlic, cover the pan with aluminum foil, and bake at 400 degrees for 1 hour. When the heads are cooked (they will become soft and mellow), set them aside and let them cool to room temperature.

Next, melt the butter over medium heat in a 12-inch skillet. And just when it starts to brown slightly, take the pan off the fire and begin rolling it around—*remember, you want the butter to "brown" not burn!* Now set it aside in a cool spot for awhile.

In another 12-inch skillet, mix the sauterne and the oyster liquor to-gether and cook it over medium heat until it reduces to one-half of its original volume. And keep stirring as it reduces—otherwise the oyster liquor will stick to the bottom of the pan.

When the oyster-wine mixture is ready, reheat the butter and begin blending the butter into the oyster-wine reduction *over medium-high heat*. At this point, you also whisk in the Dijon mustard and the softened baked garlic. Keep stirring the sauce all the time! And keep it to a gentle boil! It should become rich, creamy, and very smooth after about 5 to 10 minutes of cooking.

Next, stir into the sauce the crumbled bacon, the green onions, and the parsley and cook the mixture about 5 minutes or until the vegetables wilt slightly. Then remove the sauce from the fire and let it "set" until your oysters are prepared.

And this is how you do it!

First, pick through the oysters to remove any shell bits and preheat a baking sheet to 300 degrees. Then carefully remove the baking sheet from the oven and place the oysters on it while it's hot. Immediately, sprinkle the marjoram and the seafood seasoning over the oysters, spoon on a generous helping of the sauce, squeeze on a little lemon juice, dash on a few drops of Louisiana Hot Sauce, and top everything off with the crumbled Ritz crackers.

All that's left is to slide the pan under the broiler for about 5 or 6 minutes until the oysters curl and the sauce bubbles. Then serve piping hot with a mound of creamed potatoes and a crisp lettuce and tomato salad. Ummmmmmmmmmm!

Hints: I also suggest French bread . . . because the sauce is so good you'll definitely do some sopping! But note, however, that you don't want to pour so much oyster-wine sauce over the whole oysters that they float. You want to broil *them, not* boil *them! Oh . . . and for a little bit of extra flavor, stir a few tablespoons of bacon drippings into the sauce.*

Frank's Bronzed Fish

This dish was created as an alternative to "Blackened Redfish," and can be used with *any kind of fish you would cook in a sauce*—not just redfish! What's more, it doesn't have to be done outdoors because it produces very little if any smoke . . . you can do it at home on your stove or in your commercial kitchen . . . it's considerably lower in calories than "Blackened Redfish" . . . and best of all, it gives you all the succulence, taste, flavor, tenderness, and crispness of blackened fish . . . without all the fuss! And with the present situation concerning the overharvest of redfish and the price of the product, this dish could provide the entree you're looking for. Try it! You'll be pleased!

1 Teflon or Silverstone-coated
  skillet (12-inch size)
6 lean fish fillets (8 oz. average)*
1 tsp. oregano
2 tsp. basil
½ tsp. thyme
2 tbsp. sweet paprika

salt, white, black, and red
  pepper to taste
1 tsp. margarine per fillet
1 tbsp. chopped shallots per
  fillet
1 tbsp. white wine per fillet
¼ cup minced parsley to garnish

Start off by turning your stovetop or range to *high* and placing the skillet on the burner. It is essential that this recipe be done in a Teflon or Silverstone-coated skillet to compensate for the small amounts of oils used. Note, too, that the skillet must be heated to "hot" prior to adding the margarine (it's hot enough when a drop of water sizzles off quickly).

Meanwhile, season the fish with the herbs and spices, rubbing them into the fillets well!

At this point, add the margarine for each fillet you're going to cook, swish it around in the pan to coat the bottom, and drop in the shallots (stirring them in quickly and cooking them for about a minute or so). Then add the fish and let them cook over high heat until the margarine begins to turn them a *toasty bronze* color and the upper edges begin to turn opaque.

When they're done on one side (gently lift up with a spatula to see), flip them over and cook the other side. It is best to turn the fillets only once— otherwise they may break apart. Your fillets will be ready to serve when

---

*Catfish, flounder, croaker, drum, sheepshead, dolphin, cobia, grouper, red snapper, swordfish, tuna, and bass all "bronze" beautifully.

the meat flakes easily with a fork—which should be about 4 minutes total cooking time. Keep in mind that all this time they're cooking on "high."

When you're ready to eat, place the fish fillets on a warming platter. Then add the white wine to the hot skillet and agitate the pan briskly to de-glaze the bottom and reduce the wine. When slightly thickened, pour the sauce over the fish fillets, garnish with a sprinkling of parsley, and serve piping hot with brabant potatoes and buttered asparagus spears.

Hint: You can also use bourbon, cognac, or brandy instead of wine to vary the flavor. Experiment with them and treat your taste buds. I also suggest you top each fillet with some thinly-sliced onions and a few drops of fresh lemon juice.

This recipe can also be used to bronze *shrimp, softshell crabs, crawfish tails, and even thinly sliced cuts of beef, pork, veal, and chicken.*

Bronzed Catfish Baked in Mushroom Shrimp Sauce

Toast the catfish to a delicate crispness, bronze the mushrooms so that their natural juices are locked in, season them both with a rich mix of Cajun spices, and bake until hot and bubbly in a thick shrimpy sauce . . . and you got yourself a seafood creation that most master chefs will envy!

8 prime catfish fillets	**1 lb. peeled, butterflied shrimp**
2 tbsp. bronzing mix*	**½ cup sliced green onions**
4 tbsp. real mayonnaise	**¼ cup minced parsley**
4 tbsp. liquid margarine	**2 cans cream of shrimp soup**
½ cup fresh mushrooms,	**salt and cayenne pepper to taste**
cut in half	

First, turn your stovetop to *high* and place a 12-inch skillet on the burner. (Make a note that it is essential that you do this recipe either in a

---

*If you can't find bronzing mix at your grocery, you can create a similar taste by *lightly sprinkling* each fillet with salt, black pepper, cayenne pepper, onion powder, garlic powder, ground thyme, powdered Italian seasoning, paprika, and non-fat dry milk.

Teflon or Silverstone-coated skillet or a well-seasoned heavy aluminum frypan.) You need to compensate for the small amounts of oil you're going to use. Note, too, that the skillet must be heated to "hot" prior to adding the fish (you got it hot enough when a drop of water sizzles off quickly).

Meanwhile, season the fish with the bronzing mix (and be sure to rub it into the fillets well). Then, using a pastry brush, evenly spread a little bit of the mayonnaise on each fillet and let the fish fillets "rest" on waxed paper on the countertop for at least 15 minutes before cooking them.

At this point, add about a teaspoonful of the margarine to the skillet and swish it around to lightly oil the bottom. Then drop in about 3 fillets at a time and cook them quickly on each side (about 4 minutes per side) until they turn a toasty golden brown. Continue adding margarine and bronzing the fish until all the fillets are cooked. When they're done, take a spatula and place them side-by-side in a shallow baking pan and set the pan aside for a while.

Next, using the same skillet, drop in whatever margarine you have left and toss in the mushrooms. Then, continuously agitating the skillet, cook the mushrooms until they turn a rich toasty color. Now immediately add the shrimp, the green onions, and the parsley, reduce the heat to low, and allow the shrimp to cook until they turn pink and tender—*about 2 or 3 minutes*.

Finally, stir in the cream of shrimp soup, whisk it with a wire whip until smooth, and season it to taste with salt and cayenne pepper. Then ladle the sauce evenly over the bronzed fish and bake the fillet—*uncovered*—for about 15-20 minutes in a 375-degree oven.

When you're ready to eat, serve the fish alongside a cold, crisp salad and a hot baked potato topped with the shrimp sauce.

Hints:

1—This recipe can be done not only with catfish but with virtually any kind of lean fish, so long as the fillets average no more than about 8 ounces each.

2—Don't worry if the sauce appears too thick when you ladle it on the fish. Natural juices from the fillets will thin it out as it bakes.

Frank's Creole Crawfish

There's a recipe elsewhere in this book for *Creole Crawfish-Stuffed Bell Peppers*. And if you think the stuffing that goes into the peppers is good, wait until you try the base recipe it came from. Here it is! And I guarantee that once you fix it the first time, you'll fix it over and over again.

½ stick butter + 3 tbsp. butter	2 tbsp. Dijon mustard
1 cup small-diced white onions	2 tbsp. wine and pepper
1 cup sliced green onions	Worcestershire sauce
½ cup small-diced celery	4 tbsp. all-purpose flour
½ cup small-diced bell pepper	2 lb. crawfish tails with fat
4 cloves minced garlic	½ cup minced parsley
1 large can tomato puree (16 oz.)	juice of ½ lemon
2 cups chicken stock	salt and cayenne pepper to taste
3 bay leaves	

First, take a heavy 12-inch skillet, melt the half-stick of butter over medium-high heat, and sauté the onions, green onions, celery, bell pepper, and garlic until tender (about 5 minutes). *Just watch the garlic and don't let it burn.*

Now, transfer the vegetable mixture to a 6-quart Dutch oven, pour in the tomato puree, and mix everything together well. At this point, stir in the chicken stock, the bay leaves, the mustard, and the Worcestershire sauce. Then cover the Dutch oven, set it on the stove, turn the burner to low, and simmer the sauce mix for about 40 minutes (stirring occasionally).

While the sauce is cooking, mix the 4 tablespoons of flour into the crawfish tails. Then take the same skillet you sautéed the vegetables in, melt the 3 tablespoons of butter over high heat, and quickly stir-fry the crawfish—*you just want them to heat up, so cook them only about 2 or 3 minutes!* Now, set them aside for a while.

When the sauce is just about ready, stir in the parsley and lemon juice, season to taste with salt and cayenne pepper, and add the sautéed crawfish tails. Then set the heat to medium-high and *cook only until the sauce begins to bubble.*

At this point, take the pot off the fire and serve the crawfish piping hot over steamed buttered rice or hot buttered egg noodles! Y'all . . . we're talking *good!*

Frank's N'Awlins Fried Crawfish Tails
(Cajun Popcorn)

Light yet crisp and fully satisfying, this makes a great summertime meal when accompanied by a couple Oven-Crusted Creamer Potatoes and a sliced tomato salad with gorgonzola dressing. In fact, every summer meal should be this good!

3 eggs, well-beaten	1 tsp. garlic powder
1 cup whole milk	3 tsp. salt
2 lb. crawfish tails (with fat)	2 tsp. black pepper
2 cups all-purpose flour	1 tsp. cayenne pepper
2 tsp. onion powder	Crisco oil for frying

First, make an "eggwash" by whipping together the eggs and the whole milk until foamy. Then drop in the crawfish tails and let them "soak" for about 15 minutes.

Meanwhile, thoroughly blend the flour, onion powder, garlic powder, salt, black pepper, and cayenne to make your coating mix. Then—*a handful at a time, after shaking off the excess egg-wash*—drop the crawfish tails into the dry mix and coat each tail well.

Now, using a large-mesh strainer, remove the crawfish from the coating, shake off the excess flour, and set the coated tails on a platter to "cure" for about 5 minutes.

When you're ready to cook, add to your deep-fryer or high-sided frypan just enough Crisco oil to cover the tails. *Important—be sure to heat the oil to 375-400 degrees*.

Then, about 20 at a time, drop the coated tails into the cooking oil and stir them around to keep them from sticking together. If the temperature is right they'll fry *quickly* (about 3 or 4 minutes). And when they turn crispy and golden brown, remove them from the frypan and drain them on a couple of paper towels.

All that's left is to repeat the process until all the tails are fried. I suggest you serve them piping hot right out of the pan. But keep an eye on the cook! With these things, snacking is unavoidable!

Hint: For a thin, extra-light coating, eliminate the eggwash and coat the tails only in the seasoned flour mix.

Frank's Cajun Sauce for
Fried Crawfish Tails

While this is the principal sauce I serve with fried crawfish tails, it also goes equally well with fried shrimp, fried fish, fried oysters, and marinated crab claws. So with that in mind . . . make this stuff in big batches! You'll want to have it in the refrigerator all the time!

3 egg yolks	**2 tbsp. Dijon mustard**
2 cups Crisco oil	**2 tbsp. fresh lemon juice**
¾ cup chopped Italian olive	**1 tsp. Worcestershire sauce**
salad	**1 tbsp. Louisiana Hot Sauce**
¼ cup chopped green onions	**salt and cayenne to taste**
2 tsp. paprika	

First, drop the egg yolks into a blender or food processor and cream them together until smooth. Then, *in a thin stream with the processor running,* add the oil until it is all incorporated into the egg yolks. What you're really doing is making a mayonnaise base, so be sure to take your time combining the ingredients so that the mayonnaise doesn't break.

Next, stop the blender or food processor.

Then drop in all the remaining ingredients and fold them evenly into the base with a spatula. Now turn the processor back on and blend everything together to the consistency you desire. At this point, taste the sauce and adjust the salt and pepper to your taste.

All that's left is to dip the fried crawfish tails into the sauce and enjoy! This stuff is good served either at room temperature or chilled.

N'Awlins Oyster Fritters

Fritters are made when you take a smooth but rich batter, combine it with fruit or meat, and fry it up crunchy-crispy. These fritters—done New Orleans style with oysters—are so good . . . you may never fix oysters any other way again! Try 'em and see if you don't agree!

3 dozen oysters, cut in thirds
2½ cups oyster liquor, strained
3 cups all-purpose flour
2 tbsp. baking powder
2 tsp. salt
½ tsp. white pepper
2 eggs, slightly beaten

⅓ cup onions, finely chopped
⅔ cup green onions, finely chopped
¼ cup parsley, finely chopped
dash Louisiana Hot Sauce
1½ cups Crisco oil

Start off by draining the oysters and straining and saving the oyster liquor. And let me suggest that this dish is best when you use fresh-shucked, unwashed oysters whenever possible.

Now take a mixing bowl and sift together the flour, baking powder, salt, and pepper. It's important that you don't omit the "sifting" process—because if you do, your fritters won't be light and crunchy.

Next stir in the eggs and mix everything around lightly.

At this point, pour in the oyster liquor and mix the ingredients really well to form the fritter base. And when the consistency is smooth, toss in the onions, green onions, and parsley. And again mix everything well.

Now, fold in your cut oysters and incorporate them into the batter until the mixture is totally consistent. Add the Louisiana Hot Sauce, too, and stir it in well.

Then when you're ready to cook, heat to *hot* (375-400 degrees) just enough oil to cover the bottom of your skillet, drop the fritter base into the pan by tablespoon helpings, and fry until each fritter is golden brown on both sides.

Hints: You may have to flip them over once or twice to make sure they're cooked all the way through. Go ahead and do it: it won't affect the dish at all.

Incidentally, this recipe should make about 36 fritters and they can be served as an entree with a sautéed vegetable medley or cottage fried potatoes. But the fritters are also excellent as hors d'oeuvres or TV snacks.

Frank's N'Awlins Oyster-Fritter Sauce

Actually . . . this is more than a sauce just for your oyster fritters! It's also a great sauce for just about every kind of seafood you chow down on—boiled shrimp, fried crawfish, softshell crabs, whatever! So go ahead and whip up a batch! And whatever you don't eat, put in a Mason jar and store in the bottom of your refrigerator . . . it'll keep for weeks!

2 cups thick tomato catsup	**⅛ tsp. garlic powder**
½ cup mayonnaise	**juice of one lemon**
¼ cup horseradish	**½ tsp. white pepper**
2 tbsp. Worcestershire sauce	**2 tsp. Louisiana Hot Sauce**
½ cup finely sliced green onions	**(to taste)**
¼ cup finely chopped parsley	**salt to taste**

Very simply, in a large mixing bowl whip together all the ingredients (except the salt, pepper, and hot sauce). For best results, I suggest you use a wire whip.

Now add the salt, pepper, and hot sauce to taste and blend it in uniformly. Then cover the bowl with plastic film or aluminum foil and place it in the refrigerator for at least an hour for the flavors to "marry."

And that's all there is to it!

How to Fix Frank's N'Awlins Fried Oysters

Served with spicy coleslaw and creamed potatoes, these crispy fried oysters are some of the best you'll ever have . . . kinda like dinnertime on a Saturday night at your Momma's house. Just follow the recipe and they'll come out perfect.

2 cups cornmeal	1 tsp. black pepper
1 cup cornflour (Fish-Fry)	1 tsp. cayenne pepper
½ cup cornstarch	4 dozen fresh-shucked
1 tsp. granulated onion	unwashed oysters
½ tsp. granulated garlic	Crisco oil for frying
2 tsp. salt	

First, take a large bowl and mix together all the dry ingredients—*but mix them together thoroughly.* Then take a heavy aluminum or cast-iron skillet, place it on the burner over medium high heat, and get it hot. Then pour in enough vegetable oil to just cover the oysters while they're frying—about 3 cups.

Keep in mind that for perfect crispy oysters, the frying temperature must be somewhere between 375 and 400 degrees. A thermometer is the best way to ensure that you're at the proper frying temperature.

Next, strain the water from the oysters. Then, a few at a time, drop them into the cornmeal mix and toss them around, taking care to completely coat each oyster. (*Hint:* don't be in a hurry to take them out of the mix—remember, the oysters will continue to exude liquids once they're drained. So let them set for a minute or two in the coating.)

Then, immediately drop them into the hot oil . . . *slowly! And one at a time!* If you put too many oysters into the oil at once, the temperature will drop below 375 degrees, the frying action will stop, the cornmeal will soak up the oil, and you'll end up with soggy oysters. Yuucck!

I recommend that in a 12-inch skillet, you fry only about a dozen oysters at a batch. Drop them in, move them around gently with a slotted spoon, and fry them for about 2 to 3 minutes—turning them once or twice—until they turn a rich golden brown.

Then finally, when they're cooked, remove them from the skillet with the slotted spoon and drain them on several layers of paper towels.

Hints: Do not cover the oysters after they're fried! Don't use a dish, pot lid, aluminum foil, paper towels, or anything else in an attempt to keep the oysters hot. You should eat fried oysters as soon as they are cooked. Trying to keep them hot by covering them only traps internal steam and results in soggy oysters. Leave 'em uncovered—and keep 'em crisp!

How to Fix Frank's "N 'Awlins-Fried" Fish
(For The Perfect Fish Fry)

The Mix			
Yellow Cornmeal	2 cups	4 cups	8 cups
Corn Flour (Fish Fry)	1 cup	2 cups	4 cups
Cornstarch	½ cup	1 cup	2 cups
Onion Powder	½ tsp.	1 tsp.	3 tsp.
Garlic Powder	½ tsp.	1 tsp.	3 tsp.
Black Pepper	½ tsp.	1 tsp.	3 tsp.
Cayenne Pepper	2 tsp.	4 tsp.	3 tbsp.
Salt	3 tsp.	2 tbsp.	4 tbsp.

(Note: The spices are measured to standard proportions. You may want to increase or decrease the amounts to your tastes.)

Procedure:

1—Blend the fish fry ingredients thoroughly as per the recipe above. I suggest that since it keeps well in the refrigerator for months, you should make large batches and keep it on hand.

2—When you're ready to fry your fish (the coating mix is also excellent for frying shrimp, oysters, crawfish tails, and scallops), wet the fillets, roll them thoroughly in the dry mix, and set them aside for about 5 minutes to "rest." Do not dip the fillets into egg wash!

3—Take a skillet or frypan, pour in enough Crisco oil to come halfway up on the fillets (you can use either the vegetable or the corn oil), and heat it between 375 and 400 degrees. I recommend you use a thermometer to set the right temperature.

4—Drop the coated fish into the oil, waiting a few seconds before adding each piece. Putting too much fish into the oil all at once lowers the frying temperature too much and you end up "boiling in oil" rather than "frying."

5—Don't overcrowd the fish! Give each fillet or nugget space to fry.

6—For perfect fried fish, an 8- to 10-ounce fillet should be placed into the Crisco rounded side down and cooked for 2 minutes . . . then turned over and cooked for 1 minute . . . then turned over again and cooked for another minute. The fillet will come out crispy-crunchy on the outside and remain light and juicy on the inside.

7—Once they are fried, drain each fillet on several thicknesses of absorbent paper towels and serve them right away with fresh-squeezed lemons, sautéed onion rings, or tartar sauce.

Follow this recipe and *I promise* you the best fried fish you ever had!

Frank's Creamy Shrimp Sauce for Fried Fish

Great for spooning over fried or broiled fish, pan-sauteed oysters, baked chicken, roasted or pan-fried turkey, and just about any pasta dish. It's even good over plain French bread.

2 tbsp. Crisco oil	**1 tbsp. paprika**
½ cup finely sliced green onions	**½ cup cold shrimp stock**
3 cups chopped, peeled shrimp	**2 tbsp. cornstarch mixture**
1 cup reduced shrimp stock	**salt and white pepper to taste**
1 pint heavy whipping cream	**3 tbsp. finely chopped parsley**
2 tbsp. lemon juice	

First, take a skillet and heat the Crisco oil to medium high. Then toss in the green onions and sauté them until they wilt slightly (about 3 minutes).

Next, drop in the chopped shrimp and quickly stir-fry the pieces until they just turn pink and the juices begin to render out. *Do not overcook them or they'll get rubbery!*

At this point, turn the fire up to high and stir in the cup of shrimp stock and the whipping cream, making sure to blend the two ingredients together well. Then stir in the lemon juice, sprinkle on the paprika, and allow the mixture to cook at a *quick bubble* for about 5 minutes. (*Note:* Keep a close eye on the pot—if the heat is too high the cream will boil over the sides and make a mess.)

When you're ready to eat, mix together the cold shrimp stock and the cornstarch until smooth, and stir it quickly into the liquid in the skillet while it's bubbling.

Immediately, the cream sauce will thicken to a shiny gloss—if it's a little too thick for your liking, add a little more stock; if it's too thin, just add a little more cornstarch-shrimp stock mixture.

Finally, season the sauce to taste with the salt and white pepper and garnish it with a sprinkling of chopped parsley. To serve, ladle it generously over fried fish . . . *or anything else you wanna eat!*

Chef's Note: Using a cornstarch-water-stock mixture is an excellent way of thickening a gravy or sauce (especially when creating Oriental dishes). Just make sure you dissolve the cornstarch in cold *water or* cold *stock when you make the thickening mix. Hot water and cornstarch will lump . . . and it makes glue!*

Frank's Toasted Fish

This dish is an alternative to "Blackened Redfish," created and modified to be used with *any kind of fish*—not just redfish! It is my original formulation for what has since been renamed "Bronzed Fish."

1 12″ Teflon or Silverstone-coated skillet	6 fresh lean fish fillets
2 tsp. margarine per fillet	2 tsp. salt
1 tbsp. chopped shallots per fillet	1 tsp. black pepper
	1 tbsp. white wine per fillet

Start off by turning your stovetop or range to *high* and placing the skillet on the burner. It is essential that this recipe be done in a Teflon or Silverstone-coated skillet to compensate for the small amounts of oils used. Note, too, that the skillet must be heated to "hot" prior to adding the margarine (and you know it's hot enough when a drop of water sizzles off quickly).

At this point, add the margarine for each fillet you're going to cook, swish it around in the pan to coat the bottom, and drop in the shallots, stirring them in quickly and cooking them for about a minute or so. Then lightly season the fish fillets with salt and pepper, place them into the pan, and let them cook until the margarine begins to turn them a "toasty" color and the upper edges begin to turn opaque (about 4 minutes on each side for heavy-bodied fillets).

It is best if you turn the fillets only once—otherwise they might break apart. Your fillets will be ready to serve when the meat flakes easily with a fork. Keep in mind that all this time they're cooking on *high*.

Then when you're ready to serve them, add your white wine and swish the fillets back and forth in the pan until the alcohol burns off (about a minute or two), and the wine flavor is absorbed by the fillets.

Hint: You can also add bourbon or cognac instead of wine to vary the flavor. Experiment with them and treat your taste buds. I also suggest you top each fillet with some thinly sliced onions and a few drops of fresh lemon juice.

## CHAPTER 4

Poultry and Waterfowl

Frank's Turkey and Mushroom Italianne
(Mock Veal)

While you would ordinarily think of doing this dish with baby white veal, I can guarantee that no one will be able to tell that you substituted 69 cent per-pound sliced turkey for $9 per pound veal. Try this—it's magnificent!

10 slices of turkey breast
½ lb. fresh mushrooms, sliced
1 cup whole milk
3 eggs, slightly beaten
¼ cup Crisco oil
½ stick butter
salt and pepper to taste

Coating Mixture:

2 cups French bread crumbs
1 cup grated Romano cheese

The first thing you do is salt and pepper your turkey slices. Then make a "wash" by whipping the eggs and milk together and dip the turkey slices (one at a time) into it. Now, batter each slice thoroughly with the coating mixture and place them aside on waxed paper to "set." After each turkey slice has been coated, make your topping sauce.

Topping Sauce:

1 stick butter
1 cup finely chopped onions
3 cloves finely chopped fresh garlic
¼ cup finely chopped bell pepper
½ cup finely chopped celery
1 cup finely chopped shallots
1 cup chicken or turkey stock

2 cups heavy cream
1 tbsp. Italian seasoning
1 tsp. basil
1 large can petit pois peas
1 tbsp. finely chopped and drained pimentos
salt and white pepper to taste
1 cup finely chopped black olives
1 tsp. finely chopped parsley

First, melt the butter in a saucepan just until it begins to foam. Then "gently sauté" the onions, garlic, bell peppers, celery, and shallots, until they clear and soften. When the vegetable mix has cooked, stir in the remaining ingredients *one at a time* (except the black olives and parsley), and cook gently over a medium fire until the sauce thickens to your desired consistency (about 20 minutes).

Now go ahead and add your salt and pepper to taste . . . and *taste as you cook!* This sauce is great all by itself! Keep it simmering over a low fire (stirring occasionally) and add the parsley 3 minutes before you serve it.

To Serve the Dish . . .

In a 12-inch skillet, melt a small amount of the butter and oil together (about 2 tablespoons), bring it to high heat, and quickly stir-fry your sliced mushrooms.

Next, with the mushrooms still in the pan, bring the remaining oil-butter mix up to medium-high heat and toss in the turkey slices. Now fry them until they turn a crispy, *honey-colored* brown (about 3 minutes on each side should do it—you don't want to overcook them!).

And when you're ready to serve, ladle out some of the sauce in the bottom of a heated dinner plate, place the hot turkey slices into the sauce, and garnish them liberally with the sliced mushrooms, chopped black olives, and parsley. This is magnificent!

Hint: I suggest you serve this dish with cheese-baked New Orleans potatoes, smothered eggplant, tossed green beans, and garlic bread!

Frank's Double-Baked Thanksgiving Ducks

If this year you'd like to give a turkey a break, try fixing my "Double-Baked Thanksgiving Ducks." The nice thing about this recipe is that it's exceedingly simple and it's unlike any other baked duck dish you ever had—the insides are tender and juicy and the outside is crunchy crisp! It's the nicest thing you'll do for your tastebuds in a long time!

3 Long Island domestic ducks
   (4-5 pounds each)
salt and pepper to taste
poultry seasoning to taste

I told you this was a simple recipe! Watch this!

Take the ducks out of their plastic wrappers and dry them off with paper towels. Do not—*I repeat!*—do not try to remove any of the duck fat! It will render out when cooking!

Then merely sprinkle them inside and out with the salt, pepper, and poultry seasoning . . . and with your hands rub them down briskly and thoroughly, making sure the seasonings are forced into the duck skin.

At this point, set your oven to 450 degrees and preheat it. When the thermostat indicates the right temperature, place the ducks in a large baking pan, breast-side up (but don't let them touch!), and cook them on the middle rack of the oven for 30 minutes. Then—after a half-hour—turn them over in the pan (breast-side down) and bake them for 20 minutes more at 450 degrees. Finally, turn them back right side up and bake them for another 10 minutes.

Now . . . take them out of the oven and let them cool to room temperature (or put them in your refrigerator). When you're ready to eat, preheat the oven again to 400 degrees, put the cold ducks back into a baking pan, and slide the pan back into the oven.

Expect to bake them for about 20-30 minutes . . . what you want is for the inside to get piping hot and juicy, and the outside skin to get crispy and crunchy! Believe me—it will!

Hint: It isn't necessary to pour off the duck fat as the ducks cook the first time—I promise, the birds won't be greasy. Of course, go ahead and remove the drippings from the pan for the second baking. I suggest you use the duck drippings that fall into the pan to make duck stock or paté—it's wonderful!

Remember—"Double-Baked Ducks" are cooked unstuffed. If you want to stuff them with cornbread, andouille, oyster, or wild rice dressing, stuff them with hot-baked dressing just before you serve them (about 15 minutes).

When ready to serve, carve the breasts into slices, cut the leg and thigh off the carcass, and top with Spiced Orange Sauce (or whatever other sauce you wish to serve). One duck will serve two persons! I recommend you take the remaining duck bones, brown them in the oven, and turn them into duck stock.

Frank's New Orleans
Chicken and Dumplings

This is one of the most classic of Southern dishes—rich in flavor, tempting in texture, and easy to make. Try this recipe—following all the hints to the letter—and you'll make the best chicken and dumplings since Scarlett O'Hara had Rhett Butler over for dinner!

2 fryer chickens, cut into pieces
water to cover chicken
½ cup white wine
10 baby onions
1 large white onion, chopped
    fine
1 rib celery, chopped fine
2 carrots, diced
½ bell pepper, chopped fine
2 bay leaves

¼ tsp. marjoram
¼ tsp. thyme
2 cloves
5 cracked peppercorns
3 cups whole milk
⅓ cup flour
⅓ cup butter
salt, black pepper, and cayenne
    to taste

First, take the *unskinned* chicken pieces, drop them into a large stock pot, and measure out just enough water to cover them. Then remove the chicken pieces and set them aside.

Next, bring the water to a boil and toss in the wine, the baby onions, chopped white onions, celery, carrots, bell pepper, bay leaves, marjoram, thyme, cloves, and cracked peppercorns. Now, let the mixture boil for about 5 minutes to form a rich-flavored stock.

At this point, drop in the chicken pieces and cook them covered *at a gentle boil* until tender—about 45 minutes to 1 hour. This is also a good time to make the light butter roux you'll need to thicken the finished gravy. Just take a wire whip, mix the butter and the flour together in a skillet, and cook over medium heat until smooth (but not browned).

When the chicken is done, remove it from the pot, and let it cool enough for you to handle it. Then remove the bones and the skin, arrange the chicken meat in large chunks on a serving platter, cover it, and place it in a warm oven.

Now, while the chicken is cooking, make your dumplings. Here's what you'll need:

1½ cups of sifted all-purpose flour	**¾ cup milk**
2 tsp. baking powder	**1 cup finely chopped pre-cooked chicken**
¾ tsp. salt	**3 tbsp. finely chopped green onions**
2 tbsp. shortening	
1 egg, beaten to a froth	**1 tbsp. chopped parsley**

First, sift together the flour, baking powder, and salt. Then, with a knife or baker's tool, cut the shortening into the flour until the mixture is light and uniform. Next whip the egg and milk together until frothy and stir it into the flour mixture—*but stir only until well-blended!* Then *very gently fold* into the mixture the cup of chopped chicken, the green onions, and the parsley.

At this point, skim off all the excess fat from the chicken stock, bring it back to a gentle boil, and stir in the 3 cups of milk. Then, by spoonfuls, drop the dumplings into the boiling chicken gravy (every so often, while adding the dumplings, push them down into the gravy). When they're all in, cook at a gentle boil for 15 minutes in a tightly covered pot. *Under no circumstances do you remove the cover—if you do, the dumplings will be heavy instead of light.*

Then, when you're ready to eat, take the platter of chicken from the oven and place the dumplings all around it. Now . . . stir enough of the roux you made earlier into the hot gravy to thicken it to the consistency you want, season it with salt, black pepper, and cayenne to taste, and ladle the gravy over the platter of chicken and dumplings.

Serve with hot French bread and a crisp salad!

Notes: If you dip the spoon in the hot gravy before scooping up the dumplings, the batter mix will slide off the spoon a whole lot easier.

To make square dumplings, make your dough according to the recipe above (but use buttermilk instead of whole milk and leave out the chopped chicken, green onions, and parsley). Then knead the dough thoroughly, wrap in plastic film, and place it in the refrigerator for about 4 hours. Then roll it out "very thin" between wax paper, cut it into strips and cut the strips into 1-inch squares. Dust each dumpling lightly with extra flour and drop into boiling gravy.

Frank's Smothered Black Pot Chicken

This is one of the tastiest things you can do to a chicken . . . and easy too! And after you eat all the chicken, you're gonna need a loaf of French bread just to sop up the gravy!!!

2 spring chickens (skinned)	1 cup diced fresh carrots
2 tbsp. poultry seasoning	3 bay leaves
½ cup vegetable oil	2 tsp. sweet basil
3 large onions, sliced in rings	salt and black pepper to taste
½ cup coarsely chopped celery	3 tbsp. cornstarch + ½ cup
½ coarsely chopped fresh bell	water
pepper	2 tbsp. minced parsley
½ lb. sliced mushrooms	2 tbsp. chopped green onions
½ cup chicken stock	

Take the chickens and cut them into serving pieces, wash them thoroughly, and remove all the fat. Then season them well with salt, black pepper, and poultry seasoning.

At this point add your vegetable oil to a black cast-iron 6-quart Dutch oven and get it to the point of "just smoking." Then drop in the onions, celery, bell peppers, and mushrooms and fry them until they caramelize (turn dark brown). When the seasoning vegetables are cooked, remove them from the Dutch oven with a slotted spoon and set them aside in a strainer placed over a bowl.

Then—using the same oil you used to caramelize the seasoning vegetables—drop in and quickly fry the chicken pieces until they brown slightly. When fully seared, remove the chicken from the pot and set it aside.

Now bring the pot back to "high heat," stir in the chicken stock, and bring it to a boil. At this point you want to "deglaze" the pot (take a spoon and scrape off the bottom all the "debris" that stuck to the pot as the chicken browned). Then—*in alternating layers*—add the chicken and the sautéed vegetables back to the Dutch oven (along with the carrots, bay leaves, and sweet basil). And when all the ingredients are in, reduce the heat and simmer everything until the chicken is tender (or until the meat starts to fall away from the bone—about an hour or so).

When you're ready to eat, remove the chicken from the pot and place it on a platter. Then bring the "pot liquor" to a boil, toss in a sprinkling of parsley and green onions, stir in 3 tablespoons of cornstarch mixed with ½ cup cold water to turn the pot liquor to a smooth sauce, and ladle it over the platter of chicken.

Hints: This dish is best when served with buttered noodles and fresh homemade biscuits. It also goes great with wild rice, glazed carrots, sautéed zucchini, and a tossed spinach salad.

For an even easier version of this dish . . . Quickly sauté the seasoning vegetables until they caramelize. Then toss all the remaining ingredients into the Dutch oven (in layers), cover the pot, and slide it into a preheated 325-degree oven.

Then about an hour and a half later, take the pot from the oven, remove the cover, and place the chicken pieces on a serving platter. All that's left is to bring the gravy to a boil, thicken it with a little cornstarch mixed in cold water, spoon it over the chicken, *and eat!*

While it's cooking, you don't baste it, you don't stir it, you don't even check it! Now that's easy, y'all!

Frank's Classic Chicken Cacciatore

There's chicken in tomato sauce . . . chicken in Italian sucre . . . and chicken in marinara. And then there's "Chicken Cacciatore"—*the classic variety!* And believe me, real cacciatore is a lot more than chicken cooked in red gravy. It has a richness that comes together only after the various flavors of the ingredients marry. And here's how you do it!

1 large chicken, skinned and cut into pieces
4 tbsp. extra virgin olive oil
6 cloves whole garlic, peeled
2 cups chicken stock
1 large onion, sliced
½ medium-size bell pepper, diced
½ lb. quartered mushroom buttons

10 anchovy fillets, chopped
1½ cups dry red wine or dry sherry
4 tbsp. red wine vinegar
2 tsp. rosemary
6 sprigs fresh basil (or 1 tsp. dry basil)
½ tsp. Italian seasoning
1 can tomato paste
salt and pepper to taste

First, in a heavy Dutch oven (preferably cast-iron) heat the olive oil and sauté the chicken and garlic until lightly browned . . . (but remember to stir everything constantly so that the garlic doesn't burn!). Then remove the chicken from the pot and set it aside momentarily.

Next, take half of the chicken stock, add it to the Dutch oven over high heat, and de-glaze the pot. When all the residue is scraped off the bottom and the stock is reduced by one-half its volume, stir in the onions, bell pepper, and mushrooms and cook them until wilted (about 5 minutes).

Now place the chicken back in the pot, add the chopped anchovies, wine, wine vinegar, rosemary, basil, and Italian seasonings, and stir everything together gently.

At this point, dissolve the tomato paste in the chicken stock you have left and pour it evenly over the ingredients in the pot. Then cover the Dutch oven tightly, reduce the heat to low, and simmer gently for about 15 minutes.

Finally, taste the sauce, add the amount of salt and pepper you desire, cover the pot again and continue simmering on low for another 45 minutes to 1 hour (or until the chicken is tender).

Hints:

1—Do not leave out the anchovies! Even if you don't like anchovies put 'em in! I promise you won't taste them, but you lose the unique flavor of the dish if you eliminate them.

2—I suggest you serve the cacciatore piping hot over fettuccine noodles topped with grated Romano cheese, garlic bread, and a chilled glass of wine.

3—Once the chicken begins to cook, be sure to stir the pot gently or you'll break the meat off the bone.

4—You can make a variety of other cacciatores using this recipe by simply substituting other meats for the chicken—for example, turkey, veal, beef, pork, venison, squirrel, and rabbit all work well. Remember, cacciatore means "hunter's stew."

Spiced Orange Duck Sauce
With Grand Marnier

Ladle this over your "Double-Baked Ducks" (or any cut of poultry or pork, for that matter!) and you just won't believe the accompanying flavor you'll get! And this is so simple to make!

2 large cans of frozen orange juice	**½ cup of Grand Marnier Liqueur**
1 cup of duck or chicken stock (from drippings)	**2 tbsp. soy sauce**
	1 tsp. ground ginger
1 tsp. fresh orange zest (outer orange peel)	**2 tbsp. unsalted butter**
	1 tsp. whole cloves

In a saucepan, melt down the frozen orange juice and bring it to a "gentle boil." Then slowly stir in the stock (remember—you make this by adding a cup of water to the drippings that stuck to the pan in which you baked the ducks, the chicken, or the pork).

Continue to cook the sauce gently over *medium heat* until it begins to thicken slightly. Then add the orange zest and the Grand Marnier Liqueur and simmer the mixture until the alcohol evaporates (about 4-5 minutes).

At this point, add the soy sauce, the ground ginger, and the butter and *agitate* (do not stir!) the pan until the butter dissolves and the sauce takes on a sheen.

Finally, drop in the cloves and allow the sauce to set (covered) for about 10 minutes before ladling it over the baked ducks, chicken, or pork.

Hint: As a garnish, fresh orange slices can be cooked into the sauce and placed on the duck for presentation. If you want to make a "Sweetened Orange Sauce," stir in ¼ cup of light Karo corn syrup!

Frank's Roasted Cornish Game Hens

Take a break this year from the Christmas turkey . . . try fixing my "Oven-Roasted Cornish Game Hens." The nice thing about the little critters is they're relatively inexpensive, they're simple and easy to fix, and they're scrumptiously tender and juicy.

6 Rock Cornish game hens (one per person)
1 stick margarine (softened)
2 tbsp. salt
1 tbsp. black pepper
2 tbsp. poultry seasoning

Remember how simple the recipe was for the "Double-Baked Ducks"? Well, this recipe is just that simple. In fact, it's done practically the same way, except for the roasting technique. Here's how:

First off, completely thaw out the birds—and remember to *thaw them in the refrigerator* (it should take you 12 to 15 hours). When they're ready to cook, take the game hens out of their plastic wrappers, remove the giblets, clean the inside cavities well, and dry them off with paper towels.

Then merely sprinkle them inside and out with the salt, pepper, and poultry seasoning. And, with your hands, rub in the softened margarine. Now don't fool around—rub dem hens! Do it briskly and thoroughly, making sure the seasonings are forced into the skin.

At this point, take 4 small pieces of aluminum foil and wrap the ends of the drumsticks and wingtips. Then with a piece of butcher's twine, tie the drumsticks together.

Next, set your oven at *450 degrees* and preheat it. And when the thermostat indicates the right temperature, place the hens on a baking rack over a large baking pan (breast-side up without touching!)

All you do now is cook them for about 12-15 minutes (or until the skin turns a pretty honey-colored brown). Then turn the oven down to *300 degrees* and let them bake for another 45 minutes to an hour (or until the juices run a "beige" color—not pink—when you pierce the hens with an ice pick). I also suggest that every 15 minutes while they're cooking, you take a pastry brush and baste them with melted margarine, just to add a little extra crispyness to the outer skin.

When you think you have about 15 minutes cooking time left, take the hens out of the oven, cut away the butcher's twine, remove the foil from the wings and drumsticks so they'll brown, and stuff each game hen with *hot* wild rice dressing (cold dressing will drop the cooking temperature too much). Then put them back into the oven to finish them off.

And when you're ready to eat, generously pour on a ladle-full of green pepper jelly sauce and serve them piping hot on top of a slice of buttered toast.

Frank's Casserole Cordon Bleu

Usually, cordon bleu is recognized as chicken rolled around bacon or ham and Swiss Cheese . . . then baked and served with vegetables. But in this recipe, I've taken the chicken, ham, bacon, and Swiss, combined them with the vegetables—broccoli and carrots—and baked everything into a casserole, topped it with a creamed chicken sauce, and dished it out with red pommes petite (little potatoes). You're gonna love it!

½ lb. crumbled bacon
  (and drippings)
4 cups chopped chicken pieces
flour for dusting chicken
Crisco oil for frying
1 large finely chopped onion
½ cup finely chopped celery
½ cup coarsely chopped ham
1 cup shredded fresh carrots
1 pat butter
½ cup plain bread crumbs

3 cups fresh or frozen broccoli
  florets
2 cups shredded Swiss cheese
2 cups chicken stock (from
  chicken bones)
1 cup heavy cream
½ cup cream sherry
1 tsp. sweet basil
½ tsp. rosemary
dash thyme
salt and black pepper to taste

Start off by frying down the bacon in a hot 12-inch skillet until it turns crispy. Then drain the strips on paper towels and crumble them into small bits and pieces—*but save the drippings!*

Next, take the scraps from the chicken you de-boned and boil it into a rich stock. While you're making stock, salt and pepper the chicken parts and dust them in flour. Then drop each piece into the bacon drippings and quickly sauté them until *just tender*—remember, you're going to bake the dish so you don't want the chicken overcooked.

Now quickly stir-fry the onion, celery, ham pieces, and carrots (if you still have bacon drippings left, use it—if not, use a little Crisco oil). Then, in a large bowl, mix together all the ingredients you sautéed (along with the bacon and chicken) and set them aside so that the flavors blend.

While the cordon bleu mix is cooling, butter an 11-by-14 baking pan and lightly coat it with bread crumbs. Then, layer by layer, begin putting in the broccoli, chicken mixture, and Swiss cheese until the pan is filled.

Finally, in a saucepan, combine the heavy cream, the cream sherry, and the chicken stock (along with the basil, rosemary, and thyme), and reduce the liquid to one-half of its original volume. Then readjust your salt and pepper to taste, ladle the mixture over the broccoli and chicken casserole, and bake at 350 degrees for about 20-30 minutes or until the dish turns hot and bubbly.

Suggestions: This recipe goes great with pommes petite (which are little red potatoes you boil till tender then fry quickly in a sparse amount of Crisco oil till crunchy brown), and a crispy tossed salad topped with Caesar dressing.

Frank's N'Awlins Slow-Roasted Turkey

When it comes to cooking the holiday turkey, few recipes will turn out a prettier more tender bird than this one. Because it's roasted slowly in dry heat, unwrapped and unstuffed, you get a picture-perfect presentation; but more importantly, you get one of the juiciest turkeys you ever ate because the slow roasting bastes the bird as it cooks. Try this recipe once, and you'll never again roast a turkey any other way!

1 fresh or frozen turkey, 14-18 lb. average*	**2 tbsp. salt**
4 tbsp. poultry seasoning	**2 tbsp. black pepper**
	½ cup softened margarine

First, put the turkey in the sink under cold running water and wash it thoroughly, making sure to remove all the debris from the internal cavity. Then, with paper towels, pat the bird dry inside and out and place it onto a sheet of waxed paper on the countertop. At this point, you also want to preheat your oven to 500 degrees.

Next, season the turkey front and back, inside and out, with the poultry seasoning, salt, and pepper. And I don't mean just sprinkle it on—rub those seasonings into the bird hard! Then, with the margarine, massage the bird liberally—again both inside and out—until the margarine coats the skin completely. And be sure you put butter up under the skin too!

Now place the turkey breast-side up into a high-sided baking pan large enough to hold the bird *plus* whatever juices will be rendered out (and you will get juices!). Then tightly wrap the ends of the wing tips and drumsticks with a 4-by-4 square of aluminum foil (this keeps the tips from burning). Do not wrap the bird in foil, do not tent it, and do not put it into a baking bag! Cook it completely uncovered!

When your thermostat indicates that the oven is at 500 degrees, slide the turkey in . . . *but watch it closely.* It should brown to a honey color in about 20 minutes or less. And that's all you want it to do—just turn a honey brown.

Now, as soon as it reaches the right color (which actually seals the skin and holds in natural moisture) reduce the temperature to 200 degrees. Then slow-roast the turkey until it is tender and juicy. It should take you 40 to 50 minutes to the pound, depending upon the insulation of your oven.

After it's cooked, you may take a sheet of heavy-duty aluminum foil and cover the turkey to keep it warm and to prevent it from drying out. When you're ready to eat, place the bird onto a serving platter, move it to the table, and carve it fresh for your family and dinner guests. A gravy made from the pan drippings can be used as a topping.

----

*You can prepare either a fresh or frozen turkey this way. But if you use a frozen turkey, it *must* be thoroughly thawed out before you attempt to cook it. And I recommend that you thaw it *in the refrigerator* (it takes about 3 days). Just remember, to prevent contamination, *never, never, never thaw on the countertop, or in the sink, or at room temperature!* I also recommend that to cook the turkey to perfection you use a meat thermometer—just place it into the breast so that it doesn't touch any bone and bake until the temperature gauge reaches 185 degrees.

Frank's Back-A-Town Chicken

This has got to be one of the easiest recipes you'll ever fix! You heard of "throwing it all together"? Well . . . this is as close as you're gonna get! Yet it's as perfect for a dinner party as it is for a relaxing weekend with the family!

4 tbsp. margarine
3 large onions, thick-sliced
1 large frying chicken, cut in
 pieces
1 tbsp. poultry seasoning
2 tsp. sweet basil
2 tsp. salt
1 tsp. black pepper
1 tsp. cayenne pepper

1 lb. andouille sausage, sliced
1 cup fresh mushrooms, halved
3 carrots, peeled and chunked
½ cup celery, thinly sliced
2 cloves garlic, finely minced
½ cup green onions, chunked
½ small bell pepper, sliced
2 cups cream of chicken soup

In a heavy cast-iron Dutch oven, melt the margarine over high heat and fry the sliced onions (stirring constantly) for about 10 minutes until they turn a dark brown (caramelize).

While the onions are cooking—*and this is the only ingredient that you will precook in this recipe!*—skin the chicken, wash it well, and sprinkle each piece thoroughly with poultry seasoning, basil, salt, and black and cayenne pepper.

Next, remove all but a thin layer of caramelized onions from the Dutch oven. Then a little at a time, alternating as you go, start adding the chicken and all of the remaining ingredients (including the browned onions but not the soup) to the Dutch oven. (*Note:* Don't put any liquid in the pot! It will make it's own gravy!)

Now, preheat the oven to 350 degrees, put the lid on the Dutch oven, and bake the dish covered for about an hour and a half or until the chicken starts to fall off the bone.

Then, when you're ready to eat, remove the chicken from the Dutch oven, place it on a serving platter, and stir the cream of chicken soup into the pot liquor (*and there will be pot liquor!*). All that's left is to simmer the gravy until it is hot and bubbly and ladle it over the chicken. Uuuuummmmmmm!

Suggestion: Serve with baked potatoes, buttered mixed vegetables, crispy French bread, and chilled iced tea.

Frank's Turkey Fricassee

A "fricassee" is a Cajun stew—it's a method of cooking small pieces of poultry or meats in a braising liquid that has been thickened with a roux. The most popular form of this dish is Chicken Fricassee . . . but wait till you taste it with turkey!

1 stick margarine	**6 cloves finely chopped garlic**
¼ cup of Crisco oil	**2 bay leaves**
1 young turkey (10 lb.),	**6 cups turkey stock**
de-boned	**8 small potatoes, quartered**
½ cup all-purpose flour	**2 carrots, julienned**
2 cups coarsely chopped onions	**1 tbsp. fresh lemon juice**
½ cup coarsely chopped green	**2 tbsp. poultry seasoning**
onions	**salt, cayenne, and black pepper**
1 cup coarsely chopped celery	**to taste**
½ cup coarsely chopped bell	
pepper	

In a 6-quart black iron Dutch oven, heat the margarine-oil mixture over high heat until well-blended . . . *but do not let it burn.*

Meanwhile, cut the de-boned turkey (light and dark meat) into small serving pieces and season them with salt, black and cayenne pepper, and poultry seasoning. Now, add the pieces to the Dutch oven and quickly brown them—and you should keep them continuously moving in the pot so that they don't stick.

When they're browned, remove them from the pot and set them aside momentarily in a large bowl.

At this point—*with the heat still on high*—add your flour and make a dark brown roux. When your roux is the color you want it, toss in the chopped vegetables, stir them into the flour, and cook everything together well for about 5 minutes. Now, when your vegetables have wilted in the hot roux, toss in the turkey pieces (plus any drippings that collected in the bowl while they were set aside).

Next, add your turkey stock, lemon juice, garlic, and bay leaves, and stir them into the roux mix. This is when you should adjust the quantity of liquid to the consistency you desire—*just keep in mind that a "fricassee" should not be pasty, but it shouldn't be liquidy either.*

Now, bring the fricassee to a *quick* boil, lower the heat to simmer, put the lid on the pot, and cook slowly for 30 minutes. At this point, readjust your seasonings to taste (keeping in mind that a fricassee should be spicy!), toss in your quartered potatoes and julienned carrots, stir everything together once more, and continue cooking on low until all the flavors have married and the turkey, potatoes, and carrots are succulently tender—which should take another 30 minutes or so.

Then, when you're ready to eat, spoon the fricassee over steamed rice and serve with a compliment of succotash and hot buttered buns.

It's so good, you'll swear your family had to come from Thibodaux!

Frank's N'Awlins Cheepie Chicken

It's inexpensive (cheap, really!) . . . it's simple to fix . . . it's really Southern . . . and anybody can make it. It's kinda sweet and kinda sour, but it's tasty enough to make you kiss your mother-in-law!

5 lb. chicken wings (25 wings)	**1 cup chicken stock**
3 tbsp. poultry seasoning	**¼ cup red wine vinegar**
3 tbsp. margarine	**2 tbsp. Worcestershire sauce**
1 cup chopped onions	**2 tbsp. Dijon mustard**
½ cup chopped celery	**¾ cup molasses**
½ cup sliced green onions	**4 tbsp. honey**
½ cup chopped bell pepper	**1 tsp. cinnamon**
1 head baked garlic	**1 cup Crisco oil**
2 10 oz. cans Rotel tomatoes with chilies	**salt and pepper to taste**

First, take the chicken wings, sprinkle them liberally with the poultry seasoning and the salt and pepper, and set them aside to pick up the flavors.

Meanwhile—in a 4-quart saucepan—begin making your *Cheepie Sauce* by sautéing the onions, celery, green onions, bell pepper, and baked garlic in the margarine. You want to cook the vegetables only until they soften (which should take about 3 or 4 minutes).

Then, using a food processor, puree the Rotel tomatoes, add them to the sautéed vegetables (along with the chicken stock), and stir everything together until well-blended.

Now bring the mixture to a boil and begin adding the remaining ingredients (except the Crisco oil) *one at a time, stirring continuously.* You'll notice that the sauce will turn from a *tomato red* to *barbecue sauce brown* and begin to thicken—that's because the natural sugars in the tomato, plus the honey and molasses, are starting to caramelize. At this point, turn the fire down to simmer, cover the pot, and let the sauce cook for 15 minutes.

Then while your sauce is simmering, heat the cup of Crisco oil to medium-high in a heavy 12-inch skillet and drop in the chicken wings. Stirring constantly, fry them quickly almost all the way through (about 3 to 5 minutes). Then drop them into the sauce and simmer them at a slow bubble for another 15-20 minutes until they're done.

I suggest you serve "Frank's Cheepie Chicken" with toast points, pan-broiled potatoes, buttered green beans, and a crisp lettuce wedge topped with bleu cheese dressing.

Frank's Smothered Game Hens With Artichoke Hearts and Wild Rice

Say Rock Cornish game hens and everyone wants to pack them full of stuffing and roast them. But why not try smothering the little succulent critters in their own juices—with maybe a hint of white wine!—and some artichoke hearts? They're so good that way . . . make you slap your Momma's Momma!

6 tbsp. margarine
4 large red onions, sliced
½ cup celery, diced
¼ cup red and green bell peppers, diced
4 carrots, quartered and chunked
4 Rock Cornish game hens, quartered

3 bay leaves
1 cup artichoke hearts, drained and washed
1 cup mushrooms, sliced
1 cup white wine (Chablis)
¼ cup parsley, finely chopped
salt and black pepper to taste

The first thing you do is quarter the game hens and wash and clean them well under running water. Then pat them dry with paper towels and liberally salt and pepper them.

Next, take 3 tablespoons of the margarine, add them to a 6-quart cast-iron Dutch oven (one with a tight-fitting lid), and place it on the stovetop over high heat. When the margarine sizzles, toss in the onions and fry them down until they turn a dark brown (or until they caramelize).

At this point, quickly stir in the mushrooms and the remaining seasoning vegetables and cook them with the onions over high heat for about 3 minutes (or until they wilt). Now, with a strainer spoon, remove the vegetables from the Dutch oven and set them aside.

Next, take the remaining 3 tablespoons of margarine and add them to the Dutch oven. And on high heat again, fry the game hens until they turn brown all over and remove them from the pot.

Now, begin putting back into the pot (in layers) some of the game hens, some seasoning vegetables, some artichoke hearts—just keep adding until all the ingredients are back in the pot and mixed well. Then toss in the bay leaves and the white wine . . . *but save the parsley.*

At this point, put the lid on the Dutch oven, cut the heat down to *"low,"* and let the hens simmer for about an hour (or until very tender). *But don't overcook 'em or they'll fall apart!*

Then when you're ready to eat, serve the hens piping hot alongside wild rice (or creamed potatoes) and garnish them with the finely chopped parsley.

Note: Because you don't skin the game hens to make this dish, and you slow cook the margarine, it's common for some oils to float to the top of the pot when the dish is done. You can skim most of it off—or if you want to make the hens (and the sauce!) grease-free, simply remove them from the pot, strain the sauce, and place it in the freezer for about 30 minutes to congeal. At this point you simply lift off the solid fat, reheat the sauce (along with the hens) in a baking pan in the oven, and . . . presto! No grease, Ma!

Frank's Cajun Pot-Roasted Duck

This is one of the simplest and best tasting recipes for wild duck you'll ever get. And after you eat all the duck, you're gonna need a loaf of French bread just to sop up the gravy!!! (Incidentally . . . this recipe can also be used for rabbit, squirrel, and chicken!)

3 large wild ducks, skinned
2 tsp. salt
1 tsp. white pepper
1 tsp. black pepper
1 tsp. cayenne pepper
½ cup Crisco oil
2 large white onions, sliced
1 cup dry white wine (Chablis Blanc preferred)

3 cloves fresh garlic, chopped fine
½ fresh bell pepper, chopped coarse
1 rib fresh celery, chopped fine
3 bay leaves
1 tsp. thyme
1 tsp. sweet basil
salt to taste

First, take the ducks and cut them into serving pieces, wash them well, and remove all the fat. Then sprinkle them liberally with salt, white, black, and cayenne pepper, and rub the seasonings into the meat.

Now, take a 6-quart cast-iron Dutch oven and add the Crisco oil to it. You want to heat the oil to the point of *just smoking*. Then fry down the duck pieces until they turn nice and brown. When totally seared, remove the duck from the pot and add your onion slices. Now fry them over high heat until they *almost burn!* This is called *caramelizing,* which converts the acid in the onions to natural sugars and makes the resultant gravy rich and tasty.

When the onions are cooked, put the ducks back in the pot and mix everything together well. Then pour in the wine and mix again. Now put the lid on, reduce the heat to medium low, and let the ducks smother *for about 15 minutes*.

At this point, add the rest of the seasoning vegetables, stir in the bay leaves and spices, readjust the salt and pepper to taste, and stir everything again until evenly blended and the duck pieces are thoroughly coated. Now put the lid back on the pot, reduce the fire to *low,* and *simmer* the duck for about 45 minutes to an hour (or until the meat starts to fall away from the bone).

Hints: Watch your liquid level in the pot—forget about any excess Crisco because it will be absorbed!—and add ¼ cup at a time of water or chicken stock if needed. Keep in mind that all you want is enough liquid for gravy—you don't want duck soup! I also suggest that when you check the gravy level, you also baste the ducks.

This dish is best when served with wild rice, glazed carrots, sautéed zucchini, and a tossed spinach salad. You can garnish the duck with chopped parsley. Oh . . . and have a lot of French bread handy—the gravy is the best part!

CREATING HOLIDAY ENTREES

Goose, game hens, ham, veal pocket, crown roast, pork shoulder, venison . . . they're all excellent choices for the festive table. But for some reason or another, it always seems to be the roasted turkey or duck that usually rank the highest on the holiday popularity list. With that in mind, then, let me give you a few quick and easy chef's tips for fixing them the best you ever had!

Turkey

First and foremost, you don't have to pay a premium price to have a juicy turkey for the holidays. Because the secret to *juiciness* is not in the butter-basting, or the oil injection, or even in those little gizmos that are supposed to pop up when the bird is done. The secret is in the cooking technique.

Of course, it does help to buy a "hen" turkey instead of a "tom," because routinely the hens are tender and the toms are less tender (notice, I said less tender . . . not tough!). Because even if you end up with a tom, if you cook the old gobbler right you still got a succulent piece of poultry to feed your family.

And here's how you do it!

If the turkey is frozen, thaw him out completely. *In the refrigerator!* Not on top of the counter! Not in the sink! In the refrigerator. It should take about 3 days for an 18-pound turkey to completely defrost in the fridge. Give yourself enough time to do it right.

Next, wash him thoroughly under cold running water, being careful to remove every trace of debris from inside the cavity. After he's washed, pat him dry inside and out with absorbent paper towels.

Then sprinkle him liberally with salt and pepper, rub him all over with margarine, and douse him down good with a good grade of poultry seasoning.

Now, wrap the tips of both the drumsticks and the wings with aluminum foil, tie the drumsticks together with twine, and place him breast-side-up into a deep-sided baking pan. Then—*unstuffed and uncovered*—slide him into a preheated oven and bake him at 500 degrees until he starts to turn a nice honey-brown all over (which should take you about 20 minutes, depending upon the operation of your thermostat).

Then, when he has browned sufficiently, drop the oven temperature down to *200 degrees* and continue cooking until the bird is tender and juicy. It's not scientifically accurate, but you can figure on baking him about 35 to 40 minutes to the pound, again depending upon your oven.

I do suggest that you baste him occasionally during the last hour of the cooking process . . . but don't open the oven *at all* for the first 3 or 4 hours!

I promise, you don't have to put him in a baking bag, you don't have to wrap him in foil, and you don't have to tent him. Just fix him using this *slow-cooking* method and this Thanksgiving, Christmas, or New Years you're going to end up with a beautifully browned turkey that's the tenderest and juiciest you ever ate!

Ducks

There's something special about a couple of roasted ducks. And it doesn't make any difference whether you're a hunter and you go out and get your own, or you're a housewife and you buy them at the supermarket. Well, maybe there's one difference. On the wild duck, you remove as much fat as possible to remove the musty, gamey flavor; while on the domestic duck, you remove no fat at all because that's where the rich flavor comes from.

But the cooking technique is the same! You cook hot! Real hot! I'm talking 450 degrees here! Here's what you do!

Take the ducks, wash them well inside and out, salt and pepper them liberally (again inside and out), rub them with margarine all over, and sprinkle them generously with poultry seasoning. Then place the ducks into a shallow roasting pan, slide them onto the center rack of a preheated oven, and bake them at 450 degrees—first breast-side-up for about 25 minutes, then breast-side-down for about 20 minutes, then breast-side-up again for about 15 minutes more. See, all in all you want to cook them for about an hour—*uncovered*.

Oh—you'll have a little smoke in the oven, but don't worry about it unless you haven't cleaned your oven recently.

Remember, if you cover meats in the oven, you're really steaming them. If you leave them exposed to the dry heat, you're roasting them and making them crispy on the outside and juicy on the inside.

Now here's your cooking trick. When they've baked for the allotted time, take them out of the oven and let them cool. In fact, cover them with plastic wrap, put them in the refrigerator, and let them get *cold*. Then when you're ready to eat, put them directly from the refrigerator back into the oven again—once more at 450 degrees—and cook them breast-up for another 30-35 minutes.

The final baking does the trick. It finishes cooking the duck through and through and it turns the skin into a super-crunchy crispy delicacy. And if you take the drippings from the baking pan and turn them into a complementary sauce . . . ummmmmm!

A little wild rice or oyster dressing on the side, a few spoonfuls of candied yams, a serving or two of buttered turnips, and a slice of Mom's apple pie a la mode and you'll swear you just landed at Plymouth Rock! I mean I'm talking serious good!

Happy Holidays, y'all!

CHAPTER 5

Wild Game

Frank's Venison Velveteen

Before you announce that you don't like venison . . . try this recipe. The combination of herbs and spices, the marination in whole milk, and the slow-cook bacon wrap produces a taste treat unequalled by almost any other meat. This is gooooood!

3 large onions, cut in slices	**1 lb. sliced bacon**
1 large bell pepper, cut in rings	**4 tbsp. Frank Davis Wild Game**
2 lb. venison filet or backstrap	**Seasoning***

First, wash the venison filets in cold running water and remove *all* the fat and sinew (membranes). Then place the filets in a plastic or glass container (NO METAL), cover with whole milk, and refrigerate for at least 12 hours.

Then, when you're ready to cook:

Preheat your oven to 400 degrees, butter an 11-by-14 baking pan (to keep the seasonings from sticking to the sides and bottom), and place the onion rings and bell pepper into the pan. Now put a meat rack on top of the vegetables.

When that's done, take the venison from the fridge, pour off all the milk marinade, and pat the meat dry with a paper towel. Next, thoroughly rub down each filet with *wild game seasoning* (or use the ingredients listed below) and set them aside for about 15 minutes to "cure."

Now, taking 1 strip of bacon at a time, start on the end of each filet and wrap the bacon around the filet (kinda like wrapping gauze around your finger). Continue the process (using as much bacon as necessary) until the entire filet is inside the bacon wrap. Pin all connecting strips with toothpicks.

At this point, place the venison on top of the meat rack (over the vegetables), slide it into the oven, and bake for 15 minutes. Then turn the filets over and bake them on the other side for another 15 minutes. And finally, reduce the oven temperature to 350 degrees, and bake an additional 15 minutes.

---

*If you can't find my wild game seasoning where you shop, simply sprinkle the venison lightly with salt, black pepper, onion powder, garlic powder, granulated sugar, rubbed sage, thyme, rosemary, and non-fat dry milk.

A full 45-minute cooking time should give you a medium-well piece of meat. If you like your meat medium-rare, cook only for 30 minutes. Either way, remember that the meat will continue to cook for 20 minutes after you remove it from the oven, so allow it to set about that long before slicing.

When you're ready to eat, slice the filets into small medallions and serve with buttered spinach, glazed carrots, scalloped potatoes, and chilled burgundy wine.

TO MAKE A SAUCE FOR THE VENISON, add one can of cream of chicken soup to the drippings and vegetables left in the baking pan. Then pour the mixture into a saucepan and cook over medium-high heat until it gets to the thickness and consistency you desire. Season with salt and pepper to taste.

Frank's Roasted Venison Fantastique

Regardless of your past experiences with venison . . . regardless of how many times you said, "I don't like venison!" . . . I want you to try this recipe before you make up your mind for once and for all! Because this is the best venison you ever had!

1 venison roast (4-6 lb. average)
½ gal. whole milk
1 head fresh garlic
1 lb. meaty bacon
2 large onions, chopped fine
½ medium bell pepper, chopped
  fine

2 ribs celery, chopped fine
2 tbsp. fresh parsley, chopped
  fine
salt and pepper to taste

Start off by letting your venison roast totally defrost in the bottom of the refrigerator. Then use a real sharp paring knife and take patience to trim every bit of fat and muscle covering off the roast. *This is the most important part of the entire recipe because it greatly affects the finished dish!* Don't skimp on the trimming!

Then wash the meat thoroughly in cold running water and put it into a baking pan or deep bowl, pour the milk over it, cover it with Saran Wrap, put it in the refrigerator, and let it marinate at least overnight. And regardless of what you may have heard, *do not marinate deer (or any other wild game) in vinegar! Use milk!* The lactic acid in milk breaks down the fibers, tenderizes the meat, and removes any unwanted "gamey" flavors.

When marination is finished, discard the milk, blot the excess from the meat with paper towels, place the roast on a baking rack, pierce it with small holes, and plug the holes with garlic cloves.

Next, take half-strips of bacon and push them into the slits on top of the garlic. Do this at various spots on the roast. The process is called "barding" and it moistens the meat—remember deer (and most wild game) tend to be dry and lean, so you have to add some kind of fat to make it juicy.

At this point, take your salt and pepper and rub it into the meat well. Then still using your hands, pack all of the chopped vegetables over the top and around the sides of the roast. Finally, working with one strip at a time, lay the rest of the bacon over the vegetables to form a "cap." You can either lay the strips side by side so that they slightly overlap, or separate them slightly. When finished, pin the edges of the strips with toothpicks to hold them in position as the roast cooks.

Now place the rack (with the roast on it) inside of your baking pan and add about 2 cups of water to the bottom of the pan. Then sear the meat quickly in a preheated oven at 450 degrees (about 15 minutes), and reduce the heat to 250 degrees and cook the roast slowly (about 30 minutes to the pound—just enough to get the bacon to "render out its drippings"). When the roast turns a golden brown and *beige-colored juices* run from it when pierced with a fork, the venison is done.

Hint: Remember that the roast will continue to cook about 20 minutes after you take it from the oven. So account for that when you calculate your cooking time as to whether you want it rare, medium, or well-done. For example, if you figure your roast needs to cook for 2 hours and 20 minutes to become medium-well, remove it from the oven after 2 hours and allow it to set on the countertop for another 20 minutes. It will come out perfect! Furthermore, you'll find that the roast will slice easier if you allow it to cool for awhile after cooking.

Frank's Cajun Rabbit Sauce Piquante

You can use this easy-to-make recipe for both wild and domestic rabbit, and the amount of "piquante" you want depends on how much cayenne pepper you can handle!

2 rabbits, cut into pieces	1 can tomato paste (6-oz. size)
1 cup vegetable oil	1 tbsp. lemon juice
½ cup all-purpose flour	3 bay leaves
2 cups finely diced onions	1½ quarts water
1 cup finely diced celery	1 cup dry sherry
½ cup finely diced bell pepper	½ cup finely sliced green onions
3 cloves minced garlic	½ cup finely chopped parsley
2 cans Rotel diced tomatoes	salt, red, and black pepper to
(10-oz. size)	taste

First, wash the rabbit pieces well and remove all the fat. I also suggest that you trim away and discard the belly parts and rib bones. Then sprinkle the pieces liberally with salt, black pepper, and cayenne.

Next, in a 12-inch skillet, heat half of the vegetable oil to "hot" and quickly fry the rabbit pieces until they brown thoroughly. Then set them aside for awhile.

Now take the remainder of the vegetable oil, add it to the skillet you used to fry the rabbit, and bring it up to high heat. Then toss in the flour and make a peanut-colored French roux. *Keep stirring so that it doesn't burn!* And when it's ready, remove the skillet from the fire, mix in all the seasoning vegetables, and cook them in the hot roux until they soften (about 5 minutes). Now set the roux aside, too.

At this point, take a 6-quart Dutch oven and add it to the Rotel tomatoes and the tomato paste. Then cook the mixture together (stirring constantly) until smooth, hot, and bubbly.

Now add the lemon juice, the bay leaves, the sherry, and the water and stir everything over high heat until thoroughly blended. When the mixture comes to a slow boil, begin stirring in the roux a little at a time. (The mix will get thick, but don't worry about it—it will thin to the proper consistency as the rabbit cooks.) This is also the time to adjust your salt and pepper seasoning.

When the sauce is smooth, drop in the rabbit pieces and reduce the heat to simmer. Then cover the pot and cook over low heat for about 2 hours or until the rabbit begins to fall off the bone.

When you're ready to eat, mix in the green onions and parsley, serve the rabbit over steamed rice, ladle on a generous helping of the sauce, and sop up the drippings with crispy French bread.

Variation: Instead of simmering the sauce piquante over low heat on the stovetop . . . after you drop the rabbit into the sauce, cover the Dutch oven and slide the pot, the rabbit, and everything into the oven and bake at 325 degrees for about an hour and a half. When it's done, you'll have the richest rabbit sauce piquante you ever tasted!

Frank's Cajun-Smothered Doves

Here's a wild game delicacy you'll be proud to serve both your family and your most discriminating dinner guests. And if that weren't enough, it's extremely simple to prepare.

8 doves cleaned and split in half	**2 carrots, small diced**
salt, black and cayenne pepper	**1 tbsp. sweet basil**
to taste	**¼ cup water**
½ cup Crisco oil	**½ cup white wine (Chablis)**
2 medium onions, finely	**2 tbsp. cornstarch**
chopped	**2 tbsp. butter**
4 ribs of celery, finely chopped	**½ cup water**
½ bell pepper, finely chopped	

First, season your doves with the salt and pepper, and heat the Crisco to high in a black cast-iron Dutch oven. Then toss in the birds and quickly stir-fry them until they turn a golden brown. When they're ready, take them out of the pot, put them onto a platter, and set them aside.

Next, add the onions, celery, bell pepper, carrots, and basil to the pot and sauté the mixture until the vegetables turn soft (it should take about 4 or 5 minutes . . . and you should stir the mix constantly as it cooks).

Then add your water and wine to the pot, put the doves back in, and stir everything until the mixture coats the birds well. Now you want to cover the pot, cut the fire down to low, and simmer these babies until they're tender—which should take about 45 minutes to an hour.

When the birds are done, put them on a platter, pour the pan drippings through a fine-mesh strainer, discard the solids, and put the juices in a saucepan on top of the stove. Then bring the liquids to a boil, mix 2 tablespoons of cornstarch with about a half-cup of water, and slowly stir small amounts of the cornstarch into the dove juices. Within a few seconds you should have a succulent, semi-thick sauce. Immediately stir in 2 tablespoons of butter to give the sauce a sheen.

Then liberally pour the sauce over the doves and serve them with Cajun dirty rice, baked green beans wrapped in bacon, and a crispy romaine lettuce salad topped with French dressing. Of course, you might also want to have a loaf of hot French bread handy to sop up the juices.

Some folks say that's the best part!

HOW TO COOK WILD GAME ON THE SMOKER

Can you smoke wild game?

You bet your hunting license you can! And it's really not all that difficult to do.

Two smoking methods are standard: *hot-smoking* and *cold-smoking*. Hot smoking cooks the game at temperatures that range between 165 and 185 degrees. It is a shorter cooking method—more *cooking* than *smoking*—and it's the way most folks smoke at home. Cold smoking is the method used most often commercially. It is more *cured* than *cooked,* since it utilizes a drying process that rarely exceeds 115 degrees Fahrenheit.

But the easiest way to smoke game at home is with the *electric smoker.* It gives you hot smoke and it's the kind of cooker most common on today's market. Here is how it's done:

First, season the game with salt and pepper and rub it down thoroughly with bacon drippings. This is an important part of the smoking process; because wild game is usually lean, and unless some kind of flavored fat is added to moisten the meat as it cooks the finished dish will turn out quite tough and dry.

Next, place the meat in a shallow pan and season further with a finely diced small onion, 2 ribs of chopped celery, 1 teaspoon of garlic powder, 1 teaspoon of fresh ground black pepper, and ½ cup of good sherry. And don't cook "just-seasoned" wild game right away. Cover it tightly and put it in the refrigerator overnight so that the flavors can *marry.*

The next day, fire up the electric smoker, oil the grill or spray it with Pam, and fill the water pan. Then place the roast on the grill and put the lid on.

In an electric smoker, wild game should be smoked about 45 minutes to the pound. For instance, a 6-pound venison roast requires about 4 to 6 hours of smoking from start to finish. But be sure you seal the smoker lid tight . . . and don't keep peeking at the meat! I also suggest you don't pile on too much wood or your game will have a bitter taste. As a rule of thumb, one 2-inch square of hickory chips is more than sufficient for smoking up to 25 pounds of meat.

Properly smoked game should be tender and juicy and have a deeply-colored barbecued look.

Hints: Add a cup of sherry wine to the water in the waterpan when smoking wild ducks . . . add a large bottle of Italian salad dressing to the water in the waterpan when smoking venison . . . and add a liter of Coca-Cola or 7-Up instead of water to the waterpan when smoking pork. You don't have to use just water—go ahead and experiment with other flavorings you like when smoking rabbit, squirrel, doves, quail, and other wild game and domestic meats.

In an electric unit, recommended smoking time for ducks and rabbits is 30 minutes to the pound; for game birds it usually averages 20-25 minutes to the pound. Of course, all cooking times depend on the quality of the smoker and the influence of the air temperature outside of it—on cold days, cooking times will be much longer.

MILK—THE BEST WILD GAME
MARINADE IN THE WORLD!

I'll bet that every year when hunting season rolls around, your family expects you to rush out into the woods and come back days later with all manner of wild game dishes to serve up on the dinner table. Right?

Right!

And I'll bet, too, that your family probably complains every year that they don't like your wild game dishes because . . . *"wild game has a strong gamey taste! Yuuukkk!"*

Well, if that's your problem . . . *I can solve it for you!*

The so-called gamey flavors peculiar to squirrel, deer, ducks, rabbits, dove, moose, elk, and just about everything else that lives in Bambi's Forest can be easily removed with a *marinade*. But not just any marinade!

Sure, you can marinate with wine, beer, Italian salad dressing, Seven-Up, barbecue sauce, lemon juice, and olive oil. But remember, those are flavor additives. They *add* taste to what you're cooking.

When you marinate wild game, most of the time you want to *remove* an unwanted taste—the so-called wild taste. So, you need a *flavor extractor*. And the best flavor extractor in the whole wide world is . . . *whole milk!*

Now don't take my word for it. Try an experiment. Take a glass of whole milk (not skim or low-fat!) and place it on the top shelf of your refrigerator. Then take an onion, peel it, and place it on the bottom shelf of your refrigerator. The next morning . . . try to drink the milk! If you can, you are a better man than I am, Gunga Din!

That glass of milk will have picked up and absorbed just about every single odor in your refrigerator! Well, guess what? It does the same thing for wild game! And more!

You soak your wild game overnight in milk, and when you cook it not only are all the gamey tastes gone, the lactic acid in the milk also tenderizes the meat! You won't believe how the milk will take a tough deer roast, for example, and turn it into a cut similar to prime aged beef! But it does!

Now there's one thing you should *not* use as a marinade (and folks have been doing it for years). I'm talking about vinegar!

Don't soak your meats in vinegar!

I know they did it back in pioneer days! But that went out with highbutton shoes. You want to use vinegar? Make a salad! Put up some pickles! Wash your windows! But if you want to marinate meat . . . *use milk!*

Try it this hunting season. You got to see for yourself how well it works!

Note: Just for the record, wild game should be marinated in milk in the refrigerator preferably overnight (but not less than six hours) to achieve flavor extraction. It should also be marinated in a non-metallic container—plastic, crockery, glass, etc.

After marinating, and before cooking, pour the milk off the wild game and discard it. Then simply pat the meat dry with a paper towel, season to taste, and cook it according to your best recipe.

CHAPTER 6

Meats

Frank's Soul Ribs

Finger-food for romantics insufferably in love, deliciously tender enough for a candlelit dinner, and so full of spice it's unmistakably New Orleans, here's a recipe you can put your whole heart into. And what you get out of it is Frank's N'Awlins Soul Ribs.

3 tbsp. margarine	2 tsp. liquid smoke flavoring
3 large yellow onions, diced	1 cup Rotel tomatoes with chilies
3 tbsp. all-purpose flour (heaping)	4 cups chicken stock
3 lb. lean pork ribs	drippings from pork ribs
salt and cayenne to taste	6 medium potatoes, peeled and halved
1 cup coarsely sliced green onions	

First, take a black cast-iron Dutch oven and heat the margarine to sizzling. Then toss in the diced yellow onions and fry them over high heat—*stirring constantly*—until they turn a caramel brown (this should take about 6 minutes).

When the onions are wilted, sprinkle on the flour, stir everything together well, and continue to cook until the mixture forms a light roux. Then remove the onions from the pot and set them aside for awhile.

At this point, lay out the ribs on a sheet of waxed paper and liberally season them with salt and cayenne (a good pork seasoning can be substituted if you prefer). Then, in the same Dutch oven in which you cooked the onions, drop in the ribs and *sear* them over medium-high heat.

When they've browned, arrange them side-by-side in the Dutch oven (like jigsaw pieces), generously sprinkle them with green onions, drizzle on the liquid smoke, cover the pot, place it into a 350-degree oven, and bake for about an hour and a half (or until the rib meat starts to fall off the bones).

Now when they've cooked, remove them from the Dutch oven and set them in a shallow baking pan. Then cover them with a sheet of aluminum foil and place them back into the oven (set it on 200 degrees—you just want to keep the ribs warm).

Next, you want to drain off (and discard) all but a couple of tablespoons of the pork drippings from the pot. Then toss in the onions, turn the heat back up to high, and stir in the Rotel tomatoes and the chicken stock—stirring continuously until a smooth sauce forms. Then readjust your salt and pepper to taste, reduce the heat, drop in the potato halves, cover the pot, and simmer for about 30 minutes so that the potatoes pick up the flavors of the sauce.

When you're ready to eat, serve the ribs, the potatoes, and the sauce piping hot, with a rich bacon and green bean casserole, and lots of French bread. Uuuuuummmmmmmm!

Pete Giovenco's Exotic Sausages

Thanks to advancements in the meatcutter's art, today we can have sausages made from almost any products available to the consumer. Here are some typical examples plus a recipe (compliments of my personal butcher, Pete Giovenco) that will work for almost all of them. Go ahead! Be daring! Try them at home!

HERE ARE THE PROPER PROPORTIONS

Deer Sausage
3 lb. deer
3 lb. pork
1 cup water

Shrimp Sausage
5 lb. shrimp
3 lb. pork
½ cup water

Fish Sausage
5 lb. catfish
3 lb. pork
½ cup water

Elk Sausage
3 lb. elk
3 lb. pork
1 cup water

Turtle Sausage
3 lb. turtle
3 lb. pork
1 cup water

Alligator Sausage
3 lb. alligator
3 lb. pork
1 cup water

Rabbit Sausage
3 lb. rabbit
3 lb. pork
1 cup water

Crawfish Sausage
5 lb. crawfish
5 lb. pork
½ cup water

To the individual proportions listed above, add:

3 cups very finely diced onions
1½ cups very finely diced celery
1 cup very finely sliced green onions
½ cup very finely diced bell pepper

⅔ cup very finely chopped parsley
8 cloves minced garlic
2 tbsp. salt
2 tbsp. black pepper
2 tsp. cayenne pepper

First, place the meats (which have been cut semi-coarse) into a large mixing bowl and begin adding the water a little at a time until the mixture turns the consistency of cooked, moist oatmeal.

Then—*using your hands*—start blending in all the other ingredients, working them well into the meats until uniformly mixed. And when the consistency is just right, test your sausage mixture for seasoning . . . *but do not taste it raw! Remember . . . never eat raw pork!*

Instead, take a small dab about the size of a quarter, pop it into a skillet, and sauté it *until it's cooked*. Then taste! If you need to make any corrections to the mix, go ahead and do the adjustment. Then fry another dab and taste again. Then when it's just right, either stuff it into sausage casings or form it into patties.

See how easy it is to make your own sausage at home?

Hints and Suggestions:

1—The pork you use should be Boston butt, approximately 60 percent meat and 40 percent fat. This ratio will give you a moist sausage mixture that will be juicy when cooked.

2—Notice that less water is added to the mixture when making seafood sausages than it is in wild game (lean) sausages. That's because most seafoods contain a significant amount of water that will render out as the sausage cooks. So less water is needed when making the mix.

3—While fresh seasoning vegetables are always best, you can also substitute dried onions, garlic, celery, bell pepper, and other dehydrated herbs and spices for fresh ones and still get a delicious sausage.

Note: *If you'd rather not make your own and you want to order custom-made sausages, write or call Pete Giovenco, P.O. Box 23087, Harahan, Louisiana 70183, or call 504-469-4369.*

Frank's Andouille-Tasso Dressing
(For Stuffing a Veal Pocket)

The best way to enhance the flavor of a traditional New Orleans veal pocket is to stuff it with a cornbread dressing spiced up with andouille and tasso. And here's that recipe!

½ lb. finely chopped andouille	½ cup finely chopped celery
½ cup finely chopped tasso	½ cup sliced fresh mushrooms
4 cups chicken stock	¼ cup finely chopped parsley
1 pan cornbread (9-inch size)	¼ cup finely chopped bell
4 tbsp. margarine	pepper
1 cup finely chopped onions	2 tsp. finely chopped garlic
½ cup finely chopped green	2 tsp. salt
onions	1 tsp. black pepper

Start off by baking your cornbread to package directions (be sure you choose an unsweetened cornbread mix) and letting it cool to room temperature. Then, to a 2½ quart saucepan, bring the chicken stock to a boil, toss in the finely chopped andouille and tasso, reduce the heat, and simmer for about an hour until the meats are soft and tender.

Meanwhile, take a 12-inch skillet and melt the margarine over medium heat. Then quickly sauté the onions, green onions, celery, mushrooms, bell pepper, parsley, and garlic until all of them are just wilted—*do not overcook!*

Next, take a mixing bowl and crumble the cornbread. Then stir in the sautéed vegetable mixture and all of the meats and blend everything thoroughly.

At this point, begin adding the meat stock you made—a little at a time—to moisten the dressing. Remember . . . you want the stuffing "just moist"—not wet! And you want to taste the stuffing before adding any salt and pepper. There may already be enough in the tasso and andouille to suit you.

I recommend you allow the dressing to "rest" on the countertop (covered) for at least a half-hour before you use it—this is one of the secrets to making a really good old-time cornbread dressing. After the resting time, test the dressing once more for moisture—if it seems too dry, add more stock a little at a time.

All that's left now is to stuff the veal pocket!

Hint: You should not add salt and pepper to the dressing until after it rests.

Frank's N'Awlins Stuffed Veal Pocket

One of New Orleans' most traditional dishes, this roast used to be commonplace during the age of the neighborhood butcher shop. But today, since a veal pocket has to be custom-cut, the only way you can get one is to find an old-tyme butcher who still cuts swinging beef. And believe me . . . it's worth it!

1 veal pocket roast, about 5-7 pounds
4 cups andouille-tasso dressing
salt and pepper

First, preheat your oven to 350 degrees. Then take the roast, salt and pepper it inside and out, and stuff the hole made by the removal of the shoulder bone with the andouille-tasso dressing.

Place the roast into an 11-by-17 pan and bake at 350 degrees at 18 minutes to the pound for rare, and 25 minutes to the pound for medium-well.

Suggestions:
1—Allow the roast to cool on the countertop for about 15 minutes before slicing.
2—Convert the drippings that form in the bottom of the pan into an outstanding veal sauce by bringing them to a boil in a skillet, stirring in 4 tablespoons of green onions and 2 tablespoons of parsley, and thickening the sauce with a tablespoon of cornstarch mixed in a quarter-cup of cold water. Wait till you taste this!

Frank's Swiss-Baked Green Beans with Bacon

Looking for a nice complementary dish to go with the stuffed veal pocket? Here it is! And look how easy it is to make!

2 tbsp. sweet cream butter
2 large cans sliced green beans
½ lb. lean bacon
8 oz. imported Swiss cheese

First, take a 9-by-11 Pyrex baking dish and butter it well. Then *gently* wash and drain the green beans (you don't want to break them up), fry the bacon until it's crisp, and shred the cheese.

Now begin making layers in the baking pan—a layer of beans, a layer of crumbled-up bacon, and a layer of cheese. Repeat the process over and over until all the ingredients are used.

Then place the dish into a 350-degree oven and bake *uncovered* for about 15-20 minutes (or until the cheese has thoroughly melted and is starting to brown).

Serve piping hot!

Frank's N'Awlins Baked Beef Short-Ribs

If you never fix beef short-ribs for your family because they always come out tough and greasy, get ready for a few tricks that will change all that! Not only are the ribs something special . . . the sauce is guaranteed to make your mouth water!

8 beef short-ribs, trimmed
2 quarts water
4 tbsp. margarine
2 cups coarsely diced onions
2 cups diced carrots
½ cup finely sliced green onions
½ cup finely diced celery
¼ cup finely diced bell pepper
2 cloves minced garlic
2 cups tomato catsup

½ cup dark brown sugar
3 tbsp. white wine vinegar
1 tbsp. Worcestershire sauce
2 tbsp. Dijon mustard
1 tsp. chili powder
2 bay leaves
½ tsp. lemon zest
½ cup reduced beef stock
salt and pepper to taste

First, lay out the beef ribs on a cutting board and trim away as much of the excess fat as possible. Then place them into a shallow-sided cookie sheet and *broil* them quickly on both sides until they turn a toasty brown.

At this point, immediately transfer the ribs to a stock pot containing just enough water to cover them and *boil* them for 30 minutes "at a slow roll." Then, with a pair of tongs, place them side by side in a deep-sided baking dish and set them aside momentarily. *But don't throw away the stock!* Continue to cook it at a "slow boil" until only 2 cups are left in the pot. (This is called reduction—it concentrates the flavor and makes it rich.)

Meanwhile, in a high-sided skillet or Dutch oven, heat the margarine and sauté the onions, carrots, green onions, celery, bell pepper, and garlic until they soften. Then—*one ingredient at at time*—stir into the vegetable mixture the tomato catsup, brown sugar, wine vinegar, Worcestershire sauce, Dijon mustard, chili powder, bay leaves, and lemon zest. Now, cook the sauce over low heat for about 20 minutes (but you want to stir it constantly to keep the sugar from burning).

When the sauce is ready, skim the fat off the reduced beef stock and throw it away. Then gradually stir into the sauce enough of the beef stock to give you the consistency you desire. But don't dilute it too much, because it will thin automatically as the natural beef juices render out of the ribs as they bake.

Finally, season the sauce to taste with salt and pepper, ladle it liberally over the ribs, cover the baking pan with aluminum foil, and place in a preheated 350-degree oven for 1½ to 2 hours.

Serve piping hot with Plantation potatoes and succotash and you got an encore meal you'll want to fix at least twice a week!

Note: Instead of salt and pepper, you can add 2 or 3 teaspoons of meat seasoning (to taste) if you prefer.

Hint: If you'd like to make your own homemade barbecue sauce, just put together the sauce portion of this recipe . . . and you got yourself a winner, podnuh! It'll go great over pork ribs, steaks, chicken, brisket, and wild game.

Frank's Cajun Shredded Pork Casserole

Loaded with spicy, lean, pork strips . . . chock full of a myriad of fresh vegetables . . . gently smothered in a rich peppery sauce . . . and thoroughly blended into long-grain Louisiana rice—this is one casserole that your family will want you to make over and over again! And it's easy, too!

3 lb. lean pork loin, fat removed
2 cans Rotel tomatoes with chilies
3 small bay leaves
2 tsp. ground ginger
2 tbsp. Worcestershire sauce
½ tsp. Kitchen Bouquet
1 tbsp. flour
1 can cream of celery soup
4 tbsp. margarine
1 large onion, thickly sliced in half-rings
3 ribs celery, bias cut
3 green onions, coarsely chopped
½ small bell pepper, diced
2 cups fresh mushrooms, quartered
2 medium carrots, thinly sliced
4 cups cabbage, shredded
3 cloves garlic, minced
2 tbsp. parsley, minced
6 cups cooked rice
salt and cayenne pepper to taste

First, take the pork loin that you've trimmed of all the excess fat, remove the bones, and cut the meat lengthwise into thin strips. Then take a heavy 12-inch skillet, toss in the pork, and cook it over medium heat (stirring constantly) until each strip is completely white.

Next, stir into the sautéed pork the Rotel tomatoes, bay leaves, ginger, Worcestershire sauce, Kitchen Bouquet, and flour. Then continue cooking—*and stirring!*—until the sauce blends thoroughly and turns creamy smooth. Then add the cream of celery soup, mix it well into the sauce, reduce the heat to low, cover the skillet, and simmer the pork strips for about 20 minutes until tender.

Meanwhile, take another 12-inch skillet and heat the margarine to sizzling. Then drop in all of your vegetables—onions, celery, green onions, bell pepper, garlic, mushrooms, carrots, cabbage, and parsley—and sauté over high heat until the vegetables turn "tender crisp." *Remember, you want them softened but not overcooked—they still have to bake.* Keep them a little on the crunchy side.

When the veggies are ready, spoon them into the pork and blend all the ingredients thoroughly. Then, in a large bowl, gently fold the pork-vegetable mixture into the rice.

All that's left is to transfer the casserole into an 11-by-14 Pyrex dish, garnish the top with slices of black olives, set the oven at 325 degrees, and bake the dish uncovered for 25 minutes or until piping hot.

Hints:

1—If you want to substitute shredded chicken for the pork, go right ahead! You won't have to change anything else in the recipe. It can also be made with turkey, veal, or lean beef.

2—If you want to fix this casserole ahead of time and freeze it, freeze it before *you bake it. Then when you're ready to cook, thaw the dish in the refrigerator, cover with aluminum foil, and bake at 350 degrees for 20 minutes, then at 325 degrees for another 15 minutes.*

Frank's Fajitas

After two straight weeks of sampling just about every fajita cooked between Houston and Galveston, I decided to take the best of the best recipes, doctor them up with a little New Orleans creativity, and come up with my own fajita recipe. And here it is, amigos! Cook this up at your hacienda soon!

16 oz. Italian salad dressing	**2 tsp. black pepper**
1 cup whole milk	**4 chicken breasts, skinned and**
1 cup finely chopped onions	**de-boned**
½ small bell pepper, diced	**1 lb. flank steak, fat-trimmed**
2 tbsp. Worcestershire sauce	**2 tbsp. margarine**
1 tbsp. cumin	**2 medium-size fresh tomatoes,**
4 chili peppers, minced	**diced**
½ cup Jack Daniel's Black Label	**10 small flour tortillas**
Whiskey	**(7-inch size)**
2 tsp. salt	

In a non-metallic pan, mix together all the ingredients that make up the fajita marinade: the salad dressing, whole milk, onions, bell pepper, Worcestershire sauce, cumin, chili peppers, Jack Daniel's whiskey, salt, and black pepper. Then allow the mix to set at room temperature for about an hour so that the individual flavors will "marry."

Meanwhile, de-bone the chicken breasts, wash them well under running water, remove the skin and the excess fat, and pound them out slightly with a meat hammer. Then take the flank steak and pound it out with the hammer to about ¼-inch thickness.

After the marinade has set for the allotted time, place the chicken and the steak into it, cover the pan tightly, and refrigerate overnight.

Then when you're ready to cook, take a cast-iron skillet or heavy aluminum frypan, place it on the burner, and get it *hot*. While the skillet is heating up, begin slicing the beef and chicken—slice the beef *across the grain* in small strips, and slice the chicken *with the grain* in small strips.

Now, using a little of the margarine to keep the meats from sticking, begin frying the beef and chicken—*directly from the marinade*. You want them nice and brown, but watch them closely. Do not overcook!

When the meats are ready, add your fresh tomatoes to the skillet and de-glaze the bottom (cook until the tomatoes start to thicken). Then pour the sauce over the beef and chicken.

To serve, heat the tortillas (either in a steamer or on a plate in the microwave), place a couple pieces of beef and chicken into the tortilla, and dress with fried onions, fresh salsa, shredded cheddar cheese, guacamole, sour cream, and refried beans. A *Corona* on the side makes it complete!

Frank's Whole Baked Beef Filet

When the meal has to be extra special, this is the special meal you want to serve. The whole filet is lightly sprinkled with salt and pepper, stuffed with baked garlic, wrapped in bacon, and roasted in a hot oven till succulent and juicy. I guarantee . . . it'll please the most discriminating taste!

1 head garlic	2 tsp. black pepper
2 tbsp. olive oil	8 strips of bacon
1 whole beef filet (4 lb. trimmed)	1 can beef broth (10 oz. size)
1 tsp. salt	

First, cut the top off the head of garlic, drizzle the olive oil over the open ends, place into a shallow pie pan, cover, and bake for 1 hour at 400 degrees. Then, while the garlic is cooking, prepare your filet as follows:

Using a slicing knife, insert it lengthwise into one end of the filet and shove it straight through to the other end, making a pocket right down the middle. Then in a hot, lightly greased skillet, brown the filet quickly to seal in all the natural juices. When thoroughly seared, remove the roast from the pan and allow it to cool.

Now when you're ready to bake it, take the garlic you prepared earlier and stuff the cloves into the pocket you made in the roast with the slicing knife. Sprinkle on the salt and pepper and, one strip at a time, begin wrapping the beef with the bacon.

At this point you want to place the filet on a roasting rack, set the rack inside a baking pan (along with 1 can of beef bouillon) and slide the pan into a preheated 450-degree oven—*uncovered*.

Now cook at 450 for 20 minutes (or until the bacon browns and tightens around the filet) . . . *then reduce the heat to 325 for another 15 minutes.* This will give you a roast that comes out medium-rare. For a medium roast, just increase the 325-degree cooking time to 20 minutes. *But whatever you do . . . don't overcook a filet or it will lose all of its natural juices.*

When the roast is done, serve it with either noodles, baked potatoes, or rice, along with the natural juices that collect in the bottom of the baking pan. Pan-sautéed carrots and a crisp green salad make good side dishes.

Note: If you bake the roast without using a rack, the bacon drippings will collect in the pan and cause the roast to become greasy. To avoid this, you will have to drain off the drippings every so often. Ideally, though, the filet should be done on a rack!

I also suggest that before slicing you allow the roast to "rest" on the countertop for about 15 minutes after you remove it from the oven.

Frank's Italian Eggplant-Stuffed Veal Birds

If you *like* veal, and you *like* eggplant . . . you're gonna *love* this recipe! The eggplant bastes its way through the broasted veal, the drippings marry with the milk to create a succulent sauce, and when served with pasta and crisp salad the concoction will please the most discriminating palate!

8 thin-sliced veal chops or cutlets	**1 tsp. Italian seasoning**
4 tsp. veal seasoning (or salt and pepper)	**4 cups soft bread crumbs**
	¼ cup grated Parmesan cheese
3 small eggplants, peeled and diced	**1 raw egg**
	salt and pepper to taste
1 quart whole milk	**½ cup all-purpose flour**
1 quart salted water	**1 cup whole milk**
4 tbsp. extra-virgin olive oil	**1 cup cream of chicken soup**
1 lb. Italian sausage (pre-cooked and drained)	**(optional)**

First, place the veal chops on a cutting board and pound them out slightly with a meat hammer. Then sprinkle them liberally on both sides with the veal seasoning and set them aside.

Meanwhile, put the diced eggplant into a bowl, pour on the quart of salted water and the quart of milk, and mix the eggplant thoroughly into the marinade. Then allow the pieces to set for about a half-hour (the salt will keep the eggplant from absorbing the olive oil and the milk will eliminate the sharp taste—*the bite*—of the eggplant).

Next, drain off the milk-water. Then in a Dutch oven, heat the olive oil to "medium-hot," drop in the eggplant, and cook the diced pieces (*covered!*) until they soften—about 20 minutes or so. Halfway through the cooking process, stir in the Italian sausage, put the lid on the pot, and simmer the mixture together for another 20 minutes until well-blended.

When the eggplant is tender, stir in the Italian seasoning, the bread crumbs, and the Parmesan cheese. Then season the mix to taste with salt and pepper. After allowing the stuffing to cool slightly, crack a raw egg into the mixture and stir it in as rapidly as you can—*watch it cuz it'll cook if you're not fast!*

At this point, place the veal chops on the cutting board again. Then drop spoonfuls of the stuffing onto the center of each chop, fold the edges of the meat around the stuffing, and pin securely with toothpicks. Now, lightly dust them with the flour, place them on a cookie sheet, and broil them until they turn brown.

When the chops are seared well, remove them from the oven, place them into a glass baking dish, and add the milk. Then cover the dish, slide it into a 325-degree preheated oven, and bake it for 2 hours.

When you're ready to eat, remove the birds from the oven and skim off any excess fat that accumulated during baking. Then, with a wire whisk, whip the cream of chicken soup into the pan drippings until smooth and pour over the chops.

Serve piping hot with extra eggplant dressing, buttered pasta, and Italian salad.

Hints: I suggest you make more eggplant stuffing than you're going to need for the chops. Just take the extra, put it into a casserole dish, sprinkle the top with seasoned bread crumbs, and bake it at 375 degrees until toasty and set—about 25 minutes.

If you don't have any cream of chicken soup handy, you can thicken the pan drippings by making a little butter roux *and stirring it into the sauce. Butter roux is nothing more than equal parts of butter and flour cooked "gently" over medium heat until smooth.*

To make soft *bread crumbs, just take fresh sliced bread, break it into chunks, and run it through the food processor until fluffy.*

Note: *Do not cook the chops in a metal baking pan. The milk will pick up the taste of the metal and taint the sauce.*

Frank's Southern Holiday Glazed Ham

Fix this for your family's next holiday dinner and it'll be like dining at Tara with Rhett Butler and Scarlett O'Hara!

1 fully cooked ham (6-8 pound average)	**1 tsp. ground ginger**
1 cup brown sugar	**1 tsp. dry mustard**
½ stick real butter	**1 tbsp. paprika**
½ cup honey (clover preferred)	**10 whole peppercorns**
½ cup Coca-Cola	**1 tbsp. red wine vinegar**
1 small can frozen pineapple juice	**5 pineapple slices**
	5 whole maraschino cherries
	25 whole cloves

First, place the ham in a baking pan large enough to hold it without crowding the sides. Then put it into the refrigerator to chill.

Now, in a 12-inch skillet, melt the butter over medium heat, add the brown sugar, and cook it *gently* until it dissolves. Then—*over medium-high heat*—stir in the honey, Coca-Cola, frozen pineapple juice, ginger, mustard, paprika, peppercorns, and red wine vinegar, and keep stirring constantly until all of the ingredients have become thoroughly blended and smooth. Ideally, you should have a semi-thick sauce at this point.

Next, using a spoon or a small ladle, generously baste the ham with the sauce (it should thicken to a glaze if the ham was chilled enough). Lightly cover the ham with plastic wrap and put it back in the refrigerator for at least another hour.

When you're ready to cook (and incidentally, the ham can be pre-basted with the sauce a day in advance), preheat the oven to 325 degrees. Then take the ham from the refrigerator and score it in diagonal cuts about a half-inch apart and a half-inch deep. Now decorate it with the pineapple slices and cherries—pin the pineapple in place with toothpicks and put a cherry in the center of each slice. You also want to push 4 cloves into each pineapple slice and 1 into the cherry. At this point, generously spoon the basting sauce over the entire dressed ham (you want to use all the sauce).

Now cover the ham with a "tent" made of aluminum foil (but do not cover it tightly, otherwise the tent will steam out all the natural juices and cause it to be dry) . . . and bake it in the oven for 1 hour, basting occasionally with the marinade drippings that collect in the bottom of the pan.

Finally, remove the aluminum foil tent and bake *uncovered* for another 35-45 minutes or until beautifully glazed. Continue basting until the marinade sticks to the ham and forms a shiny crust.

When cooked, remove it from the oven, allow it to set for 15 minutes on the countertop before slicing, and serve it with generous ladle-fulls of the natural gravy. Ummmmmmmmm!

Suggestion: The ham—plus the pan drippings—goes great with creamed potatoes, pan-roasted potatoes, noodles, cornbread dressing or (if you wanna be real Southern!) grits.

Frank's Ribeye Roll-Ups
(In a Creamed Port Wine Sauce)

Rich in taste, tender in texture, and unbelievably succulent with potatoes, rice, or pasta . . . this rolled steak entree is exquisite enough for the most elegant dining, yet easy enough to serve to your family any night of the week. Try it!

The Ribeyes:

**2 ribeye steaks, pounded and
    halved**
1 small onion, julienned
1 small bell pepper, julienned
2 green onions, julienned
1 rib of celery, julienned
1 carrot, julienned
**½ lb. fresh mushrooms,
    chopped**
salt and pepper to taste

First, lay out the ribeyes on a sheet of plastic wrap. Then cover the steaks with a second sheet of wrap. Now, with a meat hammer (or a heavy skillet), pound the steaks until you flatten them to about ³⁄₁₆ to ¼ inch thick.

Next, salt and pepper them to taste (or sprinkle on your favorite meat seasonings). Then—in small portions—begin spreading on the julienned onions, green onions, celery, bell peppers, carrots, and mushrooms . . . *but do not overstuff.* Remember, just a hint of the fresh vegetables will flavor the meat very nicely. Now, tightly roll up the meat, wrapping the vegetables inside, and pin the ends in place with toothpicks.

At this point, place the roll-ups into a shallow, greased baking pan, put them into the oven, and *broil* them until they turn golden brown on both sides. You'll have to turn them over once, but be careful that you don't let the roll-ups *unroll*. Take it easy!

While the meat is cooking, begin making your wine sauce. Here are the ingredients:

Port Wine Sauce:

½ cup sliced mushrooms	1 tbsp. grey poupon mustard
2 tbsp. margarine	¼ cup heavy cream
2 cups reduced beef stock	salt and pepper to taste
⅔ cup port wine	

In a skillet, melt the margarine over high heat until it sizzles. Then toss in the sliced mushrooms and quickly stir-fry them until they turn toasty and tender (about 3 minutes or so). Then—still on high heat—pour in the beef stock, mix it into the mushrooms, and cook everything together for about 3 or 4 minutes, stirring constantly.

Next add the wine, the mustard, and the heavy cream and stir everything together until completely blended and smooth. Once again, taste for salt and pepper and correct the amount.

And now you're ready for the steak roll-ups!

Take them piping hot from the broiler, place them into the sauce you just made, remove the toothpicks, turn the fire down to medium, and simmer until fully smothered in the wine sauce—about 4 or 5 minutes.

I suggest you serve the meat and sauce over *al dente* linguine pasta, brabant potatoes, pommes petite, or buttered parsley rice, along with broccoli au gratin, sliced tomatoes with vinaigrette, toast points, and some chilled port wine. I promise y'all, British Royalty never ate this good!

Hint: I did this recipe with ribeyes to achieve tenderness. But you can do the dish with almost any cut of meat—round steak, flank steak, top sirloin—as long as you pound it well to tenderize it.

Frank's Sicilian Ossobuco

Meaning "hollowbone," ossobuco is an old traditional Italian dish made with veal shanks and a spicy tomato-flavored wine stock. It is usually done in a deep iron skillet, but it can also be cooked in the oven. This recipe is more Sicilian than Milanese because it incorporates the various flavors of New Orleans . . . which is why I'm sure you're gonna love it!

6 veal shanks, with meat	**2 cups chicken stock**
1 tsp. salt	**1 tsp. oregano**
1 tsp. black pepper	**2 tsp. sweet basil**
4 tbsp. flour	**10 anchovy strips, pureed**
3 tbsp. olive oil	**with oil**
1 cup diced onions	**2 strips of lemon peel**
4 cloves fresh-minced garlic	**½ stick of butter**
2 cups peeled tomatoes	**salt and black pepper to taste**
½ cup dry red wine	**(for sauce)**

First off, salt and pepper the veal shanks and dust them in the flour. Then place them into a greased baking pan and roast them in a 450-degree oven until lightly browned (you should turn them once to brown both sides). Set them aside.

Meanwhile, take a 6-quart Dutch oven and heat the olive oil to "hot." Then quickly sauté the onions and garlic—*just watch that the garlic doesn't burn*. Next, add the wine and the tomatoes and cook the mixture *uncovered* over medium-high heat until the liquid reduces to one-half its original volume (about 20 minutes). At this point, stir in the chicken stock (along with the oregano, basil, and anchovy puree) and reduce the volume again to one-half (about another 20 minutes). The reduction should give you a full-bodied sauce—not thick, but not watery either.

Now place the browned veal shanks into a heavy pan, generously top with the sauce, cover tightly, and bake at 350 degrees for about an hour. Then ever so gently remove the shanks (cuz they'll fall apart!) and set them on a platter in a warm oven.

Finally, put the remaining sauce (along with the lemon peel) into a skillet and bring to high heat. When the sauce is just about to boil, salt and pepper it to taste, remove it immediately from the fire, add the butter in small pieces, *agitate* (DO NOT STIR) the pan, and blend everything together until smooth and creamy.

Serve the shanks, topped with the sauce, alongside a plate of rotini pasta, garlic-sautéed zucchini, a loaf of Italian bread, and a chilled glass of wine.

Variation: Instead of baking the shanks in the oven, you can cook them on top of the stove in a skillet. But the pan must have a tight-fitting lid and the meat should cook only on the "simmer" setting—very slowly.

Frank's Kajun Kabobs

This tasty concoction is made just like ordinary shish-kabobs *except* that instead of grilling or baking them . . . you deep fry them and serve them piping hot alongside a spicy bowl of dirty rice. It's a nice variation—try it and see!

1 lb. chicken breasts, cut into pieces	½ lb. small mushrooms, buttons only
1 lb. smoked sausage, cut into discs	3 zucchini, cut into discs
1 lb. round steak, cubed	2 cups seasoned flour (all-purpose)
1 lb. pork loin, cut into medallions	3 whole eggs
1 large white onion, chunked	1 cup whole milk
3 ribs celery, cut into 1-inch lengths	Crisco oil for frying
	salt and pepper to taste

Very simply, you take about a half-dozen bamboo skewers and begin alternating the kabob ingredients on the sticks as follows: onion, chicken breast, celery, smoked sausage, mushroom, pork loin, zucchini, and round steak. Then you repeat the process until you've filled the skewer, with about a 2-inch empty space in the center.

At this point, with a pair of sharp kitchen shears, cut the skewer in half where you left the space (you want to make 2 small kabobs).

Next, salt and pepper each kabob and set it aside. Then season your flour with salt and pepper (*and season it well!*) to make a dusting mix and whip the 3 eggs into the cup of milk to make an egg wash.

Now, roll the kabob in the flour, then dip it in the egg wash, and roll it back in the flour again. At this point, *you want to allow the coated kabob to "rest" on the counter for about 3 to 5 minutes* so that the coating sticks to the vegetables and meats.

Meanwhile, in a chicken fryer or Dutch oven, heat your oil to about 375 degrees. Then one at a time, lower your kabobs into the oil and fry them until the coating turns crunchy and crispy (about 5-8 minutes).

When they're done, remove them, drain them on absorbent paper towels, and serve alongside a piping hot dish of Cajun dirty rice.

Variation: Feel free to use any meat or seafood you like for the ones I've suggested. For example, you can use shrimp instead of chicken, veal instead of pork, whatever! Just suit your own palate! Any variation will work!

Frank's German Sauerbraten

Next to wiener schnitzel, sauerbraten is one of the most recognized foods of Deutschland. And if you prepare it properly, it is tender, rich in flavor, and popular whether you're German or not! I suggest you fix up a batch at home and have your own Oktoberfest anytime you want!

2 cloves garlic	1 small sliced onion
3 lb. beef shoulder	2 bay leaves
2 tsp. salt	1 tsp. peppercorns
2 tsp. pepper	¼ cup sugar
2 tsp. garlic powder	4 tbsp. vegetable oil
2 cups apple cider vinegar	flour
2 cups water	1 cup heavy cream

First, cut the 2 cloves of garlic in half and rub the freshly-cut surfaces thoroughly over the meat. Then sprinkle the meat with salt and pepper and place it in a non-metallic bowl.

Next, add the garlic powder, vinegar, water, onion, bay leaves, peppercorns, and sugar to a 2½ quart saucepan and blend the mixture over high heat . . . *but do not let it boil.* Then, while it is still hot, pour the marinade over the meat, cover it tightly, and place it in the refrigerator for 4 to 8 days—*turning the meat each day.*

Then, when you're ready to cook, drain off the marinade, strain out all the solid ingredients, and save the liquid.

At this point, add the vegetable oil to a cast-iron Dutch oven, heat it to high, and quickly brown the meat all over. Then *carefully* pour in half of the strained vinegar solution (watch that it doesn't splatter), cover the pot, and simmer the roast until tender—it should take about 3 hours, adding more marinade as necessary to keep the liquid about ½ inch deep in the pot.

When you're ready to eat, remove the roast from the pot, place it on a platter, and slice it into serving-size pieces. Then add the remaining marinade to the pot liquor you cooked the roast in, stir in 2 tablespoons of flour for each cup of liquid, and cook the mixture over medium high heat —*stirring constantly*—until the liquor thickens to a sauce.

Finally, gradually stir in the heavy cream, cook it for 5 minutes more, and ladle it over the sliced roast.

I suggest you serve sauerbraten piping hot with boiled potatoes and German-stewed red cabbage.

Hints: If you allow the meat to cool for about 15 minutes after you take it from the black pot, it will slice easier. It is also important that you do not have more than ½ inch of marinade in the bottom of the pot as the roast cook. Too much liquid will "boil" the beef rather than "pot-roast" it.

Juice, juice, and more juice!

There's a secret to getting the maximum amount of juice from your oranges and lemons? And here's what it is!

Either drop them into a pot of water and boil them for about 5 minutes before you squeeze them . . . or place them in the microwave oven on half-power for about a minute or so. The heat actually causes the pulp pods to break and release all of their juices.

The same technique also works to help you remove the with pithe (the white membrane) from lemons and oranges when you peel them.

Frank's N'Awlins Crockpot Beef

A fast and easy way to make a rich beef stroganoff-style stew that goes great over broad egg noodles. This is one of those throw-it-together-and-forget-it-till-it's-done dishes!

2 lb. tender beef roast
½ cup all-purpose flour
½ cup burgundy or port wine
1 lb. small button mushrooms
4 carrots, peeled and quartered
2 cups finely chopped white
   onions
1 cup finely chopped celery

¼ cup finely chopped bell
   pepper
1 tsp. sweet basil
1 tbsp. Worcestershire sauce
1 cup heavy whipping cream
1 tbsp. finely chopped parsley
½ cup thinly sliced green onions
salt and pepper to taste

Start off by turning the crockpot on *high* and letting it begin heating. Meanwhile, trim all the fat off the roast (this keeps your sauce from being greasy) and cut it into one-inch diced chunks. Next, season the meat pieces liberally with salt and pepper (and be sure to use black, white, and red pepper!), dredge them lightly in the flour, and toss them into the crock pot, along with the wine and the mushrooms. *Now stir everything around well, put the lid on the pot, and forget about it for about 2 hours.*

When the pre-cooking time is up, add your seasoning vegetables (onions, celery, bell pepper), the basil, carrots, and the Worcestershire sauce. Then stir well again, put the lid back on the crockpot, and let the stew cook another 2 hours (I suggest you stir it once more in about 30 minutes).

Then to the stock base in the pot, add the heavy cream and the parsley and stir it well into the mix. Cover the pot again and let the dish cook for about another half-hour or so (or until the beef flakes easily).

When you're ready to eat, serve the beef over hot egg noodles and garnish with the sliced green onions. I also recommend a bowl of buttered green peas, a cold, crisp tossed salad, and a couple of pieces of garlic bread as side dishes.

Hint: To turn this dish into a more traditional beef stew, you simply reduce the amount of cream by one-half and add a few potatoes and a variety of diced fresh vegetables during the last hour of cooking time.

Frank's N'Awlins Meatloaf

Served very simply with creamed potatoes and buttered green peas, this classic New Orleans meatloaf is rich, full-bodied, and succulent enough for royalty. And it's easy to make!

1½ lb. lean ground beef	1 tsp. salt
1 cup seasoned bread crumbs	¼ tsp. black pepper
1 cup finely chopped onions	⅛ tsp. cayenne pepper
½ cup finely chopped celery	½ tsp. cumin
¼ cup finely chopped bell pepper	3 tbsp. grated Romano cheese
¼ cup finely chopped parsley	¼ tsp. Worcestershire sauce
2 whole eggs, beaten	3 whole hard-boiled eggs
1 cup whole milk	½ lb. bacon
1 small can V-8 juice	2 tbsp. butter or margarine

In a large bowl, use your hands and mix the ground meat, bread crumbs, onions, celery, bell pepper, and parsley until uniformly blended. Then pour in the beaten eggs, whole milk, and V-8 juice and work it thoroughly into the meat mix.

At this point, season the mixture with the salt, pepper, cumin, grated Romano, and Worcestershire and mix well again.

Now, take the butter and grease a loaf pan (one that measures 9-by-5-by-3 should work well).

Then place half of the meat mixture in the bottom of the pan, make a shallow depression down the center of the meat lengthwise, and place a strip of bacon and three hard-boiled eggs in the depression. Then cover the eggs with another strip of bacon and cap off both the eggs and bacon with the remainder of the meat mix. (*Hint: Don't be gentle here*—use your hands and knead together the top and bottom meat portions so that they join without a seam.)

Finally, put the formed meatloaf in a preheated 350-degree oven and bake until the loaf is golden brown on the outside and juicy on the inside—about 50 minutes to an hour.

Hint: You can remove excess fats from the meatloaf as it bakes by using a basting bulb. I also suggest you let the meatloaf "set" on the countertop for at least 15 minutes before slicing it.

Frank's Cajun Smothered Pork

To do this dish right, you need a lean cut of trimmed pork, a big batch of sliced yellow onions, a cast-iron Dutch oven, and whatever patience it takes to let it all cook down over a low heat until the pork falls apart. Oh . . . you're also gonna need a pot of steamed rice to serve it over— Cajun style!

3 tbsp. margarine
3 large onions, halved and sliced
½ cup sliced green onions
½ lb. fresh mushrooms,
  quartered
2 tsp. caraway seeds
4 cloves garlic, minced
3 bay leaves
3 lb. trimmed pork (Boston butt
  or loin)

2 tsp. salt
2 tsp. cayenne pepper
½ cup all-purpose flour
¼ cup water
2 tbsp. Kitchen Bouquet
¼ cup finely chopped parsley
½ cup prepared roux

First, in a 5-quart cast-iron Dutch oven, melt the margarine over high heat, toss in the sliced onions, and stir fry them until they caramelize (turn a deep brown)—this step should take you about 10 minutes. Then drop in the green onions, the caraway seeds, and the mushrooms and continue cooking over high heat for another 5 minutes until they soften.

At this point, remove the cooked vegetables from the pot and set them aside in a bowl. Now sprinkle the minced garlic and the bay leaves over the mix and stir them in well.

Now cut the pork into serving-size pieces and carefully trim away as much fat as possible. Then sprinkle each piece liberally with salt and cayenne pepper (you can substitute a good pork seasoning for the salt and pepper if you prefer) and dust each piece lightly with flour.

Then in the same Dutch oven you used to fry down the onions, turn up the heat to medium-high, drop in the pork a few pieces at a time, and lightly seal in the juices—*but do not overcook it!* You don't want to *fry* the pork—you just want to *sear* it.

Next, remove the pork pieces from the Dutch oven. Then with the heat reduced to low, begin layering your ingredients—onion mix, then pork, then onion mix, then pork—until all the ingredients are in the pot.

At this point, mix the Kitchen Bouquet with the quarter-cup of water, evenly pour it over the pork and onions, put the lid back on the pot, and simmer everything together for about an hour and a half. Oh . . . and don't peek in the pot!

Then, when the cooking time is up, gently remove the pork pieces from the pot with a pair of tongs and place them in a baking dish. Then turn up the fire to high, bring the pan liquid to a gentle boil, slowly stir in the parsley and the roux, and thicken the pan gravy to the consistency you desire. This is also the time to re-season the gravy to your taste. Cover the pot once more and simmer for about 10 minutes to cook the roux.

Finally, pour the gravy over the pork, cover the dish with a sheet of aluminum foil, slide it into a 350-degree oven, and bake it for about 20-30 minutes until piping hot and tender.

Hint: I suggest you serve this smothered pork dish with hot buttered rice, a green-bean casserole, and a frosty glass of beer. I also suggest you add a bit more cayenne than normal to make it a little piquante!

Frank's Natchitoches Spicy Meat Pies

This is the one food item that Nathan Pritikin just couldn't get the folks of Natchitoches, Louisiana to give up so that they could participate in the Pritikin Health Plan. Taste 'em . . . and you'll know why!

The Pastry Mix:

4 cups all-purpose flour
2 tsp. baking powder
½ cup Crisco shortening

2 whole eggs
2 cups whole milk

Start off by sifting the flour and the baking powder together at least twice, and preferably three times. Then, using your hands, blend in the Crisco thoroughly (you know you got it right when the flour turns crumbly). Next, add the eggs and whip them into the flour, then pour in just enough milk to make a stiff dough. When it's at the proper consistency, put it on a lightly floured surface and roll it out very thin (*actually as thin as you can get it*).

To make the crust of the meatpie, put a saucer atop the rolled-out flour, and, with a paring knife, cut out circles the same size as the saucer. This recipe, if rolled thin enough, will give you 16 pies.

The Meat Mixture:

2 tbsp. Crisco oil
2 tbsp. all-purpose flour
½ lb. lean ground pork
1½ lb. lean ground beef
2 cups extra-finely chopped
   onions
½ cup finely chopped shallots

¼ cup finely chopped bell
   peppers
½ cup finely chopped celery
2 tbsp. finely chopped parsley
1½ tsp. salt
1 tsp. cayenne (more to taste)
⅛ tsp. sweet basil

Now take a skillet and make a light brown roux with the flour and oil. Then add the vegetables, meat, and seasonings all at once and stir everything together well, making sure the roux coats all the other ingredients. At this point, reduce the heat and *gently simmer* the mixture until all the additives are cooked thoroughly. You will need to "taste" several times during the simmering process to be sure the seasonings are right. Now, after the mix is cooked, place it aside and let it cool to room temperature.

When you're ready to prepare your pies, lay out the crust and *half-fill* with the meat mix. Then fold the crust over evenly onto itself, dampen the edges slightly with water, and crimp it with a fork until well-sealed. (And don't forget to pierce the pie once in the center with the point of a paring knife. This allows excess steam to escape and keeps the crust crispy.)

Now deep-fry the pies (uncrowded) at 325 degrees until golden brown. Then place them on paper towels to drain (with the pierced side down). Serve hot with Dijon mustard sauce.

Note: Do not substitute oil for shortening in the pastry mix, otherwise the crust will crumble and fall apart. If you prefer not to fry the pies, you can bake them in the oven at 325 degrees until golden brown, but you will have to turn them over once for uniformity. Incidentally, if you want to make shrimp, crawfish, or crabmeat pies . . . use this same recipe and merely make the substitutions. It's that easy!

HOW TO MAKE CORNED BEEF
AND OTHER MEATS

Like smoking and drying, *corning* has been used for centuries as a method of curing and preserving meat. The name is somewhat misleading because the process has nothing to do with corn. The term comes from the Anglo-Saxon, where chunks of salt the size of English grain (which they called *corn*) were used to process the meats.

By using the technique of corning, stringy and tough cuts of virtually any kind of meat can be turned into a fine meal. It is especially nice for treating wild game, but, in truth, any variety of meat—wild or domestic—can be corned. And it isn't necessary to have just the brisket or top-grade cuts.

Now you should keep in mind that corning isn't one of those overnight preparations. The process—when done right—takes *15 days*. So I recommend that whenever you decide to corn meat for your family, you do several pieces at once.

The recipe below will make about 2 gallons of marinade, which is more than enough for 8 to 12 pounds of meat.

Frank's Corning Marinade

1½ cups salt	3½ tsp. sodium nitrate
½ cup sugar	1 tsp. sodium nitrite
2 tbsp. pickling spice	7 quarts warm water
1 tsp. whole cloves	1 tsp. fresh onion, minced
1 tsp. peppercorns	1 medium garlic clove, minced
3 bay leaves	1 medium lemon, sliced

First, mix all the dry ingredients together in a large crockery pot, plastic, or porcelain container. *Do not use a metal container because the chemical reaction between the ingredients and the metal can be toxic!* Incidentally, you should be able to buy sodium nitrate and sodium nitrite at your local drug store.

Now, pour in the warm water and stir until all the dry ingredients are dissolved. Next, add the onion, garlic and lemon. Then drop in the meat . . . *but make sure that it is completely submerged in the marinade so it doesn't spoil.*

At this point, cover the container and place it in your refrigerator. Then, every other day, turn the meat and stir the mix. After 15 days, the meat is corned and ready to be cooked.

THE COOKING PROCESS

First, wash the meat under cool running tap water. Then put it into a heavy-bottom stockpot and *add just enough water to cover it*. Now bring the water to a boil and spoon off the scum that will form on the surface. Next, lower the heat to *simmer* and cook the meat for 4 to 5 hours until tender.

To do a complete one-dish meal, I recommend that you add potatoes, onions, carrots, celery, bell pepper, and cabbage wedges to the stock during the last 30 minutes of the cooking process.

Corned meat should be sliced while hot—*and be sure you cut across the grain*. The meat is best when carved into thin slices. To enhance the flavor, serve it with rye bread and top it with mustard and horseradish.

*Note: If you want to store some of the uncooked meat for later use, simply transfer it directly from the marinade to a **Zip-Loc freezer bag**, along with about a cup of the marinating liquid. Then squeeze all of the air from the bag and seal it up. Corned meat will keep in your refrigerator for several weeks, but it can also be frozen for longer periods of time.*

Momma's Old N'Awlins Meat Loaf

Nothing, but nothing, matches the taste of a good ol' N'Awlins meat loaf, served up with creamed potatoes, green peas, a lettuce and tomato salad, and a Barq's root beer. And here's how you make it!

1½ lb. lean ground beef	1 tbsp. finely chopped parsley
½ cup toasted bread crumbs	1½ tsp. salt
1 large raw egg	1 tsp. black pepper
1 tbsp. sweet basil	6 strips meaty smoked bacon
⅛ tsp. oregano	3 large hard-boiled eggs
¼ tsp. thyme	2 tbsp. tomato sauce
1 cup finely chopped onion	½ cup sliced shallots
½ cup finely chopped celery	2 tbsp. flour
¼ cup finely chopped bell pepper	

Start off by putting the meat in a large mixing bowl and adding to it—*one ingredient at a time!*—all the ingredients except the last five on the list. *Do not try to shortcut this recipe by "dumping" them all together!* Your blend will not be consistent if you do. (For example: add the bread crumbs and work them in. Then add the raw egg and work it in. Then the basil. Then the oregano. And so on and so forth.) When you have the mix blended well, go ahead and separate the meat into two equal portions.

At this point, take a 6-by-9 loaf pan (one you'd use to make bread), grease the bottom and sides with margarine, pack one portion of the meat in the bottom of the pan, and run a strip of bacon on top of the meat (right down the center). Then take your hard-boiled eggs and lay them lengthwise in a row on top of the strip of bacon. I suggest you push them down slightly into the beef to keep them centered. Now top the eggs with another strip of bacon.

Then take the second portion of meat and pack it into the pan on top of the eggs and bacon. Be sure to work the meat in with your fingers so that the top and bottom layers "fuse" together. It will keep the layers from separating once the loaf is cooked. Finally, place the remaining strips of bacon on top of the loaf and tuck in the sides using a table knife.

Now preheat your oven to 350 degrees, gently ladle the tomato sauce over the meat, and bake the loaf for about 50 minutes (or until the bacon turns a crispy golden brown and the meat starts to pull away from the sides of the pan).

To make slicing easier, you should allow the loaf to "rest" on the countertop about 15 minutes before serving.

Hint: Before you serve the loaf, drain off the pan drippings into a skillet and heat them to bubbling. Then toss in about ½ cup of shallots and cook them until tender (about 3 to 4 minutes). Now, very slowly, "whisk" in the flour and simmer it over medium-high heat (stirring constantly) until you make a smooth sauce. All that's left is to slice the loaf, top it with the sauce, and have at it!

I recommend you serve this meatloaf with creamed potatoes, buttered green peas, a crisp tossed salad, a couple slices of French bread, and (if you can't get a Barq's) a frosty glass of iced tea!

New eggs—old eggs?

If you've ever wondered if there is any way to tell just how fresh eggs are when you buy them from the grocery, I've got the answer for you. And it's rather simple!

All you do is take a bowl of cold water and ease the raw eggs you want to test onto the bottom (just make sure you got enough water in the bowl to cover the eggs).

—If they lay over on their sides, they're super fresh.

—If they tend to rest on about a 45-degree angle, you can figure they're about 3 days old.

—But if they stand up perfectly straight on end, you're looking at eggs that are at least 10 days old.

By the way, if you can hear an egg sloshing around inside of its shell when you shake it . . . don't crack it! It's rotten!

More about eggs

Here are a few tips you might find helpful:

1—If you wet your knife with warm water before you try slicing hard-boiled eggs, you'll find out the yolks won't crumble so easily.

2—If you add a little bit of plain French bread crumbs to your scrambled eggs before you cook them, they'll come out lighter and improve the flavor.

3—Always add about a teaspoon of salt and a tablespoon of vinegar to the water that you use to hard-boil your eggs. You'll find that the salt will prevent the egg shells from cracking. And even if one should crack during boiling, the vinegar will quickly seal the crack.

4—It's an old wives' tale that you have to start hard-boiled eggs in cold water. If the eggs are fresh, and they are at room temperature, you can drop them directly into boiling water without them cracking. Only the old eggs will crack.

5—Whenever you poach eggs in the classical manner, be sure you have a tablespoon of vinegar in the poaching liquid. The vinegar keeps the white together and won't allow it to scatter out in the water.

6—Whenever you whip eggs (for omelets, mayonnaise, salad dressings, and meringues) always be sure you bring the eggs to room temperature first. Never use them directly from the refrigerator. Room temperature eggs beat up fluffier and with more volume.

7—According to recent U.S. Food and Drug Administration findings, it is recommended that you always store your eggs in the refrigerator. In years past, it was acceptable (and even encouraged by food experts) that eggs be kept at room temperature. This is not the case any longer. Refrigerate them!

CHAPTER 7

Vegetables

Frank's N'Awlins Vegetable Medley

I just had to pass this recipe along to you! As simple as it is to prepare, the combination of vegetables and the mingling of the flavors each contributes to the dish makes even kids crave their veggies! And it's a great accompanying dish to serve with chicken, beef, veal, pork, duck, and seafood.

4 tbsp. margarine or butter	1 cup shredded cabbage
1 cup thick-sliced zucchini	1 cup thick-sliced green onions
1 cup thick-sliced yellow squash	1 tsp. salt
1 small thick-sliced red onion	1 tsp. white pepper
1 cup thick-sliced mushrooms	2 tbsp. teriyaki sauce
1 cup julienned carrots	

Basically, all you're doing with this dish is lightly stir-frying then steaming. So you can make the vegetable medley in a 12-inch skillet, but I prefer to fix it in a 5-quart Dutch oven with a lid.

So take your pot, toss in the margarine, heat it over *high heat* until bubbles form, and quickly add the vegetables. Then with a slotted spoon, stir the mixture constantly until the vegetables are thoroughly coated with the margarine.

At this point, sprinkle on the salt, white pepper, and teriyaki sauce, mix thoroughly once again, and stir-fry for 3 minutes.

Now, cover the pot, remove it from the burner, and let it "set" for 5-10 minutes, depending upon how crispy (al dente) you want the vegetables. For a crunchy barely-cooked taste, serve them about 4 minutes after you remove the pot from the fire. For a firm-but-softened consistency, you should allow the pot to steep for about 10 minutes.

Suggestion: Don't think those are the only veggies you can put into this dish. If you like bell peppers (both red and green) toss them in! If you like broccoli, toss some in too. In other words, fix it any way your heart desires! I promise it will come out great!

Frank's Eggplant Siciliano

If you're an eggplant addict, this is one of the best eggplant dishes you'll ever fix. It's kinda like lasagne . . . only more Italian! You got to try this one, paisano!

2 tbsp. extra virgin olive oil	**1 lb. mozzarella cheese**
1 quart marinara sauce*	**2 cups grated Romano cheese**
1 large eggplant, peeled and	**1 tsp. garlic powder**
sliced	**4 tsp. basil leaves**
1 lb. Italian sausage, pan	**2 tsp. oregano**
sautéed	**black pepper to taste**

First, take a 10-by-14 glass baking pan and coat the sides and bottom with the olive oil. Then pour a cup of the marinara sauce into the pan and spread it out evenly.

Next, place a layer of the sliced eggplant in the pan (making sure to work it into the sauce). Then spread on another half-cup or so of sauce to cover the eggplant. Now *sprinkle* on some Italian sausage . . . then some mozzarella . . . then some Romano . . . then some garlic powder . . . then some basil . . . then some oregano. Just try to get the *sprinklings* as evenly distributed as possible.

At this point, ladle on another cup of the sauce, spread it around, and cover it with another layer of eggplant. Now repeat the entire process over and over again until all the ingredients are used, and top off the dish with a heavy layer of mozzarella.

Now, preheat your oven to 350 degrees, season to taste with the black pepper, and cover the dish *tightly* with heavy-duty aluminum foil. All that's left is to bake it in the upper third of your oven for about an hour (or until the eggplant is soft and tender), then cool for about 20 minutes before serving.

Hint: You can dress up this casserole any way you want to—just let your imagination be your guide. Feel free to add mushrooms, anchovies, black olives, pepperoni, or whatever other Italian—er, excuse me, Sicilian—ingredients you like.

---

*The marinara sauce recipe is elsewhere in this book.

Frank's Famous Eleven-Minute Cauliflower

If you're like me and you relish the intense flavor of fresh cauliflower cooked in its own moisture . . . then you're gonna love this dish. And it's so simple you won't believe it!

1 whole large cauliflower	**2 tbsp. sweet cream butter**
1 tbsp. water	**2 slices Velveeta cheese singles**
1 microwave dish (4 inches deep)	**salt and black pepper to taste**
1 piece of plastic wrap	

First, wash the cauliflower thoroughly, trim away the bottom leaves, and remove the stem (you want to cut it flush with the base of the cauliflower).

Then place it right-side-up in a deep microwaveable dish (along with the tablespoon of water), cover it tightly with plastic wrap, and make two or three small vent holes in the plastic.

Now place the dish into the microwave oven and cook the cauliflower on *high power* for *exactly 11 minutes*! No more—no less!

At this point, remove the wrap, cut the cauliflower into quarters, spoon on the butter, and sprinkle on your salt and pepper to taste. Then place the slices of cheese over the hot cauliflower, immediately recover it with another sheet of plastic wrap, and allow the cheese to melt.

Serve immediately!

You're not going to believe how good cauliflower can be!

Veggie tip

If you want your fresh vegetables to stay sweet and retain their rich colors when you cook them, just add a little whole milk to the water when you boil them, especially when you're cooking broccoli, cauliflower, and corn on the cob.

The broccoli will stay deep green, the cauliflower will come out pure white, and you won't believe the extra flavor you'll get in the corn!

Frank's Old New Orleans Stuffed Artichokes

If you savor the flavor of artichokes, stuffed Italian style with lots of Romano and olive oil, but you avoid making them because you think it's too much work . . . you're gonna love this super-easy way to fix Frank's Old New Orleans Stuffed Artichokes. Regardless of how you've done 'em before . . . you owe it to yourself to try this method!

1—Trim off the stalk portion of the raw artichoke as close to the leaves as you can get (and trim it straight so that it sits nice and level).

2—Then with a *very sharp* knife—an electric knife is best!—cut off the top third of the artichoke so that the upper leaves are exposed.

3—Next, wash the artichoke thoroughly, inside and out, and rub the cut edges with a piece of fresh lemon to keep the leaves from turning brown.

4—Then, using a melon baller or small teaspoon, dig out the *"choke,"* the prickly, fuzzy center of the artichoke. But remember, you just want to remove the center thistle (that's the purple part), not all the inside tender leaves.

5—Now, rinse the artichoke again, rub it once more with lemon juice, and turn it upside down on a couple of paper towels to drain. Prepare all the artichokes you plan to fix this way and set them aside momentarily. Because at this point, you're ready to stuff!

MAKING THE STUFFING MIX

For a half-dozen artichokes, you're going to need:

4 cups seasoned breadcrumbs	**2 tsp. black pepper**
3 cups imported Romano cheese	**1 lemon, sliced thinly**
1 tbsp. Italian seasonings	**6 fillets of anchovies**
2 tsp. garlic powder	**4 cups water**
1 tsp. onion powder	**1 quart extra virgin olive oil**

Simply add all the dry ingredients together in a large bowl and mix them thoroughly *with your hands* until uniformly blended.

Now, working with one artichoke at a time, place it in the bowl of stuffing mix and begin heaping the mixture over the top of the leaves. Then, just like shuffling a deck of cards, run your thumb over the leaves and allow the stuffing to drop between them until the spaces are filled. The more you stuff the leaves, the larger the artichoke will become. Do all the artichokes this way.

Incidentally, the mixture above will stuff a half-dozen artichokes nicely. To do a dozen . . . just double the recipe.

Now, lay 1 thin slice of lemon and one anchovy fillet on each artichoke and place the artichokes into a steamer pot (or seafood boiling pot with a basket) so that they just touch each other—this keeps the outer leaves from falling off. Then add about 4 cups of water to the steamer, bring it to a slow boil, and place the lid on the pot. (For best results, set the heat to about medium.)

Total cooking time is about *an hour and fifteen minutes* for medium artichokes to *an hour and a half* for large ones. *But every 15 minutes*, remove the lid carefully (WATCH THE STEAM!) and—in a thin stream—pour some of the olive oil over the top of the artichokes. Then replace the lid and continue cooking until a meat fork will pierce the artichoke through and through.

That's Frank's New Orleans Stuffed Artichokes . . . and you can serve them hot or cold.

Hints:

1—Add extra cheese to the stuffing mix if you want a heavy cheese flavor in your artichokes. Most Italians mix their stuffing to taste. I recommend you use the mixture I gave you as a base and add to it according to your tastes.

2—Don't be afraid to make more mix than you need. It freezes well in Ziploc bags and it's excellent as a coating for veal cutlets, pork chops, meatballs, chicken, and seafood.

3—To serve the artichokes hot, cook them about three-quarters of the way in the steamer, then transfer them to a baking pan, along with about a cup and a half of the steaming liquid. Then sprinkle a little extra Romano cheese over each artichoke, cover the pan tightly with aluminum foil, and bake in your oven at 325 degrees for 30 minutes.

4—Don't just stuff a few artichokes! Stuff about a dozen of 'em when you make them. Then after they cool to room temperature, wrap them in several layers of plastic film (Saran) and stash them away in your freezer! They'll keep well for up to 3 months.

Note: I stuff my artichokes "raw" as opposed to par-boiling them. I find that par-boiling causes you to lose the rich robust artichoke flavor and makes stuffing a real chore. Artichokes steamed raw with the stuffing inside locks in all the flavor! Try it!

Frank's Real N'Awlins Chili

It's beefy and robust, sticks to your ribs, peppery but not too hot, can be made with or without beans, and is usually served in a soupbowl with saltines or tortilla chips! But, even better than that . . . it's good!

2 lb. lean ground beef	**3 tbsp. all-purpose flour**
1 bottle chili powder	**1 can Contadina tomato sauce**
1 oz. cumin	** (15 oz. size)**
beef drippings	**1 can diced Rotel tomatoes with**
1 finely chopped medium bell	** chilies**
** pepper**	**2 tbsp. paprika**
3 cloves minced garlic	**2 cups of beef or chicken stock**
2 large finely diced onions	**salt and cayenne pepper to taste**
½ cup finely diced celery	

First take a 12-inch heavy aluminum skillet, heat it to medium-high, and begin sautéing the ground meat. When it is about half-cooked (some chunks are brown, some are still pink) add the chili powder and the cumin and continue to cook until the beef browns all over and most of the juices are rendered out.

When the meat is cooked, remove it from the skillet, drain off the fat (but save it), and divide the meat in half. You want to leave one half chunky, but place the other half in a food processor and chop it fine.

Then, using the drippings from the rendering process, add your bell peppers, onions, garlic, and celery and sauté the vegetables until they turn transparent. At this point, sprinkle in enough flour (you're gonna make a light roux) to absorb whatever drippings are left from sautéing the meat and vegetables. Stirring constantly, cook the roux until it begins to thicken slightly.

Now return the ground beef to the pan and add your tomato sauce, paprika, and the Rotels. Then turn the fire up to high, bring the mixture to full heat, and cook the meat and tomatoes until the roux base blends in evenly and smoothly. Then add your beef (or chicken) stock, stir it into the mixture thoroughly, and season the chili to taste with the salt and cayenne pepper.

All you do now is cover the pot and let the chili simmer for about 45 minutes (or until all the ingredients "marry" into one uniform taste). Then when you're ready to eat, liberally spoon it out in large soupbowls, garnish it with finely chopped parsley, and serve with saltine crackers.

Serving Suggestion: Chili goes best with a fresh guacamole salad and a frosty beer served in a tall glass.

Frank's Fantastic Baked Beans

Looking for a special treat to go with barbecued ribs, fried chicken, or roast beef? Try these baked beans! And I suggest you serve them with fresh corn on the cob!

4 tbsp. real butter
1 medium yellow onion, diced
½ cup finely diced celery
1 small bell pepper, diced
3 cloves garlic, minced
2 tbsp. Worcestershire sauce

1 cup hickory-flavored barbecue sauce
2 tbsp. brown sugar
¼ cup bacon bits
1 16-oz. can of pork 'n beans

First, take a 12-inch skillet and melt the butter until it comes to a sizzle (but do not let it brown). Then drop in the onions, celery, bell pepper, and garlic and sauté the mixture until it softens—*about 6-8 minutes.*

Next, add the Worcestershire sauce, the barbecue sauce, the brown sugar, and the bacon bits. And—while constantly stirring—simmer the mixture (uncovered) over low heat for 15 minutes so that all the flavors marry.

While the sauce is cooking, take a 9-by-11 Pyrex baking pan and either grease it lightly with margarine or spray it with Pam. Then place the pork 'n beans (plus the liquid they come packed in) into the pan. When your flavoring sauce is smooth and shiny, pour it over the beans and mix it in well.

Then, place the casserole into a 375-degree oven and bake the beans—uncovered—for about 35-45 minutes or until the top turns dark brown and bubbly.

Serve piping hot!

Frank's N'Awlins Scalloped Potatoes

A change from au gratin, richer than double-stuffed, more robust than brabant, and twice as tempting as butter-baked, these potatoes go great with chicken, pork, and wild game.

8 cups thin-sliced raw white potatoes	**1 cup minced onion**
6 tbsp. all-purpose flour	**½ cup finely sliced green onions**
2 tsp. salt	**½ cup finely chopped parsley**
1 tsp. black pepper	**5 cups scalded milk**
	¼ stick butter

First, take a 4-quart casserole dish and butter the bottom and sides. Then mix together well the flour, salt, and black pepper, and preheat your oven to 350 degrees.

Next, take one-third of the potatoes and make a layer on the bottom of the casserole dish. Then sprinkle the slices gently with one-third of the flour mixture. Then sprinkle on one-third of the onions, green onions, and parsley.

Repeat this process until you "layer on" all the potatoes, flour, onions, green onions, and parsley.

Now, scald the milk and melt the butter into it. And when thoroughly blended, gently pour the mixture uniformly over the layered potatoes.

At this point, cover the casserole with tight-fitting aluminum foil and bake for 30 minutes. Then uncover the dish and bake for another hour (or until the potatoes are browned and tender).

Serve 'em piping hot! And you'd better have enough for seconds!

Super-crispy French fries

Want to fix French fries so that they turn out crunchy and crispy all the time? Here's how you do it!

Just take the fries, immediately after you slice them from the potato, and place them into iced water for about a half hour before you cook them. Then pat them dry in a kitchen towel and—while still cold—drop them into deep fat. They'll come out extra crisp and crunchy every time.

By the way, if you also soak your Idaho baking potatoes in salt water for about 20 minutes before oiling and wrapping them in aluminum foil, they'll bake more rapidly and they'll taste more creamy.

Frank's Twice-Baked Stuffed Potatoes

While this recipe is intended to be a complementary dish, it can also be served as a main meal if that's what you want to do with it. Add a few ingredients here and there, and you got yourself a real gourmet treat! You gotta try it!

4 large baking potatoes	**½ cup crumbled bacon**
4 tbsp. margarine	**1 can Frito-Lay jalapeño cheese**
1 cup finely chopped onions	**dip**
½ cup finely chopped celery	**salt and black pepper to taste**
¼ cup finely chopped bell	
pepper	

First, wash the potatoes, rub them down well with Crisco vegetable oil, wrap them individually in aluminum foil, and bake them for 1 hour in a 400-degree oven until tender.

When they're done, allow them to cool for about 30 to 40 minutes. Then split them in half lengthwise, scoop out the centers, and *coarsely* mash the pulp in a large mixing bowl.

Next, in a 12-inch skillet, heat the margarine and sauté the onions, celery, and bell pepper until they wilt and turn soft. Then stir your vegetable mixture into the potato pulp, along with the half-cup of crumbled bacon. Now take your time at this point and thoroughly blend all these ingredients to a uniform consistency—*but don't mash up all the potatoes: you want to have some chunky pieces left.*

Now sprinkle in your salt and pepper and *carefully fold in* the can of cheese dip (almost as if you were trying to create a swirl effect, similar to fudge ripple ice cream). *Be sure you don't overmix!*

And when everything is blended just right, generously stuff the pulp back into the potato halves, place them onto a shallow cookie pan, and re-bake them for 10 to 15 minutes in a 450-degree oven to piping hot!

Serve with roast, grilled steaks, barbecued chicken, or fried fish for a truly N'Awlins delicacy!

Suggestions: If you want to vary the stuffing ingredients, go ahead and knock yourself out! You can use this basic recipe and substitute broccoli, shrimp, crabmeat, crawfish tails, or anything else your heart desires. You can't ruin this one!

Frank's Creole Crawfish Stuffed Bell Pepper

A combination of succulent crawfish tails, rich tomato sauce, and all the robust Creole flavor of New Orleans-sautéed vegetables blended to perfection and served over steamed buttered rice. Y'all . . . it don't get no better than this!

6 bell peppers
1 stick butter
1 cup finely chopped white
   onions
⅔ cup sliced green onions
½ cup finely chopped celery
½ cup finely chopped bell
   pepper
½ cup sliced mushrooms
3 bay leaves

1 cup chicken stock
1 can cream of mushroom soup
1 tbsp. minced garlic
2 lb. crawfish tails (with fat)
⅔ cup minced parsley
4-6 cups cooked rice
salt, black, and cayenne pepper
   to taste
1 cup seasoned bread crumbs

First, cut the bell peppers in half lengthwise, remove the seeds, and wash them well inside and out. Then place them into a steamer pot and cook them until they just begin to wilt slightly. *Do not overcook!*

Next, remove them from the steamer, shock them with cold water to stop the cooking, and place cut-side-down on paper towels to drain.

At this point, take a 12-inch skillet, melt the stick of butter over medium heat, and sauté the onions, green onions, celery, bell pepper, and mushrooms until tender (about 5 minutes). Then, to the mixture stir in the chicken stock and the mushroom soup (along with the bay leaves and garlic) and simmer over low heat until thoroughly blended and smooth.

Now, toss in the crawfish tails and cook everything together for about 5 minutes (*but do not overcook or the tails will shrink and turn rubbery*). When mixed completely, remove the bay leaves, pour the crawfish and sauce into the cooked rice (along with the parsley), and blend to a moist consistency. (*Note:* I suggest you don't add all of the sauce at one time. It is best to keep the rice mix rather dry . . . otherwise the stuffing will run when it is baked.)

Finally, season the mixture with salt and pepper to taste and stuff it into the cooled bell pepper halves. Then liberally sprinkle the tops with seasoned bread crumbs, place into a casserole dish, and bake at 350 degrees for about 30 minutes (or until the crumbs turn a toasty golden brown).

Hint: I recommend you serve the peppers with buttered carrots, a cold tomato/cucumber salad (with all the trimmings), and a glass of chilled white wine.

Frank's Pan-Sautéed Carrots au Naturel

You've had steamed carrots, carrots au gratin, and glazed carrots, huh? But if you want to try some of the best carrots you ever had . . . try these! They're tender, they're sweet, they're easy to fix, and they go with everything!

1 lb. peeled, shredded carrots
2 tbsp. butter or margarine
salt and pepper to taste

All you do is take the carrots and shred them into fine strips (you can do this with a knife, but a food shredder that you can buy at a kitchen store does a better job).

Then, in a heavy 12-inch skillet with a tight-fitting lid, heat the butter or margarine to "hot," toss in the carrots, sprinkle with salt and pepper to taste, and stir-fry them until they start to wilt slightly (this should take about 4 or 5 minutes over high heat).

At that point, turn the fire off, remove the skillet from the burner, and stir the carrots once more. Then cover the pan with the lid and let the dish "set" for 10 minutes.

When you're ready to eat, just reheat the carrots slightly and serve alongside veal, beef, chicken, fish, pork, shrimp, or anything else you like!

Simple, huh? But unbelievably good!

Frank's N'Awlins Cabbage Rolls

I've been making cabbage rolls since I was a kid! But these are not just your everyday cabbage leaves stuffed with meat and rice. The combination of seasonings along with the stir-fry cabbage that mixes into the stuffing makes them kinda special. I want you to try these and see if you don't agree!

1 large head of green cabbage	½ tsp. thyme
1 medium head of red cabbage	2 tsp. basil
½ stick butter	1 cup beef stock
2 tsp. red wine vinegar	2 cups cooked rice
1 lb. lean ground beef	1 large can tomato sauce
1 lb. lean ground pork	1 can Rotel tomatoes
1 large onion, finely diced	salt and pepper to taste
4 green onions, sliced	¼ cup grated parmesan cheese
5 cloves garlic, minced	½ cup shredded provolone
2 ribs celery, finely diced	cheese
1 tbsp. Worcestershire sauce	

First, pull off 8-10 large cabbage leaves (you can mix the red and the green cabbage to give the dish added color). Then place the leaves into a 4-quart Dutch oven or stock pot and simmer them in about an inch of boiling water for about 5 minutes until tender. *But do not overcook or they will tear apart when you try to stuff them!* Now lay them out on paper towels and allow them to drain.

Meanwhile, shred the remaining cabbage (both red and green). Then, in a 12-inch skillet, melt the butter and quickly stir-fry the cabbage. About halfway through the cooking process, add the wine vinegar and cook until most of the pungent aroma is gone. When done (and it should take about 8 minutes), set the mix aside to cool.

Next, using a 12-inch frypan, sauté the ground beef and pork together until lightly browned. Then toss in the onions, celery, green onions, garlic, thyme, basil, and Worcestershire sauce. Continue cooking until the vegetables have wilted. Then, using a strainer, drain off all the excess grease.

Now place the meat mixture back into the frypan, stir in the cooked cabbage and the beef stock, and simmer the meat mix until most of the beef stock liquid evaporates.

At this point, remove the frypan from the heat, mix in the rice, and season to taste with salt and pepper. Then fill each cabbage leaf with about a quarter-cup or so of meat stuffing and roll it up, folding the sides over to the center. Next, place each of the rolls into a lightly oiled casserole dish.

Then, with the same pan you used to sauté the meat mix, simmer the tomato sauce and Rotels together until the mixture turns hot and bubbly and begins to thicken slightly. All that's left is to ladle the sauce over the cabbage rolls, sprinkle the top with grated parmesan and provolone, and bake at 350 degrees for about an hour.

Hint: I suggest you serve the rolls with buttered parsley potatoes and crunchy cornbread. Incidentally, any extra stuffing you have left can be simmered into the tomato sauce mixture. And if you have any extra cabbage left over, place it around the cabbage rolls in the casserole dish before baking.

Frank's Oven Crusted Potatoes

You can fix potatoes hundreds of ways. But this has got to be my favorite of 'em all! Except for mashed, creamed, baked, au-gratin . . . !

2 lb. "B" size creamer potatoes	**3 egg yolks**
2 tbsp. crab boil	**salt and pepper to taste**
½ cup liquid margarine	

First, boil then peel the creamer potatoes (and remember to add the crab boil to the water to spice up the seasoning). After they're peeled, put them in your refrigerator to set for at least an hour.

Then when you're ready to cook, preheat your oven to 425 degrees, salt and pepper the potatoes, and place them onto a shallow, lightly greased cookie sheet.

Next, whip together the liquid margarine and 3 well-beaten egg yolks. And using a pastry brush, brush the egg-margarine mixture thoroughly over the potatoes. You want to coat each one of them liberally.

Now bake them in the upper half of the oven for about 20 minutes or until the outsides turn a rich, crusty, golden brown.

If you like potatoes like I do, this is almost a meal in itself!

Frank's N'Awlins Yams in Praline Sauce

I originally made this dish as a vegetable—but it's so good you can use it as a dessert! Go ahead—do what you want!

The Sweet Taters:

2 cans Louisiana yams
  (16-ounce size)
2 tbsp. real butter
½ cup chopped pecan pieces

2 tsp. cinnamon
½ tsp. salt
2 eggs (slightly beaten)

The Praline Sauce:

⅓ cup light Karo corn syrup
¾ cup dark brown sugar
  (lightly packed)
½ stick butter
⅛ tsp. salt

½ cup praline liquor
¼ tsp. vanilla
another ½ stick butter
1 cup chopped pecans

Using an 11-by-14 buttered Pyrex baking dish, start off by mashing the sweet potatoes (but leave a few chunky pieces in the mix). Then fold in— one at a time—all the remaining ingredients. When the blend is thoroughly mixed, place the dish in the oven and bake *uncovered* at 375 degrees for about 20 minutes.

While the yams are baking, make your praline sauce. Here's how you do it.

In a 3-quart saucepan, bring to a boil the Karo syrup, the brown sugar, the first half stick of butter, the salt, and the praline liquor. Then when the mix is thoroughly blended and creamy smooth, take it off the fire, stir in the vanilla, and let the sauce cool slightly.

Finally, gently stir in the second half stick of butter and the cup of pecans.

Then, when you're ready to serve the yams, pour the hot praline sauce over the potatoes in the casserole dish, take a fork and separate the potatoes lightly, and allow the sauce to seep in.

Variation #1: If you prefer not to serve the sauce as a topping you can also mix it into the yams and make it a part of the dish.

Variation #2: If you want to change the flavor of the sauce, instead of using praline liquor substitute Southern Comfort in its place. This makes the yams more of a dessert than a vegetable side-dish.

Frank's Broccoli Cauliflower Casserole

Crispy green broccoli and succulently steamed cauliflower, flavored with garlic, sautéed in olive oil, and covered in a creamy shrimp-flavored cheese sauce! For holidays or any days, this could be an entire meal in itself!

2 bunches fresh broccoli	**1 can cream of shrimp soup**
1 large head of fresh cauliflower	**½ cup heavy cream**
2 tbsp. butter	**1 cup diced Velveeta cheese**
2 tbsp. olive oil	**salt and pepper to taste**
1 cup finely chopped onion	**½ cup water plus 1 tbsp.**
4 cloves garlic, minced	**cornstarch**
¼ tsp. celery seed	**¾ cup Ritz cracker crumbs**

First, separate the cauliflower into pieces and cut the broccoli into florets. Then either steam or microwave them until they're *al dente* (tender, but still crisp). When cooked, drain the pieces and set them aside to cool.

Meanwhile, heat the butter and oil together in a 12-inch skillet and gently sauté the onions and garlic until they clear and turn soft (*but do not burn the garlic*). Then with the heat set at medium-low, stir in the celery seed, the shrimp soup, the heavy cream, and the cheese. Now simmer the mixture *gently* until the cheese is thoroughly melted and the sauce turns creamy and smooth.

At this point, taste for salt and pepper and make any adjustments you desire. Now mix together a half-cup of cold water and a tablespoon of cornstarch, stir it into the cheese sauce, and cook it over medium-high heat *only until it thickens*. Then immediately remove the skillet from the fire and set it aside for a moment.

Next, place the broccoli and cauliflower pieces into a lightly buttered 3-quart casserole dish, ladle on the melted cheese mixture, and sprinkle the top liberally with the Ritz cracker crumbs.

All that's left is to bake it in a 350-degree oven for about 15 to 20 minutes or until the top is toasty and the casserole is hot and bubbly.

Hint: Don't worry if the sauce looks exceptionally thick. As the casserole bakes, the broccoli and cauliflower will cause it to thin slightly and it will turn out just right!

Frank's Crispy Italian Fried Eggplant

This is one of the recipes I'm most proud of! It literally took me months to get it just right—crispy, tender, totally Italian, and absolutely greaseless! In other words, it's the best fried eggplant you'll ever eat!

1 gallon water	16 oz. Italian bread crumbs
3 tbsp. salt	2 tsp. Italian seasoning
2 young eggplants, peeled	1 tsp. garlic powder
3 eggs, well-beaten	1 cup grated Romano cheese
1 cup whole milk	Crisco oil for frying

First, take a container large enough to hold both of the eggplants, add the water and the salt, and mix it together until fully dissolved. Then, slice the eggplants into pieces about one-half inch thick and soak them in the salted water for at least a half-hour. *The salty water removes some of the eggplants' "bite" and prevents them from absorbing oil.*

Then, drain off the water.

Next, whip the milk and the eggs together in one bowl until foamy. Then mix the bread crumbs, Italian seasoning, garlic powder, and Romano cheese in another bowl until all are *thoroughly blended.*

Now, *a few pieces at a time,* dip the sliced eggplant into the egg wash and drop them immediately into the bread crumb mixture. And with your hands, pack the crumbs onto the eggplant until the pieces are coated well.

At this point, gently set the coated eggplant onto a sheet of waxed paper or into a baking pan and allow it to "cure" for at least 15 minutes. The trick is . . . *you want the egg mix to bind the crumbs together so that the coating doesn't fall off when the eggplants hit the hot oil.* And the only way to do this is to let the coated pieces "cure."

Finally, in a skillet, heat the Crisco oil to medium-high and fry the coated eggplants (in small batches) until they turn a toasty brown. Just be sure you give them a lot of room to cook—don't crowd them together. Your cooking time is about a minute and a half to two minutes on each side, depending on the temperature of the oil.

After cooking, drain the eggplant slices on several thicknesses of paper towels and serve them piping hot, topped with an extra sprinkling of Romano cheese.

Hints:

1—Use enough Crisco oil to almost cover *the eggplant slices without deep-frying.*

2—For a richer Italian flavor, you can use imported Extra Virgin Olive Oil instead of Crisco oil. But it will give your eggplant a heavier, more pronounced Italian taste.

3—You'll need to turn the eggplant pieces once or twice as they cook. The best way to do that is with a pair of tongs.

4—Don't take any shortcuts! The recipe won't come out right if you do!

5—Keep a good supply of the coating mix handy in the refrigerator all the time. It's also great for making meatballs, coating chicken, and stuffing artichokes.

Bacon Wrapped Green Beans

Here's a simple vegetable dish that goes well with almost any meat, fish, or fowl! And it complements just about everything on the table!

2 cans whole green beans (303 size)
1 cup of whole milk
½ lb. lean hickory-smoked bacon

How 'bout dat for simplicity, huh?

What you do is drain the green beans, *gently* wash them in cool water several times (you don't want to break them all up), and soak them in the milk for about 15 minutes (this neutralizes the canned taste and makes them mild).

Now, while the beans are marinating, take the bacon and cut each strip into three pieces.

Then, taking the raw bacon, place about 4 or 5 beans in the center of the strip and roll the bacon around them. When tightly secured, place the "bundles" into a shallow, greased, baking pan side by side.

All that's left is to bake them in a 350-degree oven until the bacon cooks and shrinks, tightening down on the beans wrapped inside (this should take about 15 minutes). The end product is a tender but crispy dinner vegetable.

Hint: To eliminate some of the bacon fat from soaking into the beans, just cook the bundles on a baking rack so that the drippings fall into the pan.

Frank's Plantation Potatoes

This is a nice combination of creamed potatoes, baked potatoes, and potatoes au gratin. And it goes great as an accompaniment with almost any main dish you serve.

8 large boiled red potatoes
2 cups finely diced onions
½ cup margarine (or butter)
2 cups grated Cheshire cheese
  (or sharp cheddar)

4 tbsp. finely chopped parsley
salt and pepper to taste

First, in a skillet, sauté the onions in a little bit of the butter until they turn a nice golden brown (caramelized). Then peel the potatoes, boil them until they are *almost done,* and set them aside to cool.

Next, slice each potato into thirds and arrange the pieces into a heavily buttered baking pan. Then mix all of the onions, half of the margarine, and half of the Cheshire or cheddar cheese into the potatoes, season with salt and pepper, cover the pan with aluminum foil, and bake in a preheated oven for 30 minutes.

Finally, when you're ready to eat, drizzle the rest of the margarine evenly over the potatoes, sprinkle the top with the remaining cheese, and place back into the oven—uncovered—until the cheese melts.

All that's left is to garnish the dish with the finely chopped parsley and serve it piping hot.

Frank's Guacamole

If you're an avocado lover . . . you're gonna love this!

¼ cup fresh minced onions
3 green chili peppers
1 medium-large tomato,
  quartered
2 ripe avocados, quartered

1½ tbsp. fresh lemon juice
1 tsp. salt
¼ tsp. white pepper
dash cumin

In a food processor, blend together the onions, chili peppers, and to-matoes until finely chopped (*but not pureed*). Then, *using a spoon,* mash the avocados into a semi-chunky paste and fold in the processed onion-chili pepper-tomato mixture.

At this point, *gently fold in* the remaining ingredients until thoroughly blended . . . *but do not over-stir and do not over-cream the avocados.* You do not want a soupy mix!

Before serving, chill in the refrigerator about 4 hours.

Suggestions: This mix is good not only as a guacamole dip or as a topping for fajitas, it makes an excellent salad dressing as well as a unique sauce for baked chicken and grilled shrimp.

Frank's German-Style Red Cabbage

You know that great-tasting, mouth-watering red cabbage they serve at all the German festivals? Well . . . here's how they make that!

2 tbsp. margarine
1 cup onions, coarsely diced
2 heads red cabbage, shredded
3 Granny Smith apples, diced
¼ cup apple cider vinegar
¼ cup water
1 tsp. granulated sugar

1 tbsp. Worcestershire sauce
2 bay leaves
2 tsp. sweet basil
2 cups shredded pork or
    knackwurst
salt and pepper to taste

First, melt the margarine in a 5-quart heavy aluminum Dutch oven and gently sauté the onions until they soften. Then drop in the shredded cabbage and the apples, mix them thoroughly with the onions and stir-fry everything for about 5 minutes or until the red cabbage begins to wilt.

Next, stir in the vinegar, the water, the sugar, the Worcestershire sauce, the bay leaves, the basil, and the knackwurst. Then combine all the ingredients thoroughly—*and I mean mix them well!*

At this point, reduce the heat to medium-low, cover the pot tightly, and smother the cabbage for about 30 minutes or so . . . stirring occasionally.

After the allotted cooking time, stir the cabbage once again, season it to taste with salt and pepper, and serve it piping hot with sauerbraten or wiener schnitzels!

Das ist wunderbar!

Hint: If you can't find good knackwurst, you can substitute two cups of lean shredded pork instead. Add it to the pot when you sauté the onions and cook it until it turns creamy white.

Frank's Southern Smothered Cabbage

If you like cabbage, especially when it's rich, crunchy, and full of flavor, I promise you that this recipe will be one of your all-time favorites from now on. Wait till you try this!

1 medium head cabbage, shredded	⅛ tsp. garlic powder
4 strips meaty bacon	½ tsp. basil
½ stick andouille sausage	1½ tsp. black pepper
3 tbsp. McCormick's Vegetable Supreme	2 tbsp. light soy sauce
	2 tsp. Teriyaki sauce
4 tbsp. finely chopped green onions	½ cup Romano cheese
	salt to taste

Start off by cutting the cabbage into quarters and removing the "knots" at the base of the head. Then shred each section to the consistency of cole slaw and set it aside for a moment.

Now take the bacon and andouille sausage, chop them into small pieces, and add it either to a 6-quart heavy aluminum Dutch oven or Chinese wok. Then quickly fry down the meats over medium-high heat until they render most of their natural oils and start to turn crisp. *Remember to stir continually as the bacon and sausage fry!*

Next, add the shredded cabbage to the pot, turn the heat up to high, and mix everything together thoroughly, making sure that all the cabbage is coated with the oil. At this point, put the cover on the pot and let the cabbage cook for about 3 minutes. *Don't worry about the slight burning that occurs on the bottom of the pot.*

Now take the cover off the pot again, add all the remaining vegetables and seasonings, and *stir, stir, stir!* The seasonings have to coat all the cabbage shreds well, otherwise the dish will lack uniformity. And when you are satisfied that you've blended everything together as best you can, put the lid back on the pot, reduce the heat to medium, and let the cabbage continue to "smother" for about 15-20 minutes or until it turns *al dente* (tender, but crispy). (*Note:* Depending on the BTU output of your stove, you may have to stir the mixture a few times during the cooking process to keep the bottom of the dish from scorching. I do!)

Finally, just before you plan to serve the cabbage, add the Romano cheese and stir it well into the mixture. This is also the time to adjust your salt content. Remember, there's going to be salt in the cheese, the Vegetable Supreme, and the soy sauce, and it has to cook into the dish before you can determine its potency. So add the salt last!

I suggest you serve this with grilled or baked pork ribs or pork chops, fresh buttered carrots, or a crisp tossed green salad with marinated artichoke hearts.

Frank's German-Style Boiled Potatoes

This potato dish goes great with almost anything. But if you want to serve German and you don't feel like potato salad or potato pancakes . . . this is real Deutsch!

8 lb. boiled creamer potatoes, peeled	**4 tbsp. finely sliced green onions**
¼ cup melted butter	**½ cup sour cream**
4 tbsp. finely chopped parsley	**⅔ cup shredded Swiss cheese**
	salt and pepper to taste

All you do is cut the potatoes in halves and place them into a buttered 11-by-14 Pyrex baking dish. Then sprinkle on the parsley, green onions, and Swiss cheese, and evenly spoon on the sour cream.

At this point, using two spoons, *gently* mix everything together well—making sure you don't break up the potatoes—and season to taste with salt and pepper. Then place the pan into a 4u0-degree preheated oven and bake for about 15-20 minutes or until hot and bubbly.

Variation: For a more elegant presentation, instead of mixing everything together in casserole fashion, you can also prepare this potato dish by layering each of the ingredients individually.

Frank's Broccoli Cheese Casserole

Rich, green, crispy broccoli flavored with garlic, sautéed in olive oil, accentuated with cheese, and covered with a creamy mushroom sauce! This could be an entire meal in itself!

**2 bunches fresh broccoli,
  chopped**
2 tbsp. butter
2 tbsp. Crisco oil
½ cup chopped onion
2 cloves garlic, minced

¼ tsp. celery seed
1 can cream of mushroom soup
1 roll garlic cheese
salt and pepper to taste
Italian-style bread crumbs

First, cut the broccoli into florets and either steam or microwave them until they're *al dente* (tender, but still crisp). When cooked, drain the pieces and set them aside to cool.

Meanwhile, heat the butter and oil together in a 12-inch skillet and gently sauté the onions and garlic until they clear and turn soft. Then with the heat set at medium-low, stir in the celery seed, the mushroom soup, and the cheese, and simmer the mixture gently until the cheese is thoroughly melted. At this point, taste the sauce for salt and pepper and make any adjustments you desire.

Next, place the broccoli into a lightly buttered 1½ quart casserole dish. Then top it with the melted cheese mixture and sprinkle it liberally with the Italian bread crumbs.

All that's left is to bake it in a 350-degree oven until the top is brown and the casserole is hot and bubbly.

That's all there is to it, y'all! And it's dynamite!

Sautéed Zucchini Julienne
With Andouille and Shrimp

Looking for a great New Orleans style vegetable dish to serve with your entrees? Try this. Or better yet . . . forget about the entrees! Just serve this! It's a meal in itself!

½ stick sweet real butter	½ cup finely chopped celery
1 lb. fresh, peeled shrimp (31-35 count)	½ cup finely chopped shallots
½ lb. sliced andouille (or smoked sausage)	6 large zucchini (julienned)
1 tsp. basil	¼ cup Romano cheese
	salt and pepper to taste

In a 12-inch skillet, melt the butter over medium-high heat and toss in the shrimp and the andouille. Then cook the mixture until the juices render out and the shrimp turn pink (about 5 minutes should do it).

Next, toss in the basil, celery, and shallots and season the pan with salt and pepper to taste. Continue to cook over medium-high heat for another 2 minutes.

At this point, drop in the zucchini and stir it around to coat it with the shrimp/andouille mixture. Then cover the skillet with a lid and reduce the heat to medium so that the shrimp/andouille stock steams the zucchini and cooks it *tender-crisp*. But note: *do not overcook!* You only want the zucchini to soften slightly; you don't want it to wilt! I suggest you peek into the skillet after about 5 minutes of "steaming time." It should be just right!

When you're ready to eat, dish up a generous helping of zucchini and shrimp, sprinkle it lightly with Romano cheese, and serve it piping hot alongside your favorite entrees.

EVERYTHING YOU NEED
TO KNOW ABOUT ONIONS

Even though you may think that Cajuns invented onions just so they could make a good pot of etouffée, the pungent and aromatic relative of the lily family actually goes as far back as ancient Egypt and the pharaohs. But just in case you are a bit confused as to which onions to use for which dishes, maybe the following will help:

• **Yellow Onions:** These are the most common onions, used whenever the recipe calls *simply* for chopped or diced onions. If you cut them in half "with the grain," they'll dice and mince a whole lot easier than trying to do it against the grain.

• **Globe Onions:** These are just large yellow onions, potent in flavor and suitable for almost any kind of cooking. They are also the ones you want to work with to make the famed *onion mums*.

• **Spanish Onions:** These are suitably substituted for yellow onions—principally used in cooking sauces, gravies, etc.

• **White (Bermuda) Onions:** These onions are often used in cooking, but because of their milder flavor they are better utilized in salads or on sandwiches (like on hamburgers and muffalettas).

• **Purple Onions:** I don't suggest you cook with purple onions when you can find yellow or white onions instead. Purple onions are soft-textured, which means they turn mushy and disintegrate when cooked. They also have a very mild flavor, which makes them the "ideal salad onion." So that's what I recommend you use them for.

• **Pearl Onions:** These are your pickling onions. Peel them by dropping them in boiling water for a few minutes and rubbing off the skins. Then "put them up" in Mason jars with vinegar and lots of spices (crab boil works great) and serve them with your Monday plate of red beans. Oh—these are also the onions you want to cook along with the corn and potatoes when you boil crawfish, crabs, and shrimp.

• **Vidalia Onions:** These are very special flat onions that come from Vidalia, Georgia, and they are so sweet and mild they can be eaten like an apple—and often are! Unfortunately, Vidalias have a very short growing season, so you should buy a good supply of them as soon as they hit the supermarket.

• **Green Onions:** These are correctly called scallions, but just about every New Orleanian will refer to them as *shallots*. I don't care what you want to call them as long as you include a half-cup or so of them (sliced thinly) in all your Cajun and Creole dishes—even if you've already used yellow onions. Incidentally, green onions are imperative if you make Cajun etouffée, courtbouillon, sauce piquante, jambalaya, gumbo, and— Oh!—Chinese food!

• **Leeks:** For all intents and purposes, let's call them jumbo-size green onions! Most New Orleans cooks rarely use them, but if you do you should use only the bottom third of the leek near the bulb (the green tops are stringy). Oh—and be sure to take them apart and wash them well because they are generally full of mud and sand. They're good minced and sautéed in sauces, and excellent in soups.

• **Shallots:** Just for the record, these are a cross between an onion and a garlic, having the flavor and characteristics of both. They look like large brown-skinned garlic cloves, and because their flavor is so mild they are best when used to make subtle sauces.

Stinky cabbage kitchen!

Do you avoid fixing cabbage and cauliflower at home because you abhor the fragrance (phew!) it gives off as it cooks? Well, have I got a few tips for you!

To keep that tell-tale stench from infiltrating every nook and cranny of your house, try this:

1—Place the peeling from an orange on top of the stove when you're cooking. The incidental heat of the stove will release the pleasing orange aroma and cover up the cabbage.

2—Next, put a slice a bread on top of the pot that you use to cook cabbage and cauliflower. The flour in the bread will absorb most of the odors as the vegetables cook.

3—And finally, when the cabbage and cauliflower begin to cook, break off one rib of celery and place it into the pot for the duration of the cooking process. The juices in the celery will neutralize the odor of the cauliflower and the cabbage. Just throw the celery away when the vegetables are cooked.

CHAPTER 8

Pasta

Frank's N'Awlins Baked Macaroni

This stuff is so good that . . . just one taste and you'll never fix macaroni and cheese out of a box again!

1 lb. cooked macaroni (#7)	1 cup light cream
2 whole eggs, well beaten	2 cups medium-sharp cheddar
¼ cup finely chopped parsley	cheese
1 stick butter	½ cup Swiss cheese
1 cup chopped onions	¾ cup Velveeta cheese
⅓ cup celery	salt and white pepper to taste

Start off by placing your cooked and drained macaroni in a buttered casserole dish and thoroughly mixing in the 2 beaten eggs and the parsley.

Then—in a saucepan—melt the butter over medium heat and sauté the onions and celery until they wilt. At this point, stir in the light cream and cook it into the butter and seasonings until blended well. Now, *a little at a time,* start adding the cheeses to the sauce (first the cheddar, then the Swiss, and finally the Velveeta). By the way, use only half of the cheddar in the sauce—the other half goes over the top of the macaroni.

Now, be sure you stir constantly as you add the cheeses so that they don't stick to the saucepan and burn. Incidentally, keep the heat on medium as you blend the sauce.

Next, season the cheese sauce with salt and white pepper to taste and pour it evenly over the macaroni. Don't be afraid to mix everything well! Then sprinkle the second cup of grated cheddar over the top of the macaroni, place in a 350-degree preheated oven, and bake for 35-45 minutes or until the cheese on top is melted and starting to brown.

Before serving, I suggest you put the entire dish under the broiler for a few minutes to toast the cheddar on top of the macaroni. Then sit back and enjoy!

Hint: For a "One-Dish Casserole," you can mix shredded chicken, shredded pork, ham, country sausage, butter sautéed shrimp, or anything else your heart desires to the macaroni (either individually or in combination) before you bake it.

Frank's Sicilian Lasagna

This isn't your weak, thrown-together, mostly-pasta lasagna you sometimes get in restaurants. The beef, mushrooms, and cheeses—generously
laced with Italian herbs and spices—are packed tightly between layers of
lasagna noodles with just enough tomato sauce to bind everything together and combine the flavors. In other words . . . "this is Italiano!"

2 lb. lean ground beef, chopped
   fine
1 cup finely chopped onions
½ cup finely chopped celery
½ cup finely chopped bell
   pepper
4 large cloves garlic, chopped
   fine
1 large can of Contadina tomato
   paste
3 cups water
2 tsp. Italian seasoning
salt and black pepper to taste
2 tbsp. margarine
1 lb. lasagna noodles, boiled
   al dente (firm)

4 cups cooked tomato gravy
   (recipe below)
2 cups shredded cheddar cheese
   (mild)
4 cups shredded mozzarella
   cheese
4 cups washed and drained
   cottage cheese
4 cups sliced mushrooms
2 cups grated Romano cheese
4 tbsp. Italian seasoning
4 tbsp. sweet basil
½ cup pitted black olives

First, take a heavy 12-inch skillet, sauté the ground beef until browned,
and set it aside. Then, make your tomato sauce by using the beef drippings
and frying down the onions, celery, bell pepper, and garlic until they
soften. Next, add the tomato paste, stir it into the vegetables, and fry it
until the color darkens slightly (about 4 to 5 minutes, being sure to stir
continuously as it cooks).

Now, add the water, the 2 teaspoons of Italian seasoning, and the salt
and pepper. Then turn down the fire, cover the pot, and let the sauce simmer for about 40 minutes.

At this point, take your lasagna pan (and you want to use a pan that you
can get about 4 layers of pasta, meat, and cheese into with about an inch
or so of free space left at the top) and grease it with the margarine.

Then, in order, lay in a layer of pasta . . . coat it with tomato sauce . . . sprinkle on some beef . . . some cheddar . . . some mozzarella . . . some cottage cheese . . . some mushrooms . . . some Romano . . . and some more tomato sauce. Then lightly sprinkle on some basil and the other 4 tablespoons of Italian seasoning and put down the next layer of pasta.

All you do then is repeat the process over and over until you have about 4 layers of pasta-meat-cheese. And when you get to the top, put on 1 more layer of pasta, coat it lightly with tomato sauce, sprinkle on a handful of mozzarella, decoratively arrange the remaining mushroom slices, and top each mushroom piece with a slice of black olives.

Now, take your hands and press down hard on the entire pan of lasagna until all the ingredients compress. Then put the lasagna into the oven and bake it—uncovered—at 350 degrees for about 20 to 30 minutes or until you can see the tomato sauce bubbling around the edges.

All that's left is to remove it from the oven and let it "set" for about 15 minutes before cutting it.

Serving Suggestion: *I recommend you serve the lasagna with garlic bread and a tossed salad made with iceberg and romaine lettuce, diced tomatoes, julienned celery and carrots, sliced black and green olives, pimientos, boiled eggs, finely chopped anchovies, a Caesar dressing, and a glass of chilled Frascati wine. Mama Mia! That's Italian!*

How to Make Frank's Pasta Alfredo
(In 8 Easy Steps)

In this classic old Italian dish, you can use shrimp, crawfish, crumbled bacon, cooked Italian sausage, sautéed calamari, sautéed shredded chicken, crabmeat, artichoke hearts, or anchovies as the main flavoring ingredient. But regardless of what variety you create . . . this is great!

1—Boil your **fettuccine noodles** until they turn *al dente*. Then rinse them in cold water, drain them well, coat them with olive oil, and set them aside.

2—Take a whole head of garlic, cut off the top just enough to expose the pods, drizzle with olive oil, wrap in aluminum foil, and bake in a 400-degree oven for about 45 minutes (or until tender and soft).

3—Take a 4-quart Dutch oven (or a high-sided skillet) and place it on medium heat. Then add to the pot:

4 tbsp. extra virgin olive oil
½ cup finely sliced green onions
3 tbsp. finely chopped parsley
1 head baked garlic

4—Sauté the parsley, green onions, and garlic in the olive oil until the onions wilt (about 3 minutes). Then turn the fire up to high and pour in **1 quart of heavy cream.** At this point, bring the cream to a *boil*. But remember to stir it continuously. Also stir in **1 heaping teaspoon of Italian seasonings** at this time.

5—Cook over high heat until the cream starts to thicken. Then gradually stir in about ¼ **stick of real butter.** Continue to stir. You want the cream nice and thick. Keep cooking—it will thicken, I promise!

6—When the cream starts to show a sheen, you have enough butter in it. Don't put in any more or the sauce will break (separate). Now this is the time when you add your main flavoring ingredient (shrimp, crawfish, chicken, etc.) . . . but you continue to cook it over high heat for several minutes.

7—Finally, stir in ½ **cup (or more to your taste) of Romano cheese,** and cook for another minute or two. Then . . .

8—Serve piping hot over your fettuccine noodles, sprinkle with a little extra parsley and some more Romano.

And that, Dawlin', is Pasta Alfredo!

Frank's Pasta and Cheese

Smoother and more creamy than baked macaroni, and ten times better than anything that comes out of a box, this dish will go great with anything from sausage to beef to poultry to pork. And it's so simple to fix, once you make it you'll probably end up making it several times a week!

1 lb. spiral (corkscrew) pasta	**1 cup heavy cream**
2 tbsp. olive oil	**¼ cup sliced black olives**
3 tbsp. butter	**3 cups diced Velveeta cheese**
⅔ cup finely chopped onions	**¼ cup parsley**
¼ cup celery	**salt and white pepper to taste**

First, take a 6-quart stockpot and boil the pasta in salted, oiled water until just tender (al dente)—*do not overcook!* Then rinse in hot water, stir in a tablespoon of olive oil to coat each piece, and set aside in a colander to drain.

Meanwhile, take a 12-inch skillet or 2-quart saucepan, melt the butter, and quickly sauté the onions and celery until they soften. Now pour in the heavy cream, mix everything together well, and turn the fire up to *high.* Then—*stirring constantly*—reduce the cream/butter mixture until it begins to thicken (about one-half its original volume).

At this point, slowly add the black olives and the Velveeta cheese and stir until the cheese melts and the sauce is thick and "velvety smooth." Finally, toss in the parsley and season the mixture with salt and pepper to taste.

Now place the drained pasta into a lightly buttered casserole dish and pour the cheese sauce evenly over the top. And with a spoon, work the cheese into the pasta until every single piece is thoroughly coated.

All that's left is to place the casserole—uncovered—into a 350-degree oven and bake until piping hot (about 15 minutes).

Hints:

1—Serve with baked chicken, breaded pork chops, fried shrimp, barbecue ribs, grilled fish, roast beef, or just about any other main dish you want to cook! It goes great with everything!

2—To make the sauce even thicker (or to hurry it along) simply mix 2 tablespoons of cornstarch with ¼ cup of whole milk and stir a little of it at a time quickly into the sauce after the cheese melts. It will thicken instantly!

HOW TO MAKE FRANK'S
MACARONI AND CHEESE SAUCE

First, boil a pound of small elbow macaroni until it is *al-dente* (just tender). Then wash and drain the pasta in a colander and place it into a buttered casserole dish.

Meanwhile, in a 12-inch skillet, melt one stick of butter over medium-high heat and sauté one large, finely chopped, yellow onion until it turns soft. Next, pour in a half-pint of heavy cream and cook the mixture over medium-high heat until it begins to thicken (about 5 minutes).

At this point, begin stirring in 6 slices of Velveeta cheese. And when the mixture is rich, smooth, and creamy, season it with salt and pepper, ladle it over the cooked macaroni, and mix it in thoroughly.

When you're ready to eat, place the casserole into a 350-degree oven and bake—uncovered—for 25 minutes or until hot and bubbly.

Serve immediately!

Chicken Fettuccine Alfredo

If you enjoyed my Crawfish Alfredo, you're sure to find this variation just as appetizing. It is rich and full flavored, zesty and tantalizing, and a dish you can serve to Italians and everybody else with pride. Serve up a dish of Chicken Alfredo . . . and you make the ones you love an offer they won't refuse!

First, boil a pound of fettuccine pasta in 4 quarts of water, to which you've added 2 teaspoons of salt and 2 tablespoons of olive oil. Be certain to cook only until *al dente*—firm, but not hard in the center. This should take about 8 minutes or so at a rapid boil!

When done, drain the pasta and rinse it thoroughly with cold water. Then pour another tablespoon of the olive oil evenly over the cooked fettuccine and stir it until every strand is coated. Now set it aside.

To make the Alfredo, you're gonna need:

4 tbsp. extra virgin olive oil	**1 quart heavy whipping cream**
½ cup finely chopped green onions	**½ stick real butter**
¼ cup finely chopped bell peppers	**1 tbsp. Italian seasoning**
6 skinned chicken breasts, julienned	**½ tsp. white pepper**
1 head baked garlic	**½ cup imported Romano cheese (grated)**
	¼ cup minced parsley
	salt to taste

In a 5-quart heavy aluminum Dutch oven, heat the olive oil until hot (it will give off a light whiff of smoke when it's ready). Then toss in and quickly sauté the green onions and the bell peppers. You want to cook them only until they soften slightly (about 3 or 4 minutes). Now remove them from the pot and set them aside for a while.

Next, drop in the julienned chicken and sauté the pieces quickly until tender—add a little more olive oil if you have to. When the chicken is cooked, toss the sautéed vegetable mixture (along with the garlic) back into the pot. Be sure to blend everything together thoroughly (but reduce the heat when you do this so that the garlic doesn't burn and turn bitter). Cook on low for 5 minutes.

At this point, pour in the heavy cream, turn the fire up to high, and begin reducing it—*stirring constantly*—until it thickens to the consistency of melted ice cream. To smooth out the sauce, once the cream begins to tighten stir in the half-stick of butter, but continue cooking until the sauce thickens to the texture of a semi-thick paste. (Keep cooking: it's gonna thicken—I promise!)

Now drop in the Italian seasoning and the white pepper, stir the mixture well, reduce the heat to low, cover the pot, and simmer the dish for about 10 minutes so that the flavors marry.

When you're ready to eat, add a couple of cups of the cooked fettuccine to the chicken/cream mixture, fold everything together in the pot to heat the pasta, and sprinkle on the Romano cheese and the parsley. Salt to taste. Now mix once more and serve piping hot with a little extra Romano, a good bottle of Frascati, and a loaf of Italian bread!

Hints: I recommend either Santa Sabina or Colavita olive oil, both of which are available at Central Grocery on Decatur Street in New Orleans.

To make baked garlic, take a whole head, cut off the top just enough to expose the pods, drizzle on some olive oil, wrap in aluminum foil, and bake in a 400-degree oven for about 45 minutes to an hour (or until soft and tender). To remove the cooked pods, just squeeze the whole head and they will pop out!

Crawfish Fettuccine Siciliana

If you have a fascination for Italian food, you're sure to find this recipe to your liking. It is rich and full flavored, zesty and tantalizing, and a dish you can serve to Italians and everybody else with pride. Ask someone to have some Crawfish Fettuccine Siciliana . . . and you make them an offer they won't refuse!

First, boil a pound of fettuccine pasta in 4 quarts of water, to which you've added 2 teaspoons of salt and 2 tablespoons of olive oil. Be certain to cook only until *al dente*—firm but not hard in the center. This should take about 8 minutes or so at a rapid boil.

When done, drain the pasta and rinse it thoroughly with cold water. Then pour another tablespoon of the olive oil evenly over the cooked fettuccine and stir it until every strand is coated. Now set it aside.

To make the "Siciliana," you will need:

¼ cup extra virgin olive oil	2 tbsp. sweet basil
¼ cup finely chopped bell peppers	1 pinch thyme
	1½ tsp. salt
½ cup finely chopped green onions	½ tsp. white pepper
	¼ tsp. black pepper
½ cup finely chopped celery	¼ tsp. cayenne pepper
1 tbsp. finely minced garlic	½ pint whipping cream
1 lb. processed crawfish tails and fat	6 tbsp. grated imported Romano cheese
2 tbsp. Italian seasoning	2 tbsp. finely chopped parsley
1 tsp. ground oregano	

In a 12-inch heavy aluminum skillet, heat the olive oil until hot (it will give off a light whiff of smoke when it's ready). Then toss in and quickly sauté the bell peppers, the green onions, celery, and garlic. You want to cook them only until they soften slightly (about 3 or 4 minutes). *Do not overcook . . . and do not burn the garlic.*

Next, add your crawfish tails and whatever liquid there is inside the plastic bag they came packaged in. This is mostly crawfish fat and it imparts a distinct flavor when sautéed into the finished dish. Over medium-high heat, cook the crawfish tails about 3 to 5 minutes until well-blended into the vegetables. (*Note:* You will have to be prepared to stir this dish constantly as it cooks!)

At this point, you will notice some juices forming in the bottom of the pan. These are the natural liquids from the tails and the softening vegetables. As soon as the juices begin to sizzle, sprinkle the dry ingredients— the Italian seasoning, oregano, basil, and thyme—over the crawfish and stir them in well. This is also the time you want to add your salt and the 3 different peppers and work them into the blend.

Now stop here momentarily to make seasoning adjustments. Taste the dish to see what you think you have to add more of! Incidentally, your cooking time here should be no longer than another 2 or 3 minutes.

Next, remove the crawfish from the pan and set them aside in a bowl, because now you want to add the whipping cream and you don't want the crawfish to overcook. And don't just pour the cream in . . . *stir it in gradually and stir constantly as you pour.* Then, when all the cream has been added, increase the heat to *high* and cook it until it begins to thicken (ideally, you want it to reach the same consistency as cold buttermilk). Cooking time is about 6-8 minutes or so.

Finally, return the crawfish to the skillet, reduce the heat to low, and gradually stir in the fettuccine you boiled earlier. Then with two forks, fold the crawfish and the pasta together until thoroughly coated with the cream sauce. Simmer everything for another minute or so to be sure the pasta is fully heated, and, just before you serve it, sprinkle the entire dish liberally with the imported Romano and the minced parsley.

Crawfish Fettuccine Siciliana should be served in soup bowls, piping hot, with a tossed Italian salad (lettuce, tomato, egg slices, black and green olives, bell peppers, mushrooms, cucumbers, olive oil, vinegar, and anchovies) and hearty pieces of fresh-baked Italian bread garnished with garlic and olive oil. I also recommend you serve this with chilled Frascati wine.

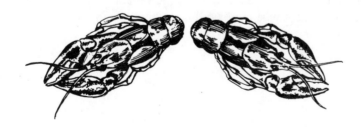

Crawfish Fettuccine Alfredo

If you have a fascination for Italian food, you're sure to find this recipe to your liking. It is rich and full-flavored, zesty and tantalizing, and a dish you can serve to Italians and everybody else with pride. Ask someone to have some Crawfish Alfredo . . . and you make them an offer they won't refuse!

First, boil a pound of fettuccine pasta in 4 quarts of water, to which you've added 2 teaspoons of salt and 2 tablespoons of olive oil. Be certain to cook only until *al dente*—firm, but not hard in the center. This should take about 8 minutes or so at a rapid boil!

When done, drain the pasta and rinse it thoroughly with cold water. Then pour another tablespoon of the olive oil evenly over the cooked fettuccine and stir it until every strand is coated. Now set it aside.

To make the Alfredo, you're gonna need:

4 tbsp. extra virgin olive oil
½ cup finely chopped green
**   onions**
¼ cup finely chopped bell
**   peppers**
1 head baked garlic
1 quart heavy whipping cream
½ stick real butter

1 tbsp. Italian seasoning
½ tsp. white pepper
2 lb. processed crawfish tails
**   and fat**
½ cup imported Romano cheese
**   (grated)**
¼ cup minced parsley
salt to taste

In a 5-quart heavy aluminum Dutch oven, heat the olive oil until hot (it will give off a light whiff of smoke when it's ready). Then toss in and quickly sauté the green onions and the bell peppers. You want to cook them only until they soften slightly (about 3 or 4 minutes).

Next, add the garlic and blend it into the vegetable mixture with a fork (but reduce the heat when you do this so that the garlic doesn't burn and turn bitter).

At this point, pour in the heavy cream, turn the fire up to high, and begin reducing it—*stirring constantly*—until it thickens to the consistency of melted ice cream. To smooth out the sauce, once the cream begins to tighten stir in the half-stick of butter, but continue cooking until the sauce thickens to the texture of a semi-thick paste. (Keep cooking: it's gonna thicken—I promise!)

Now drop in the Italian seasoning and the white pepper, along with the crawfish tails (and the crawfish fat that came in the bag they were packed in), and cook—*still stirring all the while*—for another 3 minutes or until the tails curl up slightly and the fat blends into the cream sauce. And that's all there is to it!

When you're ready to eat, add a couple of cups of the cooked fettuccine to the crawfish/cream mixture, fold everything together in the pot to heat the pasta, and sprinkle on the Romano cheese and the parsley. Salt to taste. Now mix once more and serve piping hot with a little extra Romano, a good bottle of Frascati, and a loaf of Italian bread!

Hints: I recommend either Santa Sabina or Colavita olive oil, both of which are available at Central Grocery on Decatur Street in New Orleans.

To make baked garlic, take a whole head, cut off the top just enough to expose the pods, drizzle on some olive oil, wrap in aluminum foil, and bake in a 400-degree oven for about 45 minutes to an hour (or until soft and tender). To remove the cooked pods, just squeeze the whole head and they will pop out!

Frank's Mudbugs and Macaroni

If you like crawfish etouffée and you like Crawfish Alfredo, you're going to relish the taste of this dish. It's rich, robust, smooth and creamy . . . and even better than that, you can whip up a big batch of "Mudbugs and Macaroni" in less than 5 minutes! That's how easy it is.

2 tbsp. melted margarine
1 finely diced medium yellow
   onion
2 tsp. Dijon mustard
2 tbsp. all-purpose flour
2 lb. crawfish tails (with fat)

1¼ cups chicken stock
   (if needed)
salt, cayenne, and black pepper
   to taste
¼ cup sliced green onions
1 tbsp. finely chopped parsley

First, take a heavy 12-inch skillet and heat the margarine to sizzling. Then drop in the onions and—*stirring constantly*—cook them over high heat until they wilt—about 2 minutes.

Next, with the heat still on high, stir in the mustard, sprinkle in the flour, and toss in the crawfish tails and crawfish fat. A small amount of liquids will form in the bottom of the pan—this is the base of the sauce. Now blend everything together well and cook the mixture over high heat for about 2 minutes more.

At this point, pour in the chicken stock a little at a time and quickly stir the ingredients—*still over high heat*—until a rich, creamy, smooth sauce forms. Then season the dish to taste with salt, black pepper, and cayenne (you can use a good seafood seasoning substitute if you prefer).

When you're ready to eat, garnish the pan of crawfish with the green onions and parsley and liberally ladle it into a bowl over hot buttered macaroni.

Suggestion: Serve with a crisp tossed salad, French dressing, and buttered toast points, accompanied by a tall frosty glass of iced tea.

## CHAPTER 9

Sauces and Dressings

Charlie Bruscato's Barbecue Sauce

This recipe, concocted by my father-in-law Charlie Bruscato in Monroe, Louisiana, has been responsible for more than a couple of pounds around my midriff. But that's because it perks up beef, chicken, pork, bread—anything you splash it on! This particular recipe makes a gallon of the stuff, but once prepared, it can be stored on the shelves of the pantry or placed in the refrigerator for several months. It's good!

1 cup Crisco oil	**1 can tomato sauce (6 oz. can)**
2 cups finely chopped onions	**1 pint tomato juice**
¼ cup finely minced garlic	**½ cup Karo syrup (light)**
1 cup finely minced celery	**1 cup Worcestershire sauce**
½ cup lemon juice	**32 oz. tomato catsup**
½ cup cider vinegar	**¼ cup cayenne pepper**
½ cup paprika	**(add to taste)**
2 cans tomato paste (6 oz. cans)	**enough water to make a gallon**

And here's how easy it goes together:

Add all of these ingredients to a 6-quart Dutch oven. Then cook the mixture at a slow-boil over medium-high heat for 20-25 minutes until you get a sauce that is creamy and smooth. (*Note:* It is important to continually stir the mix as it cooks and to gradually add water to achieve the consistency you desire.)

I suggest you add salt to the sauce only after it has cooked for the allotted time, since you may find that the ingredients themselves contain enough secondary salt to suit your taste. If not, the original recipe calls for 3 tablespoons . . . but this can be adjusted more or less without a significant change in quality.

When the sauce is done, set it aside and let it cool to room temperature. Then pour it into dry, tightly sealed, quart-size, "sterilized" bottles and store them in a dark, cool, dry place. It should keep well for up to 2 months.

Frank's Marinara Sauce

Traditional marinara sauce calls for oil, garlic, slices of fresh peeled tomatoes, and fresh basil, cooked for about 20 minutes. This recipe includes all the traditional ingredients, plus a little extra touch of Italiana.

4 tbsp. Extra Virgin Olive Oil	**1 small onion, finely chopped**
6 garlic cloves, baked and	**6 anchovy fillets**
pureed*	**2 tsp. sweet basil**
2 cans Italian peeled tomatoes	**½ tsp. oregano**
(303 size)	**1 strip lemon peel**
1 6-oz. can tomato paste	**2 tsp. black pepper**

In a 5-quart Dutch oven, heat the olive oil and gently blend in the puréed garlic until smooth. Then add both the peeled tomatoes and the tomato paste, along with the onions and anchovy fillets, and cook over medium heat until the mixture begins to reduce and thicken. (Incidentally, I recommend you purée the anchovies before stirring them into the sauce.)

Now, add the sweet basil, oregano, and lemon peel and stir everything together well. Then cover the pot, reduce the heat to low, and simmer for about 45 minutes.

At this point, add the black pepper and season the sauce with salt to taste (it may not need any, depending upon the saltiness of the anchovies). Then cover and simmer for another 15 minutes.

Marinara sauce goes great with fish, scallops, shrimp, broiled chicken, veal, eggplant, and pasta.

Hint: Fresh tomatoes produce an outstanding marinara. So if you want to use fresh tomatoes, put about a half-dozen of them into a pot of boiling water for 10-15 seconds until the skin can be easily peeled off. Then discard the skins, cut the tomatoes into small dice, and add the pieces to the Dutch oven. Then add your tomato paste and cook uncovered until the mixture starts to thicken. Fantastico!

---

*The recipe for Italian baked garlic is elsewhere in this book.

Green Pepper Jelly Sauce

Slightly tart, semi-sweet, and full of peppery spice, this recipe was taught to me by a lady named Lou White. It goes well over any kind of pork or poultry, and it is exceptionally good on Cornish game hens.

2 cups seeded bell peppers, coarsely chopped	1¾ cups apple cider vinegar
5 whole green jalapeño peppers, coarsely chopped	7 cups granulated sugar
	¼ tsp. salt
2 whole red jalapeño peppers, coarsely chopped	¾ tsp. green food color
	2 pouches Certo gel

First, take the bell peppers and the jalapeños and drop them into a food processor—along with 1 cup of the apple cider vinegar—and chop them up until they're cut into small slivers. Then pour the mix into a deep-sided pot (a 6-quart heavy aluminum Dutch oven works great).

Next, take the other three-quarters cup of apple cider vinegar and rinse out the food processor. Then add that to the pot and stir it into the pepper mix well.

At this point, add the salt, sugar, and food color and mix everything together thoroughly. Then turn up the heat to high and bring the mixture to a boil, *stirring constantly for a minute and a half!*

Now stir in the Certo . . . and when the mixture comes back to a "hard boil" cook it for exactly 2 minutes. And you want to *stir, stir, stir!*

After 2 minutes, remove the jelly from the heat, skim off the foam that floats to the top, and pack the jelly into small, sterilized Mason jars. Seal them at once—but do not refrigerate. Allow them to cool to room temperature then store them in your pantry. They will keep well for up to 6 months.

Hints: The jelly, by itself, makes a great condiment to serve with grilled beef, barbecued chicken, red beans, baked fish, fried shrimp, double-baked duck and just about anything else you want to perk up!

To turn the jelly into a sauce to serve over chicken, pork, and game hens, mix ½ cup of the jelly with ¼ cup of heavy cream and heat til smooth! You won't believe how wonderful!

Note: This recipe makes about 6 small jars of jelly.

Frank's Oyster Rice Dressing

Let's face it . . . the most popular dressing in grand old New Orleans—
especially around holiday season—is oyster dressing. But instead of the
old traditional style, this year try "oyster rice." It has a unique flavor that
goes with almost any entree you cook. And it's good, too!

6 cups cooked rice	6 dozen fresh-shucked oysters
1 stick real butter	plus liquor
½ pint sliced mushrooms	2 tsp. seafood or poultry
2 cups finely chopped onions	seasoning
1 cup finely chopped celery	2 tsp. basil
½ cup finely chopped bell	1 tsp. black pepper
pepper	pinch thyme
3 cloves finely chopped garlic	1½ tsp. salt (if necessary)
½ cup thinly sliced green onion	2 tbsp. finely chopped parsley
tops	

In a 12-inch heavy aluminum skillet, melt the butter over medium heat
and sauté the mushrooms, onions, celery, bell pepper, garlic, and green
onion tops until all of them are soft and tender. The one thing to remember
is to keep the butter hot, but don't let it burn. And keep stirring the mixture
to cook it uniformly.

Next, chop the oysters and gradually stir them into the vegetable-butter
mixture. Notice I said *"gradually stir in."* The reason for this is that you
do not want to reduce the heat—lowering the heat will cause the oysters to
cook too slowly . . . and slow cooking releases too much of the oyster
water and makes them rubbery.

At this point, cook the oysters for about 4 minutes, stirring all the
while. And when the ingredients are well-mixed, stir in the seafood or
poultry seasoning, basil, pepper, thyme, and salt. (About the salt—check
your oysters to see if they are naturally salty before adding the amount
listed in the recipe.) You should begin tasting the dressing immediately as
it cooks and make whatever adjustments are necessary.

Now cover the pot, lower the heat, and simmer for about 5 minutes to
allow time for the flavors to thoroughly blend (this is one of the secrets to
making a really good oyster dressing).

After the simmering process is done, remove the pan from the fire and fold the oyster mixture into the cooked rice thoroughly. I recommend that you use a slotted spoon to add the *oysters and the seasoning vegetables* first, then add the liquids as necessary to make a moist (not wet!) rice dressing.

Finally, spoon the mixed dressing into a buttered casserole dish, cover with aluminum foil, drizzle with melted butter, and bake about 30 minutes in a 350-degree oven until piping hot! Sprinkle with parsley and serve.

Frank's Sweet and Sour Sauce
(And Other Oriental Sauces)

If you like the sweet and sour sauce that they serve in the good Chinese restaurants . . . here's how you make it at home!

½ cup water
¼ cup red wine vinegar
¼ cup granulated sugar
4 ounces plum jelly

2 tbsp. soy sauce
2 tbsp. cornstarch
¼ cup cold water

In a heavy saucepan, mix together over medium heat the water, red wine vinegar, and the granulated sugar.

Then, when the sugar dissolves and the mixture comes to a *slow boil,* add the plum jelly and the soy sauce. Continue to cook and stir constantly over medium heat until the jelly dissolves and becomes smooth and the strong vinegar aroma disappears.

Then to thicken the sauce, mix the cornstarch and water together in a small bowl, add it gradually to the saucepan, and cook it over medium heat for 1 minute (or until the sauce reaches the consistency you desire).

Variations:
1—To make a peppery sweet and sour sauce, add 2 tablespoons of crushed red pepper flakes to the saucepan when you stir in the plum jelly.

2—To make a minty sweet and sour sauce, follow the recipe to the letter but substitute 4 ounces of mint jelly for the plum jelly.

3—To make yellow Chinese hot sauce, follow the recipe to the letter but substitute undiluted frozen pineapple juice for the jelly, eliminate the granulated sugar, and substitute white pepper for the crushed red pepper flakes. But watch this stuff! It gets hot!

Frank's Dirty Wild Rice Dressing

No dressing goes better with Rock Cornish game hens than one made with wild rice. And when you take that dressing one step further—Cajun-style—and turn it into a dirty wild rice . . . it's like being back home on the bayou for Christmas!

2 cups wild rice (regular or converted)	**1 cup finely chopped onions**
2 tsp. salt	**6 whole green onions, chopped fine**
½ stick real butter	**4 tbsp. finely chopped parsley**
1 cup sliced mushrooms	**¼ tsp. thyme**
¼ cup peanut oil	**drippings from roasted game hens**
giblets from six Rock Cornish game hens	**salt and cayenne pepper to taste**

First off, add your 2 cups of wild rice to a gallon of boiling water that's been seasoned with 2 teaspoons of salt and cook it till *just tender* (about 12 minutes). Now be sure you don't *overcook* because it will be stuffed inside the game hens and finished off in the oven. When it's done, drain it in a collander and set it aside.

While the rice is cooking, grind (or finely chop in a food processor) the gizzards and livers from the game hens and set them aside too. Now keep in mind that if the hens you bought were short a few giblets, you can always add a half-cup or so of chicken livers to make up the difference.

Next, melt the half stick of butter in a skillet and gently sauté the mushrooms until they turn tender. Then remove them from the pan, add the peanut oil to the butter drippings that came from the mushrooms, and quickly fry down the chopped giblets. And when the giblets turn brown, toss the cooked mushrooms back in, along with the onions, green onions, parsley, and thyme, and "gently simmer" the mixture—covered—until the gizzards are tender (which should take about 30 to 45 minutes).

Now, add the giblet mixture to the wild rice, blend everything together thoroughly, and season to taste with salt and cayenne. At this point, you need to put the dressing into a buttered casserole dish, cover it with aluminum foil, and hold it until you're ready to stuff the hens.

But before you stuff—and here's the *coup de grace*—take some of the drippings that came from the game hens while they were roasting and mix it into the dressing. You want to add just enough to "moisten" the rice.

Reminder: Just be sure you heat the dressing to at least 250 degrees in the oven before stuffing it into the game hens.

Frank's Cornbread Dressing

Whether it be Thanksgiving, Christmas, New Year's, or just another weekend, this dressing (which goes great with turkey, chicken, pork, and veal) will make your mouth run water two blocks away! And it's so easy to make, anybody can do it!

3 cups poultry giblets
2 pans cornbread (9-inch size)
½ cup real sweet cream butter
2 cups finely chopped onions
1 cup finely chopped celery
1 tbsp. finely chopped parsley
½ cup finely chopped bell
  pepper
1 tsp. finely chopped garlic

¼ cup thinly sliced shallots
  (tops)
2 tsp. poultry seasoning
2 tsp. basil
1 tsp. black pepper
pinch thyme
1½ tsp. salt
2 cups poultry stock

Start off by finely chopping all your giblets from the poultry you will be using (capon, Cornish game hen, turkey, or chicken) and adding them to 2 quarts of water in a stock pot. Also add the neck bone—it gives excellent flavor and can be picked later for the meat. To the water, toss in 2 diced carrots, 1 small finely chopped onion, and one-half teaspoon each of salt and black pepper.

Now boil the ingredients rapidly for 5 minutes . . . then turn the heat down to medium and "reduce" the stock for about an hour (you want to go from about *2 quarts to 2 cups*). Just allow the stock to evaporate until you get to this point.

It is also at this point that you want to bake your cornbread. Two 9-inch pans will do nicely. Just use the recipe on the package you buy . . . but remember to buy a brand containing little or no sugar.

After the cornbread is baked, set it aside to cool. Then crumble it into small pieces.

Now, in a 4-quart Dutch oven melt the butter over medium heat and sauté the onions, celery, bell pepper, parsley, garlic, and shallots until all of them are tender. The one thing to remember is to keep the butter hot but don't let it burn. Keep stirring your ingredients together to cook them uniformly.

Next, stir in the chopped giblets and the meat you picked from the neck bone. Cook them gently on low heat for about 2 minutes, stirring constantly. When the ingredients are well-mixed, stir in the poultry seasoning, basil, pepper, thyme, and salt.

Then take the bowl you crumbled the cornbread in and add the giblets and seasonings to it. *Stir everything together so that it blends thoroughly!* Then begin adding the stock you made—a little at a time—to moisten the dressing. At this point you should begin "tasting" and make whatever adjustments are necessary. Remember, you want the stuffing "just moist"— not wet!

For the richest flavor, I recommend you allow the mix to "rest" on the countertop (covered) for at least a half-hour before you use it. I also recommend you stir the mix at least every 10 minutes to re-blend the ingredients. This is one of the secrets to making a really good old-time cornbread dressing.

After the resting time, test the dressing again for moisture. If it's too dry for your taste (remember, it will absorb stock while it sits), add more stock a little at a time.

Go ahead and take some liberties with the recipe: you can add flair and creative touches to suit your taste. For example, you might want to sauté about a half-pound of fresh mushrooms and fold them into the stuffing. Or you can make the dish spicier by tossing in some cayenne pepper. You be the judge.

All that you still have to decide is how you plan to use the dressing. It can be stuffed into birds (from chicken to doves to ducks to Cornish game hens), or baked into a rich casserole at 350 degrees until lightly brown and used as a side-dish stuffing with roast pork, fried chicken, veal, etc.

It's great stuff no matter how you serve it. But I do suggest you serve it hot.

Pyracantha Jelly

Pyracantha means "thorn bush," which correctly describes this Eurasian thorny evergreen or half-evergreen shrub of the rose family. But, contrary to what you've heard over the years, *pyracantha berries are not poisonous!* Many forms of wildlife down through the years have used pyracantha berries as their primary source of food. And if you prepare them properly, you'll create some of the best jelly this side of mayhaw. Here's the recipe:

Pick the berries when they are deep red, wash them well, and remove all the stems. Then, for each pound of pyracantha berries you have, add one cup of water to a large pot, drop the berries in, and boil them rapidly for 20 to 25 minutes or until the pomes pop open.

Then drain them immediately in a bag made of outing flannel or several thicknesses of cheesecloth. And when the dripping has almost stopped, press the berry bag and capture the juices. *The juice is the product you use to make your pyracantha jelly!*

Here Are the Jelly Ingredients:

7 cups sugar	1 box Sure-Jel
3 cups pyracantha juice	5 tbsp. vinegar
juice of two lemons	

Simply bring the sugar, pyracantha juice, and lemon juice (all mixed together well) to a boil in a 6-quart pot. Then, according to the directions for making jelly on the side of the Sure-Jel package, add the Sure-Jel and the vinegar to the pot and boil the combinations for 2 minutes. Then pour the reddish mixture into sterilized jars and cap them with wax.

You can serve your fresh pyracantha jelly over buttered rolls or biscuits for breakfast, in a sandwich for snacks, over Philadelphia brand cream cheese as hors d'oeuvres, or as an accompaniment to meat or poultry. It's truly Southern!

Note: This recipe was perfected by Mildred Swift, home economist for the Louisiana State University Extension Service and host of KNOE-TV's cooking show. It has been kitchen tested!

Frank's Cornbread-Andouille Dressing

If you like the taste of old-fashioned cornbread dressing, and you like the spicyness of good Cajun andouille . . . wait till you combine them into one dish and blend the flavors! It's one of those stuffings you'll make over and over again!

1½ lb. andouille sausage
2 cups giblets (duck or chicken)
2 quarts water
2 pans cornbread (9-by-13 size)
2 carrots, diced
½ cup real sweet cream butter
2 cups finely chopped onions
1 cup finely chopped celery
2 tbsp. finely chopped parsley
¼ cup finely chopped bell
   pepper

1 tsp. finely chopped garlic
¼ cup thinly sliced shallot tops
2 tsp. poultry seasoning
2 tsp. sweet basil
1 tsp. black pepper
pinch thyme
1½ tsp. salt
2 cups giblet-andouille stock

Start off by finely chopping the andouille sausage and all the giblets from the poultry you will be using (capon, Cornish game hen, turkey, duck, or chicken). Then add both the giblets and sausage to 2 quarts of water in a stock pot. Also add the neck bone—it gives excellent flavor and can be picked later for the meat. To the water, toss in 2 diced carrots, 1 small finely chopped onion, and ½ teaspoon each of salt and black pepper.

Now, boil the ingredients rapidly for 30 minutes, then turn the heat down to medium and "reduce" the stock for about an hour (you want to get from about *2 quarts to 2 cups*). In other words, allow the stock to evaporate until you get to this point.

It's also at this point that you want to bake your cornbread. Two 9-inch pans will do nicely. Just use the recipe on the package you buy . . . *but buy one without sugar!* After the cornbread is baked, set it aside to cool. Then crumble it into small pieces.

In a 4-quart Dutch oven, melt your butter over medium heat and sauté the onions, celery, bell pepper, parsley, garlic, and shallot tops until all of them are tender. The one thing to remember is to keep the butter just hot enough so that it doesn't burn. Keep stirring your ingredients together to cook them uniformly.

Next, stir in the chopped giblets, the meat you picked from the neck bone, and the andouille. Cook them gently on low heat for about 5 minutes, stirring all the while. When everything is well-mixed, stir in the poultry seasoning, the basil, thyme, and salt. Be careful with the pepper—usually, andouille is peppery to start with.

Then take the bowl you crumbled the cornbread in and add the giblets, andouille, and seasonings to it. *Again . . . stir everything together so that it blends thoroughly!* Then begin adding the stock you made—a little at a time—to moisten the dressing. Remember, you want the stuffing "just moist"—not wet! You don't have to use all the stock! At this point you should begin "tasting" and making whatever seasoning adjustments are necessary.

Finally, spoon the dressing into a buttered 11-by-16 baking pan, place it in a preheated 400-degree oven, and bake it uncovered until it turns a pretty honey brown (about 30-40 minutes).

Hint: For the richest flavor, I recommend you allow the dressing to "rest" on the countertop (covered) for at least a half hour before you use it. I also recommend you stir the mix at least every 10 minutes while it cooks to re-blend the ingredients. This is one of the secrets to making a really good old-time cornbread-andouille dressing.

All that you still have to decide is how you plan to use the dressing. It can be stuffed into birds (from chicken to doves to ducks to Cornish game hens) . . . or used as a side-dish stuffing with roast pork, fried chicken, veal, etc. It's great stuff no matter how you serve it. But I do suggest you serve it hot.

Frank's Thanksgiving Oyster Dressing

Let's face it . . . the most popular dressing in grand old New Orleans—especially around holiday season—is oyster dressing. But most folks unfamiliar with it think it's too hard to make. Not true, cher! All you do is follow this recipe to the letter and you got yourself a winner!

½ cup real sweet cream butter
½ cup finely chopped smoked
   sausage
2 cups finely chopped onions
1 cup finely chopped celery
1 tbsp. finely chopped parsley
½ cup finely chopped bell
   pepper
1 tsp. finely chopped garlic
¼ cup thinly sliced green onion
   tops

6 dozen chopped oysters plus
   liquor
1 tsp. poultry seasoning
2 tsp. basil
1 tsp. black pepper
pinch thyme
1 whole egg (lightly beaten)
1½ tsp. salt
3 cups unseasoned bread
   crumbs (coarse)

In a large black iron Dutch oven, melt the butter over medium heat and sauté the smoked sausage, onions, celery, parsley, bell pepper, garlic, and green onion tops until all of them are tender. The one thing to remember is to keep the butter hot but don't let it burn. Keep stirring the mixture to cook it uniformly.

Next, gradually stir in the chopped oysters. Notice I said *"gradually stir in."* The reason for this is that you do not want to reduce the heat. Lowering the heat will cause excessive water to be released from the oysters and you'll have to add too many bread crumbs to the finished dish.

Cook the oysters gently for about 4 minutes, stirring all the while. When the ingredients are well-mixed, stir in the poultry seasoning, basil, black pepper, thyme, and salt. (About the salt—check your oysters to see if they are naturally salty before adding the prescribed amount. You may have to reduce the salt if nature has provided her own.) At this point you should begin tasting the dressing and make whatever adjustments are necessary.

Now cover the pot, lower the heat, and simmer for about 5 minutes to allow time for the flavors to thoroughly blend. This is one of the secrets to making a really good oyster dressing.

After the simmering process is done, remove the pot from the fire and begin stirring in the bread crumbs a little at a time. Note that you do not have to add all 3 cups. If you want your dressing moist, stop adding crumbs when you get to the texture you desire. If you want a drier stuffing, add all 3 cups—even more if your taste and needs dictate.

When, in your estimation, the stuffing is ready (it should be the consistency of cool oatmeal), go ahead and rapidly stir in the egg to tie everything together. Then cover it for a few minutes to let it *set up*. This is where the body comes in—it's how the final blending brings out full flavor. And you can make adjustments at this point by moistening the dish with the oyster liquor . . . that's why you saved it.

The only thing you still have to decide is how you plan to use the dressing. It can be stuffed into birds (from chicken to doves to ducks to Cornish game hens) and baked, or it can be used as a side-dish stuffing for seafood (flounder, red snapper, or trout), or set out as a topping for canapes at a party. It's great stuff no matter how you serve it. But I do suggest you serve it hot.

If you plan to use the dressing as a casserole side-dish without stuffing it into your ducks, spoon it out in a buttered casserole dish, lightly sprinkle with more bread crumbs, top with butter, and bake about 20 minutes in a 350-degree oven.

Frank's Gorgonzola Dressing

Here's a salad dressing that's gonna blow you away! It ranks as the all-time favorite of my television production staff!

½ cup creamed cottage cheese	3 tbsp. sliced green onions
⅔ cup diced gorgonzola cheese	2 tsp. black pepper
½ cup extra virgin olive oil	⅔ cup whole milk
2 tbsp. red wine vinegar	salt to taste
1 tbsp. chopped parsley	

First, combine the cottage cheese and the gorgonzola in a food processor until smooth. Then—*with the processor running*—begin adding the olive oil in a thin steady stream to cream the mixture.

Now, *one ingredient at a time with the processor running,* add the vinegar, chopped parsley, green onions, and black pepper . . . and then blend in just enough milk to thin the mix to salad dressing consistency.

All that's left is to chill the dressing and serve over tomatoes, cucumbers, spinach, or tossed green salad.

Hint: Add salt only after you taste the dressing. You may not need any!

Frank's N'Awlins Vinaigrette Dressing

Here's a rich and spicy salad dressing that's a cut above plain Italian oil and vinegar. See if you don't like it!

¼ cup red wine vinegar	1 tbsp. Worcestershire sauce
2 tbsp. finely chopped parsley	1 hard-boiled egg yolk
3 tbsp. Dijon mustard	1 cup extra virgin olive oil
juice of one-half lemon	salt and black pepper to taste

Using either a food processor or a wire whip, mix together everything *except the olive oil and the salt and pepper* in a large bowl until creamed.

Then—constantly mixing, either with a wire whip or the blade of the food processor—slowly add the oil in a thin stream until the dressing is smooth and creamy. (*Note:* If you pour the oil in too quickly, the dressing will "break" and separate.)

All that's left is to season it to taste with salt and pepper, chill for at least an hour in the refrigerator, and serve over tossed salad, sliced tomatoes, diced avocados, fresh spinach, or any other dish that calls of a light but aromatic dressing.

I promise . . . you won't use plain oil and vinegar ever again!

Blackened bananas?

Being the master chef he is, Paul Prudhomme cannot only "blacken" redfish, he can blacken anything and make it taste good. But even Paul draws the line on blackened bananas, peaches, and apples.

So to keep your bananas, peaches, and apples from discoloring, just dip them quickly into a water and lemon juice mixture as soon as you peel them. I promise you, the citric acid won't let them darken and turn black.

Frank's Mexican Salsa

Great for serving with fajitas and for dipping with nachos.

1 large can whole tomatoes
 (303 size)
1 large can tomato sauce
 (303 size)
5 chili pepper, minced
3 pods fresh garlic, minced
½ cup chopped onions

¼ cup fresh bell pepper
1 fresh jalapeño pepper, sliced
 thin
¼ cup vegetable oil
1 tbsp. red wine vinegar
salt to taste

In a food processor, blend together the whole tomatoes, tomato sauce, chili peppers, garlic, onions, jalapeños, and bell pepper until roughly blended. But note: do not cut them to the "puree" stage—you still want small bits of onions, tomatoes, and bell pepper in the mix.

When thoroughly blended, stir in the vegetable oil and the vinegar and season with salt to taste.

Before serving, allow the salsa to marinate in the refrigerator for at least 4 hours. But keep in mind that the longer the mixture sets, the more spicy and flavorful it becomes.

Note: This salsa will keep fresh in the refrigerator for about 2 weeks.

## CHAPTER 10

Breads

Frank's Crunchy Homemade Buttermilk Biscuits

If you like homemade biscuits that you don't have to roll out, that are light and fluffy on the inside, and that are crispy-crunchy on the outside . . . then you're gonna love my N'Awlins buttermilk biscuits. They go with everything!

3 cups all-purpose flour	1 cup buttermilk
2 level tbsp. of baking powder	¼ cup water plus 2 tbsp.
½ tsp. salt	
1 stick softened butter (or ½ cup Butter Crisco)	

First, preheat your oven to 450 degrees (preferably on the convection heat setting).

Then, in a large bowl, mix together thoroughly the flour, baking powder, and salt. Now pour the mixture into a sifter and sift it into another bowl.

Next, using your hands, work the butter into the flour mixture until it becomes crumbly, almost the consistency of cornmeal.

At this point, add the buttermilk and the water to the flour-butter mix (keeping in mind that you may have to reduce some of the water, depending upon the amount of gluten in the flour). With a spoon, you want to stir the liquids into the flour until the mixture is moist and semi-sticky *but not wet!*

Finally, drop tablespoon-size dollops of the dough onto a well-greased cookie sheet and bake for approximately 15 minutes or so until golden brown.

These are the easiest and best tasting biscuits you will ever eat!

Hint: Instead of using a cookie sheet, you may also drop the dough into greased muffin tins and make a batch of biscuit muffins that will go with almost any main dish you serve. By the way . . . this recipe will make about a dozen muffins.

Frank's Real N'Awlins French Bread

It isn't the old, closely-guarded New Orleans traditional recipe . . . but it's doggone good when served piping hot right out of the oven!

3 tbsp. sugar
2½ tsp. salt
1 package dry yeast
5 to 5½ cups all-purpose flour,
   divided
1½ cups milk

½ cup water
3 tbsp. softened butter or
   margarine plus
1 egg, well-beaten with 2 tbsp.
   water

First, in a large bowl mix together well the sugar, salt, yeast, and two cups of the flour. Then set it aside.

Next, in a saucepan, combine the milk, water, and butter and cook the mixture over *low heat* until the butter melts. It is important to stir the mix occasionally and watch that the milk doesn't scorch. When well-blended, cool the mix to 120-130 degrees.

At this point, gradually add the milk mix to the flour, using an electric mixer (preferably with dough hooks) on high speed. During the process, gradually add ¾ cup of flour, beating it in well. Then, a little at a time, stir in enough of the remaining flour to make a soft dough.

Now, turn the dough out onto a floured surface and knead it until smooth and elastic (about 10 minutes). Shape the dough into a ball and place it in a well-greased bowl, turning it a couple of times to grease the top. Then cover the bowl with plastic wrap and let the dough rise (at 85 degrees) for 1 hour or until doubled in bulk. Now punch the dough down, turn it out onto a floured surface, and knead it lightly 4 or 5 times.

When you're ready to make bread, divide the dough in half and roll each portion of it into a 13-by-8-inch rectangle on a lightly floured surface. Then roll the dough *jellyroll fashion,* starting at the long edge and pressing firmly to eliminate all the air pockets. Now pinch the ends and the seams together to seal them, and place the loaves seam-side-down into a well-greased baking sheet.

Cover each loaf with plastic wrap and let it rise in a warm place (85 degrees), free from drafts, about 45 minutes or until doubled in bulk. Next, using a sharp knife, carefully make diagonal slits about ¼ inch deep down the length of the loaves.

At this point, brush the egg-water mixture evenly over the loaves (taking care not to let any of it drip on the baking sheet). Then bake at 400 degrees for 20-25 minutes or until the loaves sound hollow when tapped. When done, cool on wire racks.

Frank's Beer Bread

This is the recipe that caused such a rage the first time I did it on my radio show. But remember . . . you must follow the directions to the letter or the dough will come out heavy instead of crisp. Done right, though, it's some of the best quick bread you ever had!

3 cups self-rising flour   **2 tbsp. butter**
3 tbsp. granulated sugar
1 12-oz. can of your favorite beer
 (warm)

All you do is mix everything *except the butter* together in a large bowl until the ingredients are perfectly blended. But do not overmix the dough—you just want it smooth. Then grease and flour a 9-by-6 loaf pan (or dust it with Baker's Joy) and put the blended mixture into the pan.

Next, melt the butter and pour it over the dough—just dribble it over—don't push it into the mix. Then cover the dough with plastic wrap and let it stand on the countertop at room temperature for 5 minutes to rise.

After the allotted time, put the pan in a preheated oven at 375 degrees and bake the bread for 45 to 50 minutes until golden brown and crusty on the top.

And that's all there is to it! I recommend you eat it right out of the oven, piping hot. You talk about good!

Variations: You can also put the mix into muffin tins to make individual breads . . . or you can put raisins or bananas into the mix to make raisin bread or banana bread . . . or you can toss in butter-sautéed apples and cinnamon to make great breakfast treats. The variety is up to you and your imagination!

Frank's Braided Italian Bread

It isn't as good as your old Sicilian grandmother used to make, but I doubt that you'll turn it down when it comes piping hot out of the oven!

3 tbsp. sugar	½ cup water
2½ tsp. salt	3 tbsp. softened butter or
1 package dry yeast	margarine plus
5 to 5½ cups all-purpose flour,	1 egg, well beaten with 2 tbsp.
divided	milk
1½ cups milk	2 tbsp. sesame seeds

First . . . in a large bowl mix together well the sugar, salt, yeast, and 2 cups of the flour. Then set it aside.

Next, in a saucepan, combine the milk, water, and butter and cook the mixture over *low heat* until the butter melts. It is important to stir the mix occasionally and watch that the milk doesn't scorch. When well-blended, cool the mix to 120-130 degrees.

At this point, gradually add the milk mix to the flour, using an electric mixer (preferably with dough hooks) on high speed. During the process, gradually add ¾ cup of flour, beating it in well too. Then gradually stir in enough of the remaining flour to make a soft dough.

Now, turn the dough out onto a floured surface and knead it until smooth and elastic (about 10 minutes). Shape the dough into a ball and place it in a well-greased bowl, turning it a couple of times to grease the top. Then cover the bowl with plastic wrap and let the dough rise (at 85 degrees) for 1 hour or until doubled in bulk. Now punch the dough down, turn it out onto a floured surface, and knead it lightly 4 or 5 times.

When you're ready to make bread, divide the dough in thirds and shape each third into a 20-inch strip. Then place the strips on a greased baking sheet (don't stretch them!) and pinch the ends together at one end to seal.

Now braid the strips, one over the other. And when completely braided, pinch the loose ends together and tuck them under.

Next, cover the loaf with plastic wrap and let it rise in a warm place (85 degrees), free from drafts, for about 45 minutes or until doubled in bulk.

At this point, brush the egg-milk mixture evenly over the loaf (taking care not to let any of it drip on the baking sheet) and sprinkle liberally with sesame seeds. Then bake at 350 degrees for 25-30 minutes or until the loaf sounds hollow when tapped. When done, cool on wire racks.

Hint: To keep the bread from overbrowning, shield the loaf with a tent made of aluminum foil.

Frank's Old-Fashioned Loaf Bread

Loaf bread is the most basic of all the yeast breads.

3 tbsp. sugar
2½ tsp. salt
1 package dry yeast
5 to 5½ cups all-purpose flour, divided
1½ cups milk

½ cup water
3 tbsp. softened butter or margarine plus
2 tbsp. melted butter or margarine

First, in a large bowl mix together well the sugar, salt, yeast, and 2 cups of the flour. Then set it aside.

Next, in a saucepan, combine the milk, water, and butter and cook the mixture over *low heat* until the butter melts. It is important to stir the mix occasionally and watch that the milk doesn't scorch. When well-blended, cool the mix to 120-130 degrees.

At this point, gradually add the milk mix to the flour, using an electric mixer (preferably with dough hooks) on high speed. During the process, gradually add ¾ cup of flour, beating it in well. Then, a little at a time, stir in enough of the remaining flour to make a soft dough.

Now, turn the dough out onto a floured surface and knead it until smooth and elastic (about 10 minutes). Shape the dough into a ball and place it in a well-greased bowl, turning a couple of times to grease the top. Then cover the bowl with plastic wrap and let the dough rise (at 85 degrees) for 1 hour or until doubled in bulk. Now punch the dough down, turn it out onto a floured surface, and knead it lightly 4 or 5 times.

When you're ready to make bread, divide the dough in half and roll each portion of it into a 14-by-17-inch rectangle on a lightly floured surface. Then roll the dough *jellyroll fashion,* starting at the narrow edge and pressing firmly to eliminate all air pockets. Now pinch the ends and the seams together to seal, and place the dough seam-side-down into 2 well-greased 9-by-5-by-3-inch loafpans.

Cover each loaf with plastic wrap and let it rise in a warm place (85 degrees), free from drafts, 1 hour or until doubled in bulk. Then bake at 375 degrees for 35 to 45 minutes or until loaves sound hollow when tapped.

When done, remove the bread from the pans immediately, brush the tops of the loaves with melted butter, and cool on wire racks.

Franco's Pane Italiano
(Frank's Italian Bread)

While United Bakery on St. Bernard Avenue makes the best Italian bread in the City of New Orleans, you might want to make your own sometime soon. If you do, try this recipe, paisano! It's like eating in Roma!

1¾ cups pure water*	4 tbsp. cornmeal
1 tbsp. real butter	2 tbsp. olive oil
1 tbsp. granulated sugar	1 tbsp. toasted sesame seeds
2 tsp. salt	1 egg white
2 pkgs. Fleischmann's dry yeast	1 tbsp. water
5 cups all-purpose flour, divided in cups	

Start off by bringing the water to a boil in a saucepan and adding the butter to it, stirring it around constantly until it melts. Then remove the pan from the fire and allow the liquid to cool to "lukewarm" (that's 110 degrees on your thermometer).

While the butter-water mixture is cooling, *use your hands* and blend together in a large bowl the sugar, salt, yeast, and 2 cups of the flour—*and*

---

*I suggest you use a good bottled water when making this bread. The chemicals that most metropolitan areas use for purifying tap water often give bread an off-taste and produce inconsistent quality.

make sure it's blended together well. Proper rising and proofing won't take place unless all these ingredients are uniformly mixed.

Now gradually begin adding the 2 cups of flour to the lukewarm butter-water mix, beating it constantly on the low-speed setting of an electric mixer until it becomes moist. Then increase the mixer speed to medium and beat for *exactly 2 minutes.*

At this point, add another half-cup of flour and beat 2 more minutes. Then add another half-cup and beat 2 more minutes. See, you want to continue adding the remaining flour a little at a time until you make a soft dough that is slightly sticky. Not wet and pasty! Just sticky!

Now put the dough on a heavily floured pastry board (or a cutting board covered with waxed paper) and knead it with the heel of your hand until it turns smooth and elastic (it's going to take all of 10 minutes to get it just right). Then when it's ready, divide the dough in half, cover each portion with a towel, and let it rest in a warm place (80 degrees Fahrenheit) for 20 minutes. (*Note:* A gas oven with a pilot light lit usually stays at 80 degrees and is an ideal spot for proofing bread).

While the dough is resting, grease a cookie sheet and sprinkle it with your cornmeal.

Now go back to your pastry board, and this time you want it "lightly floured." Take the risen dough, punch it down, knead it slightly, and roll out the 2 halves into 10-by-15-inch rectangles. Then roll up the rectangles in jelly-roll style, beginning at the wide edge. Put the 2 pieces (seam-side down) on the cookie sheet you just greased, turn the edges under, brush the tops with olive oil, and sprinkle with sesame seeds.

At this point you want to cover the loaves loosely with plastic wrap and put them in the refrigerator for at least 2 hours. This is an important part of the "curing process"—*do not short-step this procedure!*

Now take the loaves from the refrigerator, uncover them, and let them stand at room temperature for 10 minutes. Then take a knife and cut several diagonal cross-hatch marks in the top of each loaf (about an inch deep) and bake in a preheated 400-degree oven for 20 minutes. And finally, to glaze the bread, mix your egg white and water well, brush the top of the loaves, sprinkle on a few more sesame seeds, and bake for another 5 minutes.

And Mama Mia! That's Italian! *Bella molte bene!*

Frank's N'Awlins Dinner Rolls

The perfect breads to make for your next dinner party . . . or whenever you have a hankering for the real homemade stuff!

3 tbsp. sugar
2½ tsp. salt
1 package dry yeast
5 to 5½ cups all-purpose flour,
   divided
1½ cups milk
½ cup water

3 tbsp. softened butter or
   margarine plus
2 tbsp. melted butter or
   margarine
1 egg, well-beaten with 2 tbsp.
   milk

First . . . in a large bowl mix together well the sugar, salt, yeast, and 2 cups of the flour. Then set it aside.

Next, in a saucepan, combine the milk, water, and butter and cook the mixture over *low heat* until the butter melts. It is important to stir the mix occasionally and watch that the milk doesn't scorch. When well-blended, cool the mix to 120-130 degrees.

At this point, gradually add the milk mix to the flour, using an electric mixer (preferably with dough hooks) on high speed. During the process, gradually add ¾ cup of flour, beating it in well, too. Then gradually stir in enough of the remaining flour to make a soft dough.

Now, turn the dough out onto a floured surface and knead it until smooth and elastic (about 10 minutes). Now shape the dough into a ball and place it in a well-greased bowl, turning to grease the top. Cover the bowl with plastic wrap and let the dough rise (at 85 degrees) for 1 hour or until doubled in bulk. Now punch the dough down, turn it out onto a floured surface, and knead it lightly 4 or 5 times.

When you're ready to make bread, use kitchen shears to cut the dough into baking portions without stretching it. Then roll each piece into 1½-inch balls and place in 2 well-greased 9-inch baking square pans.

Cover the pans with plastic wrap and let the rolls rise in a warm place (85 degrees), free from drafts, about 35 minutes or until doubled in bulk.

At this point, brush the egg-milk mixture evenly over the loaf (taking care not to let any of it drip on the baking sheet). Then bake at 375 degrees for 15 minutes or until golden brown. When done, drizzle on the melted butter and cool the bread on wire racks.

Note: This recipe makes about 3½ dozen rolls.

Frank's Homemade English Muffins

Excellent for breakfast with eggs and bacon or whenever you want to savor the real *homemade* taste!

3 tbsp. sugar	**1½ cups milk**
2½ tsp. salt	**½ cup water**
1 package dry yeast	**3 tbsp. softened butter or**
5 to 5½ cups all-purpose flour,	**margarine plus**
divided	**1 cup cornmeal**

First . . . in a large bowl mix together well the sugar, salt, yeast, and 2 cups of the flour. Then set it aside.

Next, in a saucepan, combine the milk, water, and butter and cook the mixture over *low heat* until the butter melts. It is important to stir the mix occasionally and watch that the milk doesn't scorch. When well-blended, cool the mix to 120-130 degrees.

At this point, gradually add the milk mix to the flour, using an electric mixer (preferably with dough hooks) on high speed. During the process, gradually add ¾ cup of flour, beating it in well, too. Then gradually stir in enough of the remaining flour to make a soft dough.

Now, turn the dough out onto a floured surface and knead it until smooth and elastic (about 10 minutes). Now shape the dough into a ball and place it in a well-greased bowl, turning to grease the top. Cover the bowl with plastic wrap and let the dough rise (at 85 degrees) for 1 hour or until doubled in bulk. Now punch the dough down, turn it out onto a floured surface, and knead it lightly 4 or 5 times. At this point, you're ready to make bread!

When you're ready to make bake, divide the dough in half. Turn out one half onto a smooth surface heavily sprinkled with cornmeal, and—using the palms of your hands—pat it into a circle about a half-inch thick. Now cut the dough carefully into rounds using a 2¾-inch biscuit cutter. *But be careful—leftover dough cannot be reused.*

At this point, sprinkle 2 baking sheets with cornmeal, and transfer the dough rounds to the sheets, placing them 2 inches apart with the cornmeal side down.

Cover the muffins with plastic wrap and let the rolls rise in a warm place (85 degrees), free from drafts, about 30 minutes or until doubled in bulk.

Then, using a wide spatula, transfer the muffins to a preheated, lightly greased electric skillet set at 360 degrees—*cornmeal side down*. Cook 5 to 6 minutes or until browned, then turn and cook 5 to 6 minutes more. When done, cool the muffins on wire racks.

Note: This recipe makes about 16 English muffins.

FRANK'S HOMEMADE BREAD RECIPE
HELPFUL HINTS

THE RAPID MIX METHOD—mixing the yeast with all the dry ingredients before adding liquid ingredients. This process eliminates the need to dissolve the yeast first.

YOU NEED A THERMOMETER TO MAKE BREAD—it is essential to *measure* the temperature of the liquid ingredients. Liquids too hot will kill the yeast and keep the bread from rising. Liquids too cold will stunt the rising of the bread.

Note—the proper temperature for adding liquids is between 120-130 degrees.

ALWAYS KNEAD THE DOUGH for about 10 minutes. Here's the proper procedure: On a floured surface, using floured hands, lift the dough furthest from you, fold it over, and knead with the heel of your hand. Make a quarter-turn and repeat the process. If at any point the dough tries to stick, add a slight amount of extra flour.

After kneading, roll the dough in a ball, place in a well-greased bowl, cover with plastic wrap, and let the dough rise for 1 hour or until doubled in bulk. Then press your index finger about a half-inch into the dough. If the indentation remains, the dough is ready.

PROOF BREAD AT 85 DEGREES. A gas oven with a pilot light (lighted) or an electric oven containing a large pan of hot water usually proofs at 85 degrees. Just keep the oven draft free.

ALWAYS COOL FRESH-BAKED BREAD ON A RACK. If you leave it in the pan in which it was baked, moisture will collect along the sides and the bread will become "gummy."

STORE FRESH-BAKED BREAD IN KRAFT-TYPE PAPER. Never wrap it in plastic film or put it in plastic bags unless you plan to freeze it. Paper allows the bread to breathe and keeps it fresh and crisp.

CHAPTER 11

Desserts

Frank's Fresh-Apple Walnut Pie

If you're like me, once you cook all the main dishes for Thanksgiving and Christmas, by the time you get around to making dessert you want something extra simple . . . but good! And I've got it for you! Try this—your guests will think you worked on it for days! And it's not as sweet as other pies.

1 Pet-Ritz deep dish pie shell
8 fresh apples, sliced (use the
   apple you like best)
1 stick unsalted butter (melted)
4 tsp. ground cinnamon
1 cup granulated sugar (or
   brown sugar)

2 cups chopped walnuts
1 tbsp. fresh lemon juice
dash allspice
eggwash (1 egg-2 tbsp. water)

Start off by defrosting the pie shells—you're going to need to leave one in the pan, but remove the other one and roll it out flat with a rolling pin. Then go ahead and peel, core, and thinly slice your apples. (Incidentally, to keep them from turning brown until you place them in the pie shell, soak them in a water-sugar-lemon juice solution.)

Now . . . preheat your oven to 350 degrees.

While the oven is heating, take the pie shell, add a couple tablespoons of butter to it, sprinkle on some cinnamon, a pinch of allspice, and about 2 tablespoons of sugar. Then put in a layer of sliced apples and a layer of chopped walnuts. Repeat the process again—more butter, cinnamon, sugar, allspice, apples, and walnuts. Do this over and over again until you have a pie that's heaped high with fresh apples and walnuts.

Finally, cut the top crust of the pie shell into half-inch strips and begin placing them in lattice-fashion over the apples and walnuts. Be sure to weave them in and out of each other to lock the strips in place. When finished, use a fork to burnish the dough together at the pan edge.

All that's left is to brush the top crust with the eggwash and bake the pie until the apples cook and the crust turns a golden brown.

Hint: Oh—I suggest you serve this pie a la mode with French vanilla Frusen Gladje, Blue Belle, or Haagen Dazs ice cream. Forget the calories!

Frank's Black Pot Christmas Cake

Here's the perfect dessert to top off any holiday meal! But if you make it at Christmas time, remember to leave a slice on the kitchen table for Santa Claus!

1 cup self-rising flour	1 cup diced candied fruitcake
1 cup whole milk	mix
1 cup brown sugar	2 cups strained sliced peaches
3 tbsp. peach brandy	½ pint heavy cream (ice-cold)
1 stick of real butter, softened	1 cup red currant jelly (melted)

First, take a 12-inch cast-iron skillet, place it into your oven, and pre-heat it to 350 degrees. And while it's heating, take a large bowl and mix together the flour, the milk, the sugar, and the peach brandy. (But be real careful not to *overwork* the mixture—you just want it smooth and free of lumps.)

Next, remove the skillet from the oven (carefully—it's hot!) and toss in the stick of butter, constantly agitating the pan until the butter is fully melted and sizzling. At this point, pour in the sugar-flour-milk mixture and spread it around evenly. Then immediately on top of the batter, ar-range the peach slices in a loose semi-circle and sprinkle on the diced fruit-cake mix.

Now put the skillet back into the oven and bake the cake at 350 degrees for about 45 minutes.

Make a note here! You're going to notice that as the cake bakes, the fruits will sink into the batter and the cake will rise to the top, forming a crust.

When that happens and the cake begins to brown (which should be about 25 minutes into the baking process), remove it from the oven and liberally brush the top with additional melted butter. This is going to give you a rich crunchy-crisp coating.

Suggestions: When it's done, allow it to cool for about 15 to 20 minutes before serving . . . *and you should spoon it out of the skillet to serve*—don't try to slice it. For a real treat, take a large salad dish, ladle about 4 tablespoons of ice-cold heavy cream on the bottom, spoon the cake over the cream, and top it off with a tablespoon or two of melted red currant jelly.

Frank's Bananas St. Luke

Combine bananas with crushed pineapple, maraschino cherries, and chopped walnuts, place over Blue Belle ice cream, and top with a buttery Southern Comfort sauce and fresh whipped cream . . . and you've got a dessert especially created for Father Adrian Hall's annual Fais-Do-Do at St. Luke's Church.

½ stick real butter
1 cup brown sugar
1 tsp. cinnamon
2 tsp. vanilla
dash nutmeg
⅔ cup Southern Comfort
   liqueur
6 ripe bananas, peeled and
   sliced

1 cup crushed pineapple,
   drained
1 cup sliced maraschino cherries
2 cups chopped walnuts
½ cup shredded coconut
2 cups fresh whipped cream

First, take a 2½-quart heavy aluminum saucepan and melt the butter over medium heat until it begins to foam. Then gradually add the brown sugar and gently stir it until it thoroughly dissolves.

Next, *carefully* stir in the liqueur (it will flame up if poured in too quickly!), along with the cinnamon, the vanilla and the nutmeg, and blend everything completely over medium heat. Cook for about 5 minutes—stirring constantly—until smooth.

Finally, drop the bananas into the sauce and simmer them for a couple of minutes until they soften. Then serve some of the bananas, plus a generous helping of the sauce, in a small bowl over a heaping scoop of vanilla ice cream, and top with the pineapple, cherries, walnuts, coconut, and whipped cream.

Hints: To increase flavor intensity even more, cook the juices from the pineapple and the cherries into the Southern Comfort sauce. Add them when you add the liqueur.

Frank's Old New Orleans Bread Pudding
(With Rum Walnut Sauce)

Of all the classic desserts we have in New Orleans, few can compare with "Bread Pudding." And when you top *this* bread pudding with *this* rum-walnut sauce . . . Babe, you got something special! See if you don't agree!

1 tbsp. margarine	¼ tsp. nutmeg
1 loaf semi-stale French bread	6 cups whole milk, scalded
8 eggs, beaten well	1 stick butter, melted
1½ cups granulated sugar	2 cups raisins
2 tbsp. vanilla	1 large apple, peeled and diced
2 tbsp. ground cinnamon	

First, grease an 11-by-14 Pyrex baking pan with the margarine, break the French bread into small chunks, and place them into the pan.

Next, take a large mixing bowl and a whisk and make an egg custard by creaming together the eggs and the sugar until smooth. Then whip in the vanilla, cinnamon, and nutmeg until thoroughly mixed into the custard. Now stir in the whole milk and the butter and blend until thoroughly uniform.

At this point, pour the egg-milk mixture over the bread chunks and, using your fingers, work it into the bread until the pieces soften. Then evenly sprinkle on the raisins and diced apple. And again with your fingers, gently push them into the softened bread.

Finally, sprinkle a little more cinnamon over the top of the pudding and bake in a preheated 325-degree oven for about an hour (or until a rich honey brown).

This bread pudding is great served both warm or chilled, especially when it's topped with rum walnut sauce.

Frank's Rum Walnut Sauce
for Bread Pudding

Here's a quick and easy sauce that you can make for bread pudding . . . or pound cake . . . or waffles . . . or fried bananas . . . or pancakes or as a topping for Frusen Gladje ice cream! In fact, it'll go on almost anything!

1 stick butter	zest of one lemon (outer peel)
1½ cups brown sugar	dash cinnamon
2 tsp. vanilla	¾ cup dark rum
1 cup finely chopped walnuts	

First, melt the butter over medium heat in a 3½ quart sauce pan, stir in the brown sugar, and cook until the sugar melts. Then quickly stir in the lemon zest, the vanilla, the walnuts, and the cinnamon and cook gently until all the ingredients blend thoroughly.

Then just before you're ready to serve, slowly pour in the rum, stir it quickly into a smooth sauce, and cook it for about 3 minutes to drive off the alcohol and marry the flavors.

It's just that simple!

Note: I suggest that you use this recipe to experiment with liqueurs other than rum. For example, you can try Grand Marnier, Galliano, Kahlua, Peach Brandy, Southern Comfort, Amaretto, and a wide variety of others. It's just a matter of letting your imagination be your guide.

Hate soggy cream pies?

If you want to prevent your pie crusts from becoming soggy when you make cream pies, just sprinkle the bottom crust with powdered sugar! It works!

Charlie's Chocolate Marble Rum Pie

This is a recipe hand carried to me by Charles McMahon. He created it one afternoon while suffering from a severe case of sweet-tooth and chocolate attack! And was it worth it!!

The Crust:

1½ cups crushed Oreo cookies
  (middle removed)

1 tsp. granulated sugar
¼ cup unsalted butter

The Chocolate Mix:

1 envelope unflavored gelatin
⅛ tsp. salt
¼ cup granulated sugar
2 egg yolks, unbeaten
¼ cup rum (light or dark)

1 cup heavy whipping cream
12 oz. semi-sweet chocolate
  chips
2 egg whites, beaten until foamy
1 cup granulated sugar

The Cream Mix:

1 cup heavy cream
1 tbsp. Warren Leruth Vanilla

¼ cup granulated sugar

Start off making a super Oreo cookie pie crust by mixing 1½ cups of crushed Oreo cookie crumbs with ¼ cup of unsalted butter and 1 teaspoon of sugar. (The cookies can be crumbled fine in a food processor or under a rolling pin.) Shape the crust by working it well with your fingers until it holds together in a paste. Then press it out evenly over the bottom and sides of a 9-inch pan and bake it at 350 degrees for about 8 minutes (or until firm!).

Next, make the chocolate filling by mixing together the envelope of gelatin, the ⅛ teaspoon salt, and the quarter-cup of sugar and putting the mixture in the top of a double boiler. Then one ingredient at a time, gently stir in the egg yolks, the rum, and the heavy cream, and cook the mixture over boiling water—*stirring constantly*—until it "slightly thickens."

When it begins to thicken, remove the filling from the heat and fold in the chocolate chips until they are well incorporated into the mix. Now cool the chocolate mixture until it thickens . . . *but don't let it set!*

At this point, take the beaten, foamy egg whites and add the cup of sugar to them. You want to beat this mixture until it forms stiff peaks. Now fold the egg white mixture *gently* into the thickened chocolate mixture and cool until it thickens again *(it must be very thick without it being set!)*.

Finally, whip the second cup of heavy cream with the vanilla and another ¼ cup of sugar until it "firms." And here comes the *"marbling process"* . . . you alternate the chocolate mixture and the cream mixture into the pie shell, and swirl them together with a spoon or spatula (being sure to keep the two colors separate!).

All that's left is to refrigerate the pie until it sets—preferably overnight! If you can wait that long!

Warning: If you're a chocolate lover you're gonna drool over this pie! It's creamy and smooth and rich and wonderful!

N'Awlins Blueberry Cream Cheese Crumble

Combine a carton of Creole cream cheese with a batch of plump juicy blueberries and top it with a crunchy sugary crust . . . and you've got an easy New Orleans dessert fit for royalty!

1 tbsp. butter	11 oz. Creole cream cheese
1 pint fresh blueberries	½ cup granulated sugar
(washed)	¾ stick real butter (softened)
3 tbsp. lemon juice	another ½ cup granulated sugar
2 tbsp. Triple Sec	1 cup self-rising flour

First, take the tablespoon of butter and thoroughly grease a shallow 9-by-9 glass baking pan—bottom and sides.

Then place the fresh blueberries in a small bowl and stir in the lemon juice, the Triple Sec, and the Creole cream cheese. *Be sure all the berries are coated with the mixture, but be careful not to break up the cream cheese too much.* Now evenly sprinkle ½ cup of granulated sugar over the mix and let it "set" for about 15 minutes.

Next, in a large bowl, combine the second ½ cup of sugar with the flour and "cut" the butter into the mix until it reaches a crusty crumbly consistency. (Ideally, you want to use a food processor for this, but two table knives also work well.) Now sprinkle the topping over the blueberries.

At this point you're ready to bake the *crumble* at 350 degrees for 45 minutes (or until the crust turns a golden brown).

Suggestion: This dish is good served either hot or cold. But to add extra richness and elegance, try it nestled into a bed of whipped cream and topped with French vanilla ice cream and a tad more Triple Sec.

Mary Clare's Blueberry Crunch

This is one of the tastiest desserts you can concoct with fresh fruit . . . and one of the simplest ones to prepare. Telling you about this dish doesn't do it justice—you gotta taste it for yourself! Meet you in the kitchen!

2 cups fresh, washed blueberries   **⅔ cup all-purpose flour**
2 tbsp. margarine   **another ⅓ cup granulated sugar**
⅓ cup granulated sugar   **¼ cup softened butter**

First, wash the blueberries under cold, running water. Then—while they're still wet—put them into a 9-by-9 Pyrex baking dish that has been greased with the margarine.

Next, sprinkle the first ⅓ cup of sugar evenly over the berries and mix it in gently with a spoon *(but you want each berry coated well)*.

While the fruit is marinating, take a separate bowl and mix together the flour, the second ⅓ cup of sugar, and the butter. This works best if you use two table knives to "cut" the ingredients into each other. All you want to do is form a crumbly topping that resembles granola.

Finally, sprinkle the topping over the berries (working a little of it into the fruit) and bake in a preheated oven at 350 degrees for about 30 minutes or until the top turns a crispy brown.

Hints: I recommend you serve this dessert hot, topped with either French vanilla ice cream or fresh whipped cream! And if you don't happen to have any blueberries handy, you can also substitute any fresh fruit *that will make its own juices when cooked (blackberries, strawberries, raspberries, figs, peaches, nectarines, apples, and so forth).*

Frank's Favorite Microwave Divinity

I've often said "on the air" that one of my favorite forms of candy is "Divinity." So one Saturday when I was doing my radio show, a listener called in this recipe and told me to try it! I did! It tasted like it came from a professional candy kitchen! But you can do it in your microwave!

2 cups granulated sugar	**2 egg whites**
⅛ tsp. salt	**1 tsp. vanilla**
½ cup light Karo corn syrup	**2 cups coarsely chopped pecans**
⅓ cup water	

First, take a large Pyrex bowl (preferably 4-6 cup size) and mix together the sugar, salt, Karo corn syrup, and water until it is fully blended. Then slide it into your microwave oven and cook it on *high*—uncovered—*for exactly 3 minutes.*

Now remove the bowl from the oven and stir the mixture *thoroughly.* When you have it well-mixed, put it back in the microwave and cook it on *high* again—uncovered—*8 to 10 minutes* or until a teaspoonful dropped in very cold water forms a small hard ball (this is about 260 degrees on your candy thermometer, just in case you want to check it).

While the sugar is cooking in the microwave, beat the egg whites in a large, chilled, stainless steel bowl until they form stiff peaks. Then take the cooked sugar-base from the microwave and pour it *in a thin stream* over the egg whites while you beat them at the high-speed setting of your electric mixer.

After all the sugar is whipped in, pour in the vanilla and continue beating until the candy mix holds its shape and begins to lose its sheen (this should take you about 5 minutes).

Now you're going to have to work fast, but when you have the candy formed, *gently fold* in the pecans. Then turn out tablespoon-size servings on waxed paper and let them set up. That's all there is to it, y'all.

Incidentally, this recipe will make about 30 pieces of spoon-size divinity. And you talk about good!

Frank's Pig-Out Pudding Pie

This is the dessert your friends probably call "Out-Of-This-World-Cake." Well, I've done a little doctoring up here and there, changed it from a cake to a pie, added a few more calories, and given it a more accurate name . . . because this is so good you will "pig-out!"

Crust:

1 stick real butter
⅓ cup powdered sugar

1 cup sifted all-purpose flour
1 cup chopped pecans

Soften the stick of butter to room temperature and add to it the powdered sugar and the flour. Then cream it all together until well-blended. Now toss in the pecans and, with your hands, distribute them equally through the mix.

Next, with your fingers spread the mixture over the bottom of a 12-inch pie pan into an even thin crust. You'll have to work at it a bit, and it may appear that you're going to run short . . . but there's enough to spread out.

Now bake the crust for 20 minutes in a preheated 325-degree oven until slightly brown. Then set it aside to cool.

At this point, begin preparing your ingredients for the fillings. Here's what you're going to need:

First Layer:

1 8-oz. Philadelphia cream
 cheese
1 cup powdered sugar

1 cup fresh whipped cream
½ teaspoon real vanilla

Using an electric mixer, cream all these ingredients together until they are blended thoroughly. Then spread it over the baked crust.

Second Layer:

1 small package vanilla instant
 pudding
1 small package chocolate
 instant pudding

3 cups cold whole milk
 (not low-fat)

Stir everything together in a bowl. Then whip the mixture to a smooth consistency with an electric beater until thick. Now spread this over the previous layer.

THIRD LAYER: Finally, spread about 2 cups of whipping cream over the pudding layer. Then, using your cheese shredder, shave 1 Hershey bar or Baker's bittersweet over the top of the whipped cream, sprinkle on a few finely chopped pecans, and garnish with half-cherries.

Come to think of it . . . top it any way you want to! Then refrigerate it overnight—if you can wait that long to eat it!

Frank's Chocolate Coconut Pecan Pie

Chocolate pie is super! Pecan pie is exceptional! But when you put them both together and toss in a little coconut to make Frank's Southern Chocolate Coconut Pecan Pie . . . you'd better go lock up the bulldog! Cuz' this will make him break his chain!

3 eggs, lightly beaten
1 cup Karo dark corn syrup
3 tbsp. vanilla extract
⅛ tsp. salt
1 cup granulated sugar
¼ cup melted butter
2 oz. Baker's unsweetened
    chocolate

¼ cup shredded coconut
1 cup broken pecan parts
1 cup pecan halves
1 deep-dish unbaked Pet-Ritz
    9″ pastry shell

Start off with a bowl large enough to hold the lightly beaten eggs, Karo syrup, vanilla extract, salt, and sugar. Then put all these ingredients in the bowl and mix them thoroughly.

Next, take a small skillet and melt down the butter and the chocolate over *very low heat,* stirring constantly as the chocolate dissolves. Once the consistency is smooth, pour the mix into the bowl with the eggs and syrup and "thoroughly blend" everything evenly.

Now, toss in the chopped pecans and the shredded coconut and—using a tablespoon—work them both into the filling base. I suggest you don't hurry this part of the recipe—you want to make sure the uniformity is just right. Next, pour the mixture into the unbaked pie shell and smooth it around. Then take "half" of the pecan halves and lay them evenly on top of the filling.

Now here's where the creativity comes in! Again take your tablespoon and gently push the halves into the filling so that they stop about halfway down. Take your time—don't rush! And when you've finished, put the rest of the pecans evenly over the top of the pie. *But don't push these in!* As the pie bakes, they'll settle in by themselves.

All that's left now is to bake this masterpiece in a 350-degree oven for about 50 minutes . . . and it's done! I do suggest you let it cool for about 20 minutes before you slice it. Oh—and when you serve it, top it with a healthy scoop of Haagen Dazs or Frusen Gladje vanilla ice cream!

That's style, y'all!

Hint: You may have excess dough around the edges after you fill the pie shell. For a nice presentation, turn a teaspoon upside down, scallop the edge of the dough, and fold it over into the filling. It bakes into "points" and looks pretty.

New Orleans Apple Crisp

If you like apples and you'd like a quick and easy apple dessert to serve with almost anything . . . put this dish together. You can even make it at the last minute!

4 cups tart apples, chopped and sliced	**1 cup white or brown sugar**
½ cup water	**1 tsp. cinnamon**
¾ cup flour	**2 tbsp. lemon juice**
	½ cup butter

The first thing you do is arrange the apples in a 9-inch buttered baking dish. Then pour the water over the apples.

Next, blend the flour, sugar, cinnamon, lemon juice, and butter with the pastry hooks of your kitchen mixer until it forms the consistency of granola and sprinkle it over top of the apples.

All that's left is to bake the dessert for about 30 minutes in a preheated 350-degree oven until the top turns crisp and honey brown.

I told you it was simple, huh?

Hint: Incidentally, I suggest you serve the apple crisp piping hot right out of the oven and top it with French vanilla Haagen Dazs, Blue Belle, or Frusen Gladje.

Coconut Raisin-Nut Clusters

For the fastest and easiest chocolate candy you ever made (and ever tasted!) . . . follow this recipe:

1 8-oz. can sweetened condensed milk	**1 cup chopped pecans**
1 large bag Nestle's chocolate chips	**1 lb. raisins**
	½ cup coconut, shredded and toasted

First, take a 3-quart saucepan and heat the condensed milk to just bubbling. Then—*over medium heat*—add the whole bag of chocolate chips and stir them until they are fully melted.

At this point, reduce the heat to low and stir in the pecans and raisins until each piece is fully coated with the chocolate. *Immediately remove from the burner!*

Then, when the candy is mixed well, drop teaspoon-size portions on a sheet of wax paper, top each one with a dab of toasted coconut, and let it set up. This is great stuff!

Hint: To toast coconut, place it in a thin layer on a shallow cookie sheet and bake it in the oven at 300 degrees for about 15 minutes or until it turns a honey brown.

Ruth's Country-Style Black Pot Blueberries

Without a doubt, one of the finest kitchen assistants I ever worked with is a lady named Ruth Tannehill. She not only stood behind the cameras and prepared my ingredients for television every Tuesday morning . . . but occasionally, she shared one of her special recipes with me. This is one of them! And I guarantee you're gonna love it!

1 cup granulated sugar	**1 pint of fresh blueberries (washed)**
1 cup self-rising flour	**½ pint heavy cream (ice-cold)**
1 cup whole milk	**1 cup red currant jelly (melted)**
1 stick of real butter	

First, take a heavy 12-inch cast-iron black skillet and preheat it in the oven to 350 degrees.

Then, while the skillet is heating, take a large bowl and mix together *with a wire whip* the sugar, self-rising flour, and whole milk until thoroughly blended. (But be real careful not to *overwork* the mixture—you just want it smooth and free of lumps).

Next, remove the skillet from the oven (carefully—it's hot!) and toss in the stick of butter, constantly agitating the pan until the butter is fully melted and sizzling. At this point, pour in the sugar-flour-milk mixture and spread it around evenly. Then immediately on top of the mixture, add the fresh blueberries—*evenly.* Now put the skillet back into the oven—*uncovered*—and bake at 350 degrees for 45 minutes.

Make a note here! You're going to notice that as the cake bakes, the berries will sink into the mix and the mix will rise to the top, forming a cake crust. So when the cake begins to brown (which should take about 25 minutes), remove it from the oven briefly and liberally brush the top with additional melted butter. This is going to give you a rich crunchy-crisp coating.

Suggestions: When it's done, allow it to cool for about 15 to 20 minutes before serving . . . and you should spoon it out of the skillet to serve— don't try to slice it. For a real treat, take a large salad dish, ladle about 4 tablespoons of ice-cold heavy cream on the bottom, spoon the cake over the cream, and top it off with a tablespoon or two of melted red currant jelly. Lord! You talk about sinful!

Variation: Instead of blueberries, you can substitute any other kind of juicy fruit you desire—peeled peaches, peeled plums, strawberries, blackberries, peeled pears . . . or you can use a variety of canned fruits (just drain off all of the liquids first). The truth of the matter is this dessert will turn out great regardless of what you use as a filling.

## CHAPTER 12

Lagniappe

Lagniappe Delight

In New Orleans, *lagniappe* is that little bit extra. Well, when you ask what do you do with the handful of extra bits and pieces of meats and vegetables that we all stash away in the refrigerator as leftovers . . . you turn them into a dish I call "Lagniappe Delight." And you do it with a wok, a couple cans of soup, and a little bit of creativity.

YOU CAN USE ANY OR ALL OF THESE INGREDIENTS IN ANY COMBINATION

3 boneless thinly sliced chicken breasts
2 small thinly sliced steaks
4 thinly sliced pork chops

4 thinly sliced veal cutlets
3 cups of raw shrimp, coarse-chopped

AND THEN YOU'RE GOING TO NEED:

1 cup celery, bias-cut
1 large onion, quartered and separated
½ bell pepper, sliced
1 cup mushrooms, thick-sliced

1 cup fresh broccoli florets
1 large carrot, bias cut or julienned
2 coarse-chopped green onions
3 cloves minced garlic

Or you can use any other vegetables you like—crookneck squash, zucchini, cabbage, green beans, snow peas—whatever.

YOU WILL ALSO NEED:

2 tbsp. cornstarch
4 tbsp. soy sauce
4 tbsp. Crisco oil
2 cans chicken broth
2 tsp. ground ginger

1 tsp. ground mustard
2 tsp. white pepper
1 can of Campbell's creamy chicken mushroom soup

And now you're ready to cook.

First, take the meats you've decided to use and lay them out on a plate. Then sprinkle them lightly with cornstarch and drizzle on the soy sauce. Now, with your fingers, mix everything together until the meat is thoroughly coated.

At this point, heat the wok (and if you don't have a wok you can use a heavy 6-quart Dutch oven), add the Crisco oil, and drop in the meats gently so that the oil doesn't splatter on you. Remember, all you want to do is "stir-fry" the meats until just cooked. Then, with a strainer, remove them from the wok and set them aside.

Now toss in all the vegetables and stir-fry them too—*but not too much!* You just want them "tender-crisp," not cooked! They are going to finish cooking in the steaming liquids you're about to add.

So when the vegetables have richened in color and begun to turn tender, place the meats back in the wok and stir everything together well until uniformly blended. Keep in mind that you're cooking all this on the "high" setting on the stove. *You're cooking hot!*—so you're going to have to keep stirring constantly. It should take about 3 minutes if the temperature is right.

Next, pour in the 2 cans of chicken broth, along with the ginger, mustard, and white pepper to taste, and stir everything again. Then cover for about 3 or 4 minutes so that the broth braises the meats and vegetables.

Finally, add the can of creamy chicken mushroom soup and stir it in well. At this point, the soup should combine with the broth and create a rich creamy sauce. One more time, taste the dish and add a little extra soy sauce if you want to. You can also add a little white wine if you'd like at this time.

Then serve the "Lagniappe Delight" over steamed rice or vermicelli pasta along with toast wedges and a tossed green salad with vinaigrette dressing. I promise—you'll love it!

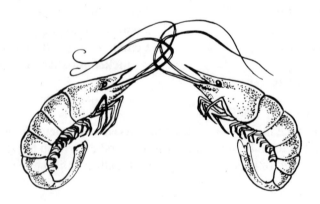

Frank's Cajun White Beans and Shrimp

This old Cajun dish is extremely popular down on the bayous of southeast Louisiana where it is packed as a "hot lunch" into Thermos bottles and taken aboard the shrimp boats. But whether you're a shrimper or not . . . you're gonna love this recipe because it's easy to fix and unbelievably tasty!

2 lb. fresh shrimp	1 tsp. thyme
4 tbsp. margarine	1 tbsp. sweet basil
8 strips lean bacon	4 bay leaves
2 cups diced onions	8 cups shrimp stock (from
1 cup diced celery	heads/shells)
1 lb. white beans (Navy or	1 tbsp. crab boil
Great Northerns)	salt and black pepper to taste
1 tsp. garlic powder	

First, rinse the shrimp well under cold running water. Then peel, devein, and butterfly them and set them aside.

Next, take the shrimp heads and shells, place them on a pizza pan, drizzle on the 4 tablespoons of margarine, and bake them until toasty (about 15 minutes) in a preheated 450-degree oven.

When done, add the heads and shells (plus whatever juices accumulate in the bottom of the pan) to a stock pot containing 10 cups of water. Bring the mixture to a rapid boil, then reduce the heat to "simmer" and cook for about an hour until you have approximately 8 cups of stock left. Now strain and save the liquid and discard the shells.

Meanwhile, take a 6-quart Dutch oven and put it on the fire. Then sauté the bacon, onion, and celery together until the vegetables turn brown. Next, toss in the beans, garlic powder, thyme, sweet basil, and bay leaves and mix everything thoroughly. (Incidentally, the fire is on "high" during this entire cooking process.)

At this point, pour in the shrimp stock and the crab boil and stir the pot well, making sure the mixture is uniformly blended. Then bring the beans to a boil . . . *but immediately reduce to a simmer, cover the pot, and cook until rich and creamy* (about 3 hours). Stir the pot occasionally.

Finally, about 20 minutes before you're ready to eat, stir the butterflied shrimp into the beans, season to taste with salt and pepper, cover the pot again, and *simmer* until they turn pink and tender. *Do not overcook the shrimp or they will turn rubbery and mealy.*

Serve piping hot over steamed rice, accompanied by a crisp tossed salad and lots of buttered French bread.

Hint: This recipe also works well with lentils and lima beans, but the cooking time is much shorter.

Frank's Cajun Jambalaya
(New Orleans Gourmet Style)

Nothing—but nothing!—beats a good plate of spicy, seasoned jambalaya. And this recipe is the hardest to beat because it's loaded with all the good things New Orleanians love—sausage, chicken, andouille, and shrimp! You gotta try it!

½ cup bacon drippings or
  margarine
1 lb. smoked sausage, diced
½ lb. andouille, diced
½ lb. tasso
½ lb. bacon, crumbled
2 cups julienned chicken
  (or turkey)
2 large onions, coarsely chopped
1 medium bell pepper, chopped
  fine
6 ribs celery, coarsely chopped
4 garlic cloves, finely minced

3 cups long grained rice
2 8 oz. cans Rotel tomatoes
2 cups beef stock
2 tsp. Kitchen Bouquet
½ tsp. thyme
2 tsp. chili powder
black pepper to taste
cayenne pepper to taste
salt to taste
2 lb. peeled shrimp
12 green onions, sliced
½ cup minced parsley

To make a really good pot of jambalaya, you're going to need a well-seasoned black cast-iron Dutch oven with a tight-fitting lid. And for this recipe, an 8-quart pot is perfect!

So take the pot, put it on the burner over high heat, and pour in the bacon drippings (or margarine). Then toss in the smoked sausage, andouille, tasso, and crumbled bacon and stir-fry the meats until the smoked sausage turns light brown (it should take about 8 minutes or so).

Now, drop in the julienned chicken and stir-fry it until every strip loses its translucency (turns white). Then immediately add the onions, bell pepper, celery, and garlic, reduce the heat to medium-high, and cook the vegetables until they soften.

At this point, pour in the rice. And you want to stir it thoroughly into the seasoning vegetables and meats until every single grain is moistened—*about 4 to 5 minutes.*

Next, add the tomatoes, beef stock, Kitchen Bouquet, thyme, and chili powder, blend everything together well, and bring the mixture to a slow boil. When this happens, taste the liquids and season the dish *to taste* with salt, black, and cayenne pepper. Just remember that you're going to have to season a little on the "heavy side" because the rice will absorb much of the seasonings as it cooks, and you still have a couple pounds of shrimp to mix in. *So be sure to taste carefully!*

When everything is just right, reduce the heat as low as it will go, put the lid on the pot, and simmer the jambalaya for about an hour. This "slow cooking" process allows each grain of rice to cook evenly, puff properly, and pick up the combination of flavors. If the heat is too high, the rice will stick to the bottom of the pot and turn mushy.

Then when the jambalaya is done, about 5 minutes before you're ready to eat stir in the raw shrimp, green onions, and parsley, put the lid back on the pot, and continue to simmer the jambalaya over *low heat* until the shrimp turn pink.

I suggest that before you serve the dish, you fluff the rice slightly. I also suggest that you serve the dish alongside crispy buttered French bread and ice-cold beer.

Chef's Hints:

1—Under no circumstances should you remove the cover from the pot during the slow-cooking process. If you do, you'll release steam you need to cook the rice . . . your rice will turn out hard in the center . . . and your jambalaya will be dry instead of moist. Don't peek in the pot!

2—If you don't feel that your stove-top will cook the jambalaya slowly enough, put the cover on the pot (after you mix the liquids in), set your oven at 300 degrees, put the pot into the oven, and bake *the dish for about 45 minutes. It will come out perfect!*

Frank's Creole Baked Eggs and N'Awlins Fried Grits With Ham and Red-Eye Gravy

Now here's a breakfast that will stick with you all day long! In fact, it's so good I wouldn't be surprised if you fixed it for lunch . . . or dinner . . . or even a late-night supper!

The Eggs:

3 tbsp. butter or margarine
1 cup sliced bell pepper
  (half-rings)
2 cups sliced mushrooms
2 cups sliced onions (half-rings)
¾ cup sliced green onions

¾ cup coarsely chopped celery
½ cup Rotel tomatoes with
  chilies
6 fresh eggs
salt and pepper to taste

In a 12-inch heavy aluminum skillet, melt the butter or margarine to the point of bubbling. Then toss in all of the vegetables—bell pepper, mushrooms, onions, green onions, and celery—and sauté the mixture until it wilts. At this point, stir in the Rotel tomatoes, turn up the heat to high, and cook until most of the tomato liquid evaporates and the vegetable mixture becomes soft and tender.

Next, transfer the vegetables to a 9-by-12 Pyrex baking dish and place the dish into a preheated 375-degree oven for 10 minutes. Then—*carefully!*—remove the heated dish from the oven and gently crack the 6 eggs evenly over the vegetables (but don't break the yolks).

Now all you do is lightly sprinkle the eggs with salt and black pepper to taste and slide the dish back into the oven to bake. Remember that since the Pyrex dish was hot to begin with, the eggs will start to cook immediately. So keep a close eye on them—8 to 10 minutes should be all it takes to firm up the whites and the yolks. You don't want to overcook them or they'll turn rubbery.

When they're ready, take a spatula and scoop out the eggs and the seasoning vegetables on which they're sitting.

The Ham and Red-Eye Gravy:

6 slices of ham (¼ inch thick)
2 tbsp. margarine
¼ cup strong fresh-brewed
  coffee

2 tbsp. paprika
salt and black pepper to taste

In a heavy preheated skillet, fry the ham slices in the margarine over medium heat until they start to brown. Don't worry about the juices that come from the ham and the ham pieces that stick to the bottom of the pan—this is the base for your red-eye gravy.

Now when the ham is cooked, set the slices on a platter for a while. Then stir in the coffee and the paprika, bring the mixture to a boil, and (with a spoon) deglaze the bottom of the skillet. You want to scrape up every bit of whatever is stuck. Finally, when the gravy is thoroughly blended, mix in a little salt and pepper to taste, set it aside, and keep it warm.

The Fried Grits:

2 cups water	**salt and black pepper to taste**
½ cup quick grits (not instant)	**½ cup shredded Colby cheese**
3 tbsp. butter or margarine	**½ cup crumbled bacon bits**

In a 3-quart Dutch oven, bring the water to a boil and stir in the grits. When the water comes back to a boil, mix in the butter, reduce the heat to low, and cook the grits for about 5 minutes (be sure to stir them occasionally). Season to taste with salt and pepper.

When they're done, remove the pot from the fire, put a cover on it, and let the grits "set up" for about 3 minutes. Then mix in the cheese and the bacon bits, put the cover back on the pot, and allow the grits to "set" again for about 5 minutes.

Then, when they're cool enough to handle, drop them into a 12-compartment muffin tin and let them cool until they hold their shape (or you can refrigerate them to speed up the process if you're in a hurry).

Now, when you're ready to eat, just unmold the grits from the muffin tin, drop them into a hot, lightly buttered skillet, and quickly fry them on both sides until they become a toasty brown.

All that's left is to dish out the ham, the eggs, and the grits, cover them liberally with a couple ladle-fuls of the red-eye gravy, and serve everything alongside a toasted, buttered English muffin. *Y'all, you're eating one of the best breakfasts you ever had!*

Variation: If you don't have a muffin tin, you can spread the cooked grits out evenly on a thin baking sheet, let them cool to set, and slice them into squares or cut out circles with a drinking glass dipped in hop water. At that point, it's just a matter of frying them hot and toasty brown.

Frank's Ol' N'Awlins Hogshead Cheese

As soon as the weather turns chilly, the first thing I do is clear a spot in my kitchen and begin the annual ritual of making one of my favorite New Orleans foods—Creole Daube Glace (more commonly known as *hogshead cheese!*). Of all the recipes I've tried, I like the one Vincent Messina taught me (of course, I've made a few modifications). So even if you have never tried making hogshead cheese before, you can do this one. And it really tastes "Naturally N'Awlins!"

6 lb. fresh raw pigs feet
4 lb. Boston butt, cut in chunks
¼ cup salt
1 3 oz. bag of crab boil
3 ribs coarsely chopped celery
½ sliced lemon
8 bay leaves
1 medium onion, diced

½ green bell pepper, coarsely chopped
1/2 red bell pepper, coarsely chopped
6 cloves minced garlic
1 tsp. rosemary
2 tsp. basil

Plus:

2 bunches coarsely chopped shallots
1 cup finely chopped parsley
1 tbsp. pork seasoning

3 tsp. crushed red pepper (to taste)
4 tbsp. paprika

First, drop the pigs feet and the pork butt (cut into large chunks) into a 12-quart stock pot and add enough water to cover the meat—about 1½ gallons should do it. When the water begins to boil, a foam will form on the surface—*skim it off!*

When you've removed as much foam as possible, add the salt, crab boil, celery, lemon, bay leaves, onion, bell pepper, garlic, rosemary, and basil, and continue to cook the meats on a medium setting—*skimming as necessary*—until the pigs feet are tender. This should take about 3 hours or so. Just remember, the bottom line is you want the meats to be "super tender."

When the meat appears to fall off the bone, turn off the fire. Now remove and drain the meat and set it aside to cool. Then strain the cooking liquid through a collander and set it aside to cool too. While the liquid is cooling, pick as much meat from the pigs feet as possible and chop it into small pieces with a knife. Then remove all the fat from the pork butt and pull the meat shreds apart with your fingers.

By now, the fat from the boiled pork should have come to the surface of the cooking liquid. Skim off as much as you can!

Next, put both meats back into the liquid, bring it to a boil once again, and toss in the shallots, pork seasoning, crushed red pepper, and parsley. Immediately, reduce the heat to "low" and simmer the mixture for 15 minutes (or until the shallots are soft). You can also add the paprika now to reach the color you desire.

When the shallots and parsley are wilted, take the pot off the fire and allow it to cool slightly. Again, skim off whatever fat has collected on the surface and pour out the "cheese" into molds. All that's left is to refrigerate the molds overnight to set.

When you're ready to eat, unmold the hogshead cheese, slice, and serve with saltine crackers and chilled white wine.

Now that's . . . Naturally N'Awlins!

Hints:

1—If you want to make hogshead cheese without using the animal fats found in pigs' feet, you can substitute Knox unflavored gelatin and a few 10½ ounce cans of beef broth. Just use a 1:1 ratio (1 broth, 1 gelatin), bring the broth to a boil, stir in the gelatin, and fold in the other pre-cooked ingredients. How much "gelatin-broth" you need depends on how much meat you use and how much hogshead cheese you want to make.

*2—The cheese can be hardened in any kind of mold you want to use . . . **as long as it's glass!** I prefer Pyrex baking pans, meatloaf pans, Bundt pans, and small cereal bowls.*

3—To avoid having unwanted flavors in your hogshead cheese, I suggest you use bottled water when cooking the pigs feet and Boston butt.

Frank's Tamale-Taco Pie

This is one of the easiest—*and tastiest!*—casseroles you'll ever fix . . . and if you like Mexican as much as I do, you'll probably end up fixing it several times a week!

3 tbsp. margarine
2 cups onions, diced
1 cup green onions, sliced
1 cup fresh mushrooms, sliced
2 lb. ground meat
2 cans Rotel tomatoes
   (with chilies)
2 pods fresh garlic, minced
4 tsp. chili powder
3 tsp. cumin

2 tsp. Worcestershire sauce
1½ tsp. salt
1 dozen taco or tortilla chips
   (broken)
black pepper to taste
2 cans black beans
2 cups shredded cheddar cheese
1 cup sour cream
1½ cups cornbread mix

Start off by melting the margarine in a 4-quart Dutch oven and sautéing—*on high heat*—the onions, mushrooms, and green onions until they soften (about 4 minutes). Then toss in the ground meat and cook—again over high heat—until the beef has fully browned.

At this point, strain the meat and set it aside, remove all the juices from the pot, put the pot back on the burner, and add to it the 2 cans of Rotel tomatoes. Now cook the tomatoes about 3 minutes on high heat, or until the liquid begins to reduce slightly.

Next, put the meat back into the pot and add to it the garlic, chili powder, cumin, Worcestershire sauce, salt, and pepper. Now stir everything together well and simmer the meat mixture (with the cover on the pot) for about 5 minutes. While the ground meat is cooking, butter an 11-by-14 Pyrex baking dish and sprinkle the broken taco chips evenly on the bottom. Then take a small bowl and make your cornbread mix. Set both aside temporarily.

Now, remove the cover from the pot and stir in the black beans (liquid as well as beans). *But make sure the beans are fully blended into the meat.* Again cover the pot and simmer the mixture for 2 more minutes.

All that's left now is to spoon out the meat mixture over the taco chips, spread the sour cream over the meat with a spatula, sprinkle the shredded cheddar cheese over the sour cream, and pour the cornbread mixture over everything, making sure it is evenly distributed.

Then bake in a preheated 450-degree oven for 15-20 minutes or until the cornbread is golden brown.

Hint: I suggest you place a bed of shredded lettuce and diced tomatoes on a dinner plate and serve the pie over the lettuce and tomatoes. It not only tastes great, it's quite appetizing too and can be used not only as a dinner entree but as a party dish as well.

Real New Orleans Hot Tamales

I've eaten lots of hot tamales in my day . . . and I've tried a lot of hot tamale recipes. But when it comes to making them at home, it's tough to beat my brother Augie's recipe! I want you to try it! You won't believe how easy it is!

3 lb. lean ground meat
2 cups Ballard cornbread mix
1 X-large onion, chopped fine
1 10 oz. can Rotel tomatoes with chilies
1 envelope Two-Alarm chili mix
1 16 oz. can peeled tomatoes, chopped

1 2.5 oz. can Mexican-style chili powder
1 tsp. cumin (heaping)
3 cups water
salt and cayenne pepper to taste

Start off by sautéing the ground beef and the onions in a 5-quart Dutch oven until the beef browns and the onions become wilted and tender. At this point, strain the meat and drain off all but a couple tablespoons of the beef drippings. *But keep it in reserve—you'll need it later.*

Then place the beef back into the Dutch oven, turn up the heat to high, and mix into the meat the Rotel tomatoes, the chili mix, the peeled tomatoes, the chili powder, the cumin, the water, and the salt and cayenne pepper. Now, bring the mixture to a "slow boil" . . . *but as soon as the boil begins,* reduce the heat to low and simmer everything together (with the cover on the pot) for about 45 minutes to an hour.

Next, strain the meat again from the juices (but save the juices). Then put the beef back into the pot once more and thoroughly stir in the cornbread mix *plus 1 cup* of the meat drippings you saved from the sautéing process.

At this point taste the mixture and adjust the spicyness of the tamales by adding either more chili powder or cayenne pepper. Then mix everything together extremely well once again . . . and note—*you want the tamale mixture to be moist and pasty, but not runny and wet*. Now allow the mixture to cool down enough to handle it.

Finally, place about a tablespoon of the meat-stuffing into the center of a moistened tamale paper, roll the paper around the tamale, and put the rolled tamales into a deep steamer pot.

Then gently ladle over the tamales *all* the juices and drippings you reserved during the entire preparation process and simmer everything on *low* for about 45 minutes!

When you're ready to eat, serve the tamales piping hot New Orleans style (which is on top of newspaper with a Barq's root beer on the side and a box of saltine crackers!).

Note: I suggest that whenever you decide to make this recipe you make a batch to eat right away and another batch to stash in the freezer. That way, anytime you get a hankering for hot tamales . . . it's just a matter of heating 'em up!

How to Make Sweetened Condensed Milk

1 cup boiling water
2 cups granulated sugar
2 cups non-fat dry milk

½ cup butter-flavored Crisco
shortening

This is real simple to make, and it does taste just like the commercially-prepared product. So whenever you find yourself needing condensed milk for a recipe and you don't have time to run to the store . . .

All you do is put all the ingredients into a food processor and blend them together until the mixture turns rich and creamy. That's all there is to it!

Incidentally, this recipe will make a full quart of sweetened condensed milk and will store in your refrigerator for weeks.

Frank's Non-Alcoholic Holiday Egg Nog

This is the crowning touch to a festive holiday party. And whether or not you relish the taste of egg nog, you'll want to make some of this to serve to your special guests!

2 pints half-and-half
2 cups whole milk
2 tsp. vanilla
5 whole eggs

2 tbsp. sugar
⅛ tsp. cloves
fresh nutmeg nut

The first thing you do is take a bowl and beat the eggs together until they are a creamy yellow. Then gradually whip in the whole milk until the mixture turns frothy.

Next, mix in the vanilla, cloves, and sugar and blend everything together well. At this point, stir in the half-and-half. Then grind about a third of a whole nutmeg nut and stir it into the mixture.

Finally, refrigerate the nog until thoroughly chilled. Then pour it into stemmed glasses, top with a dollop of fresh whipped cream, and serve as a cordial.

Frank's Old New Orleans High-Spirited Holiday Egg Nog

Here's another egg nog recipe I like . . . but make a note that this one has a little more than just a kick to it!

4 cups whole milk	**2 tsp. vanilla**
2 large cans Pet evaporated milk	**2 tbsp. rum extract**
8 egg yolks	**1 tsp. nutmeg**
1 can Magnolia condensed milk	**1 jigger rum per serving**
¼ tsp. salt	

Start off by mixing the whole milk and the evaporated milk in a saucepan and scalding it. Then beat the yolks, condensed milk, and salt together until the blend is smooth. Now gradually add the scalded milk to the mixture, stirring it constantly as you pour.

Next, stir in the vanilla, the rum extract, and the nutmeg. And with an electric mixer, whip all the ingredients thoroughly.

At this point, the egg nog can be served hot and spiked with a jigger of rum per serving, or it can be laced with rum to taste, chilled in the refrigerator, and served cold in frosty glasses. Either way, make a batch for the holidays! It keeps well in the refrigerator for up to 2 weeks.

Note: If you'd rather serve this egg nog without adding the liquor . . . go ahead! I personally like it better without it!

TRICKS FOR CUTTING BACK
ON SALT IN YOUR DIET

The experts call it a "dietary trend."

But for a long time high blood pressure and heart patients have been trying to take the advice of the American Medical Association and reduce the amount of salt in their diets. Of course, I don't have to tell you that kicking the *salt habit,* especially in a city that cooks like New Orleans, can be a very bland affair. But there are a few tricks you can use to make cutting back on sodium chloride a little more palatable.

Let me tell you up front that I've never tasted any good *salt substitutes*—most of the commercial stuff you find on the market contains "potassium." And as far as your taste buds are concerned, potassium is *not* a substitute for sodium.

So that means that if you have to cut back on your salt intake, you got to find something that will do what salt does—bring out the natural flavor in foods.

Fortunately, there are about four very good natural flavor *enhancers*— parsley, celery, lemon, and wine. If you add parsley to your food—and do it about at the end of the cooking process—you release some of the aromatics which in turn release and accentuate natural flavor.

Then there's celery. It's a good natural enhancer—in fact, it does an unbelievable job of covering the blandness of unsalted foods. Lemon, too, is another good old standby. It can be juiced and added to your dishes during the cooking process, rubbed on the surface of your foods before cooking, or squeezed over your food after cooking.

But of all those, *wine*—perhaps because there are some natural salts in vino—is probably the best flavor enhancer you can use as a substitute for salt. Wine acids perk up the ingredients, and the essence of the grapes makes just about everything you cook taste a little better.

Yet, the bottom line is . . . *salt is salt* and *substitutes are substitutes.* So there's no way outside of a vivid imagination that you're gonna make parsley, celery, lemon, and wine taste like sodium chloride. The best you can do is cut back on the salt, increase your herbs and spices, and begin looking for natural flavors. I promise you, you'll learn to cultivate (and appreciate) a whole new taste experience.

HOW TO SEASON THOSE BLACK
CAST-IRON POTS

When it comes to fixing those old New Orleans recipes, nothing beats cooking in the old black cast-iron. But to get those dishes to come out right, the cast-iron first has to be properly "seasoned." And since I'm forever being asked how to do that . . . let me show you.

You're going to need a good steel wool soap pad, lots of running water, a roll of strong paper towels, a pound of lard, and a barbecue pit or oven.

First, scrub the pot four or five times with the soap pad to get it really clean and to remove whatever rust spots have formed. Then rinse it—and I mean rinse it well! Get out every bubble of soap. Then, after you dry it, wipe on your first thin, even layer of lard—inside, outside, handle, and cover. Then you place it into a preheated barbecue pit or oven set to give you about 200 degrees of even heating. And then you cook the cast-iron until it stops smoking and the burned in lard sticks to the metal.

At this point, you let the pot cool enough so that you can handle it. Then you put on another coat of lard . . . put it back into the oven . . . and cook some more. The one thing you want to make sure of is that you don't let any puddles of oil form in the bottom of the pot. The layers have to be applied thinly and evenly to season the surface properly or the "seasoning" will chip off.

Then after you've repeated the process about a dozen times, you end up with a deep black coating on your cast-iron that will cook as good as any other piece of cookware you own. If foods ever stick, all you do is scrub the spot with salt and oil and wipe it out with a paper towel.

And that's how you season the old New Orleans black pot.

CHAPTER 13

Frank's Handy Kitchen Tables

CANDY MAKER'S SUGAR
COOKING CHART

Regardless of whether you're making divinity, pralines, fudge, or your brother-in-law's favorite peanut brittle, it is important that you work at the right temperature when you make candy. Just so you won't have to guess—and have your peanut brittle turn out like caramel with peanuts in it—here is your candymaker's temperature chart.

230-234 Degrees	Thread Stage
234-244 Degrees	Soft Ball Stage
244-250 Degrees	Firm Ball Stage
250-270 Degrees	Hard Ball Stage
270-300 Degrees	Soft Crack Stage
300-310 Degrees	Hard Crack Stage

MEASUREMENT EQUIVALENTS

3 teaspoons	=	1 tablespoon
4 tablespoons	=	¼ cup
8 tablespoons	=	½ cup
12 tablespoons	=	¾ cup
16 tablespoons	=	1 cup
½ pint	=	1 cup
1 pint	=	2 cups
1 quart	=	4 cups
1 quart	=	2 pints
2 quarts	=	½ gallon
4 quarts	=	1 gallon
4 ounces	=	½ cup
4 ounces	=	¼ pound
8 ounces	=	1 cup
8 ounces	=	½ pound
16 ounces	=	2 cups
16 ounces	=	1 pint
16 ounces	=	1 pound
32 ounces	=	1 quart

64 ounces = ½ gallon

128 ounces = 1 gallon

1 ounce (liquid) = 2 tablespoons

2 ounces (liquid) = 4 tablespoons

2 cups of liquid = 1 pound

COMMON INGREDIENT WEIGHTS

1 pound cornmeal = 3 cups

1 pound cornstarch = 3 cups

1 pound all-purpose flour = 4 cups

23 soda crackers = 1 cup

15 graham crackers = 1 cup

1 medium lemon = 2½ tablespoons lemon juice

1 medium lemon = 1 tablespoon grated zest

1 medium orange = 3 tablespoons orange juice

1 stick butter = ½ cup

8 egg whites = 1 cup (approximately)

16 egg yolks = 1 cup (approximately)

1 cup raw pasta = 2 cups cooked pasta

12 ounces uncooked spaghetti = 6½ cups cooked spaghetti

1 cup raw long-grain rice = 4 cups cooked rice

1 cup soft bread crumbs = 2 slices fresh bread

2 sticks butter = 1 cup

1 pound butter = 2 cups

1 cup whipping cream = 2 cups whipped cream

4 ounces block cheese = 1 cup shredded cheese

1 pound block cheese = 4 cups shredded cheese

¼ pound shelled nuts = 1 cup chopped nuts

1 pound shelled nuts = 4 cups chopped nuts

1 pound granulated sugar = 2 cups

1 pound powdered sugar = 3½ cups

HOW MUCH IS IN THOSE
STANDARD CANS?

If you want to be more proficient in the kitchen, take a moment or two to memorize how much is in each of the cans you find on your grocery store shelves. You'll save a lot of time by not having to measure ingredients.

Picnic Size	1¼ cups
# 300 Size	1¾ cups
# 303 Size	2 cups
# 1 Tall Size	2 cups
# 2 Size	2½ cups
# 2½ Size	3½ cups
# 3 Size	4 cups
# 5 Size	7⅓ cups
# 10 Size	13 cups

WHAT'S THE CORRECT TEMPERATURE
FOR SERVING WINE?

Dry Red Wine	60-65 Degrees
Rosé Wine	55-60 Degrees
Dry White Wine	55-60 Degrees
Semi-Dry White Wine	50-55 Degrees
Sweet Sherry/Sauternes	50-55 Degrees
Dry Sherry	45-50 Degrees
Vintage Champagne	50-55 Degrees
New Champagnes	45-50 Degrees
Cold Duck/Sparkling Wines	45-50 Degrees

RECOMMENDED BAKING CHART

Just in case you get confused and you're not quite sure what oven temperature to use when you're cooking your favorite recipes, here's an easy reference chart I've put together.

Food Item	Degrees F.	Minutes
White Bread	400	45-60
Cornbread	425	20-25
Angelfood Cake	350	40-45
Layer Cake	350	30-35
Pound Cake	325	60-80
Drop Cookies	375	10-12
Brownies	400	25-30
Muffins	425	15-20
Pie Shell	450	10-12
Double Crust Pie	425	30-35
Casseroles (Uncooked)	350	60-90
Casseroles (Pre-cooked)	350	35-40
Baked Fish (Fillets)	400	20-25
Baked Fish (Whole)	400	12 per pound
Baked Chicken (Cut Up)	350	60-80
Baked Chicken (Whole)	350	40 per lb.
Beef Roast (Rare)	325	25 per lb.
Beef Roast (Medium)	325	30 per lb.
Beef Roast (Well Done)	325	35 per lb.
Ham	325	30 per lb.
Roast Lamb (Leg)	300	35 per lb.
Pork Roast	300	45 per lb.
Roast Duck	See Double Baked Duck Recipe	
Turkey	See Frank's Slow-Roasted Turkey	

OVEN TEMPERATURES

250-300 Degrees .... Slow Oven

300-325 Degrees .... Moderately Slow Oven

325-350 Degrees .... Moderate Oven

350-375 Degrees .... Moderately Quick Oven

375-400 Degrees .... Moderately Hot Oven

425-450 Degrees .... Hot Oven

475-500 Degrees .... Very Hot Oven

CHART OF INTERNAL
COOKING TEMPERATURES

People tell me all the time, "Frank, I can never tell when my meat dishes are done! Is there a trick to it?"

Yes, there is! It's called a *food thermometer.*

And it is the only method that is certain to give you correct and consistent results time and time again. What's more, the thermometer guarantees that when the meat you cook reaches the temperature on the chart, the internal heat has killed *all* present and harmful bacteria and the meat is safe to eat.

So let me make a suggestion, buy yourself a good food thermometer . . . and use it!

How to Use the Thermometer

The thermometer should be inserted into the thickest part of the meat to a point where the tip of the thermometer is ¾ inch past the center of the roast, *but not in contact with bone, fat, or gristle.* I also suggest you invest in a good quality thermometer—Taylor/Sybron makes an accurate, yet inexpensive one, available at most kitchen shops.

Meat Is Cooked When Food Thermometer
Reaches This Temperature

Beef Rib Roast (Rare) .... 140 Degrees

Beef Rib Roast (Medium) .... 160 Degrees

Beef Rib Roast (Well-Done) .... 170 Degrees

Beef Rump (Boneless—Well-Done) .... 170 Degrees

Venison Roast (Rare)	140 Degrees
Venison Roast (Medium)	160 Degrees
Venison Roast (Well-Done)	170 Degrees
Veal Roast	170 Degrees
Lamb Roast	177 Degrees
Pork Roast	170 Degrees
Smoked Ham (Whole—Raw)	160 Degrees
Smoked Picnic Ham	170 Degrees
Baked Ham (Cured)	140 Degrees
Baked Chicken	185 Degrees
Baked Turkey	185 Degrees
Baked Goose	185 Degrees
Baked Duck	185 Degrees

Notes:

1—Remember that your roast will continue to cook about 20 minutes on the countertop after you take it from the oven.

2—Pork cooked to 170 degrees may still have a pinkish tint when sliced. But don't be reluctant to serve it. At 170 degrees, you can be assured it is thoroughly cooked.

QUANTITY COOKING

Planning a big family get-together? A super weekend party? You'll need to refer to this chart to find out just how many groceries you'll have to buy for your guests.

Item	25 People	50 People	100 People
Coffee	1 pound	2 pounds	3 pounds
Cream	1 quart	2 quarts	3 quarts
Sugar	1 pound	2 pounds	4 pounds
Milk	2 gallons	4 gallons	8 gallons
Fruit Juice	1 #10 can	2 #10 cans	4 #10 cans
Soup	2 gallons	4 gallons	6 gallons
Oysters	2 gallons	4 gallons	8 gallons
Oysters (Half-Shell)	2 sacks	4 sacks	8 sacks

Hot Dogs	8 pounds	16 pounds	32 pounds
Meat Loaf	6 pounds	12 pounds	24 pounds
Ham	10 pounds	20 pounds	40 pounds
Roast Beef	10 pounds	20 pounds	40 pounds
Roast Pork	10 pounds	20 pounds	40 pounds
Hamburger (Raw)	10 pounds	20 pounds	40 pounds
Potatoes (Raw)	10 pounds	20 pounds	40 pounds
Vegetables	7 pounds	14 pounds	28 pounds
Vegetables	2 #10 cans	4 #10 cans	6 #10 cans
Pork 'N' Beans	2 gallons	4 gallons	6 gallons
Cauliflower	5 pounds	10 pounds	20 pounds
Cole Slaw	6 pounds	12 pounds	24 pounds
Sliced Carrots	9 pounds	18 pounds	36 pounds
French Bread	10 loaves	20 loaves	40 loaves
Sliced Bread	5 loaves	10 loaves	20 loaves
Dinner Rolls	50	100	200
Butter	4 pounds	8 pounds	16 pounds
Potato Salad	4 quarts	8 quarts	16 quarts
Fruit Salad	4 quarts	8 quarts	16 quarts
Lettuce	6 heads	12 heads	24 heads
Fresh Tomatoes	8 pounds	16 pounds	32 pounds
Salad Dressing	2 quarts	4 quarts	8 quarts
Apple Pie	5	10	20
Layer Cake	3	6	12
Ice Cream	3 gallons	6 gallons	12 gallons

The Naturally N'Awlins Language of Cooking

I'll bet you've heard just about every one of these terms . . . but do you really know what they mean when you're talking "Naturally N'Awlins"? Let's see:

• **A La:** A dish termed "Something a la . . ." means "Something in the style of." For example, Crawfish a la Frank would mean crawfish done the way Frank does them. "Beef a la Westwego" would mean beef done the way they do it in Westwego. But you know that, huh?

• **A La King:** A dish made with ham, chicken, turkey, tuna, shrimp, crawfish, lobster, or you-name-it wherein a rich white sauce (created in the French roux style with butter, flour, and milk) contains butter, sliced mushrooms, chopped bell pepper, and pimientos.

• **Al Dente:** In Italian, it means "to the tooth." In New Orleans, it means *not overcooked*. I recommend that you learn to cook *al dente* (just till it's done), especially when you cook rice and pasta. Neither should be soft and mushy! Each should be "cooked," but each should still offer the tiny least bit of resistance when chewed. When it does . . . it's perfect!

• **Amandine:** In New Orleans, this is any dish—but usually fish or chicken—that is served topped with a sauce containing slivered, toasted almonds. Also called almondine.

• **Andouille:** Pronounced "an-dew-ee," this is a hard, peppery Cajun sausage that's used for seasoning rices, stuffings, dressings, jambalayas, and gumbos.

255

- **Antipasto:** If you translate it literally from the Italian, it means "what you eat before the meal." Traditionally, it consists of nothing more than appetizers served in very small portions—typically thinly sliced salami or prosciutto ham, melon chunks, black olives on provolone cheese, anchovies on artichoke leaves, miniature meatballs, crispy-fried eggplant, pickled banana peppers, or anything else that's *Italiano!*

- **Aspic:** This is a transparent jelly, usually made from a meat stock, which has been boiled down (reduced) to gel and become firm when chilled. The most common aspic used in New Orleans is tomato aspic.

- **Au Gratin:** A dish that is "bubbly and crusty." And to do that the food you prepare must be sprinkled either with fresh or toasted bread crumbs, or with some kind of cheese that will crust (usually Parmesan sprinkled with butter). So essentially, *au gratin* doesn't mean "cheesy;" it means "bubbly and crusty." It just so happens that some cheeses turn crusty. Now if you want a sauce with your au gratin, traditionally you would use a white sauce (French butter roux and milk).

- **Au Jus:** This is the highly-flavored natural pan drippings from beef, veal, and chicken, usually served without a thickener as a gravy. The best au jus are those that are skimmed of all excess fat.

- **Bake:** This is nothing more than cooking by dry heat—either covered or uncovered—in an oven.

- **Barbecue:** While the strictest definition means "to broil whole on a revolving frame" (as in a suckling pig, or a hindquarter of venison, or a beef brisket), in old New Orleans to "barbecue" usually means *to cook steaks or hamburgers or chicken on a barbecue grill over gas or coals*. And if you want the most liberal of definitions, "barbecued shrimp" is not *barbecued* at all . . . it's baked in an oven, submerged in a buttery sauce. A matter of semantics?

- **Batter:** A batter is a rich, creamy blend of flour and some type of liquid (water or stock) that can be beaten, whipped, or stirred and used to coat chicken, fish, shrimp, crawfish, oysters, and chicken-fried steaks.

- **Bearnaise:** This is your basic hollandaise sauce that has been spiced up with wine, shallots, and various herbs.

- **Bechamel Sauce:** This is your basic white sauce, made by blending together butter, flour, and whole milk and cooking it until it turns a creamy smooth texture. Of course, in New Orleans you can bet it will also be flavored with a selected number of fresh vegetable seasonings, herbs, and spices.

- **Bias-Cut:** The technique of slicing meats and vegetables on a 45-degree angle against the grain, so that more of the flavor surface is exposed to cooking. A bias cut is used primarily in Oriental stir-frying and is intended to help foods cook faster.

- **Bienville:** As in "Oysters Bienville," these are fresh-shucked Louisiana oysters that are nestled into a rich and spicy dark roux-base sauce and baked in a hot oven until bubbly.

- **Bisque:** A good New Orleans bisque is nothing more than a rich, thick creamy soup, usually made with some type of seafood (more commonly crab, oyster, artichoke, or crawfish). Keep in mind, though, that in the Crescent City oyster and artichoke bisques are usually "cream based," while crab and crawfish bisques are tomato based.

- **Blacken:** A Cajun cooking technique made popular by Chef Paul Prudhomme, initially for redfish and later for a number of other foods. It requires the use of a heavy cast-iron skillet heated to *white hot*. Done properly, foods to be blackened are first liberally coated with herbs and spices, then dipped into real melted butter, and then dropped into the *dry* cast-iron pan until they take on a charred *(not burned!)* appearance. Because blackened foods cook extremely fast and tend to smoke a lot, I recommend you cook them outdoors. Veal, beef, pork, fish, and chicken are the foods most commonly blackened.

- **Boil:** Basically, this is cooking in water at or above 212 degrees, so that large bubbles rise from the bottom of the pot and continually agitate the liquid. Now, while the natives of many states boast about their boiled chicken and boiled beef, the only food New Orleanians really get excited about boiling are shrimp, crabs, and crawfish . . . and boiling water in the Crescent City is *always* highly-seasoned with salt, cayenne, herbs, spices, onions, celery, garlic, and lemons, along with a complement of creamer potatoes, corn-on-the-cob, and country-smoked sausage.

- **Boudin:** Pronounced "boo-dan," this is a Cajun *entree* sausage made with rice, pork, a small amount of liver, a blend of fresh seasoning vegetables, a mixture of herbs and spices, and just the right touch of salt and cayenne pepper. Now, originally, you could buy both white boudin (rice) and red boudin (blood sausage); but government regulations today prohibit the sale of blood sausage, which means that unless you make it yourself, you'll probably be limited only to the white variety. Incidentally, boudin is best when it is baked uncovered or steamed and served with sunny-side-up eggs for breakfast.

- **Bouillabaisse:** Classically, this is a special of France, not New Orleans. Authentically, real bouillabaisse is a chowder made from very select varieties of fish and wine. Real new Orleanians would just as soon have a good spicy Creole or Cajun *courtbouillon,* made with catfish or redfish, and served up with steamed rice.

- **Braise:** The cooking procedure by which meats are first browned thoroughly in hot oil, then covered and slowly and gently simmered in a very small amount of concentrated highly-flavored stock.

- **Broil:** A method of cooking whereby the food is exposed *directly to the source of heat.* For example, in *oven broiling* the heat is close to and directly over the food; in *pan broiling* the food is directly touching the hot surface of the skillet; and in *grill-broiling* (grilling) the food is suspended on a metal grate directly over the coals or flames.

- **Bronze:** A cooking technique I created as an alternative to "blackening." It requires the use of a well-seasoned skillet or non-stick-coated pan, a small amount of margarine, and a moderately high cooking temperature. When foods are bronzed, they are seared on each side and quickly cooked, practically in their own juices. As opposed to *blackening,* foods that are *bronzed* are "toast-colored," contain considerably less fat and oil, are lower in calories and cholesterol, and smoke only slightly (which means they can be done indoors). Thin cuts of veal, beef, pork, chicken, turkey, fish, shrimp, and soft-shell crab, as well as mushrooms and other vegetables, are the foods most commonly bronzed.

- **Calas:** This is an old traditional New Orleans dish (usually eaten every Mardi Gras and at Holy Communion breakfasts) that can be traced back to the early 1800s. Softened, overcooked rice is combined with eggs, flour, sugar, salt, milk, and nutmeg, beaten until smooth, dropped by tablespoons into deep hot oil, fried until golden brown, and served with powdered sugar. But you got to eat calas as soon as they come out of the skillet, because once they get cold . . . they get greasy.

- **Caramelization:** This is the process of converting the acids in onions (and other seasoning vegetables) to natural sugars by quickly stir-frying them over very high heat in small amounts of vegetable, peanut, or olive oil. Caramelization makes foods taste sweeter.

- **Clarifying:** This is the process of removing the milk solids (the white particles) from the liquid fat in melted butter. A special strainer cup makes the task easy. Most often, clarified butter is used as a gourmet condiment for sautéing delicate dishes and for *dipping* seafood (like lobster and king crab).

- **Cochon Du Lait:** This is the classical *roast suckling pig,* the one you usually see with the apple in its mouth. When cochon du lait is done in New Orleans, it takes on all of the authentic Cajun characteristics—liberally spiced and highly seasoned and cooked slowly for a long time to make it almost greaseless. In other words, it's magnificent! And it's the perfect entree for a big party!

- **Coddle:** A technique whereby a food is slowly and gently cooked in a plain (or flavored) liquid that is forever kept just below the boiling point; i.e. to "coddle" an egg.

- **Couche-Couche:** In African and Eastern cuisines, the proper spelling is *couscous,* and it is made by cooking semolina flour into a spiced paste. But in New Orleans, the recipe of Creole origin is preferred, which means that couche-couche is a crusty breakfast-type cornmeal dish usually served with milk and sugar or with pure cane syrup and a platter of crisp bacon on the side.

- **Courtbouillon:** This is *our* spicy (and often peppery) fish stew. It is usually made with catfish or redfish; but when those species aren't available it's not uncommon to find just about any other kind of Louisiana fish simmering in the pot. Good courtbouillon combines both a rich tomato stock with a peanut-colored Cajun roux as its base.

- **Cracklings:** Cajun in origin, cracklings are the spicy pork rinds that are left after the fat has been rendered and fried out of small strips of pork skin. In New Orleans, real hog cracklings are snacks that are relished with cold beer during Saints football games.

- **Cream:** This is the technique of stirring, whipping, or beating food until it becomes smooth, soft, and fluffy. For example, whipping together sugar and shortening into an icing is called "creaming" the mixture. By the same token, whipping supersaturated amounts of butter and heavy cream into mashed potatoes is called "creaming" potatoes.

- **Cream Sauce:** This is an ultra-rich, highly flavored sauce made from the reduction of heavy whipping cream. Basically, plain whipping cream is poured into a skillet, brought to a moderate boil, and cooked until it thickens to a desired consistency. It is then seasoned to taste with salt, white pepper, Romano cheese, paprika, garlic powder, onion powder, concentrated flavoring, green onion tops, and parsley. It is the basis for Pasta Alfredo, Crawfish Au Gratin, Crabmeat Imperial, and numerous other New Orleans gourmet dishes.

• **Creole:** While it is a subject of continuing dispute, it is safe to say that "Creole food" originated in south Louisiana and is any recipe that has the combined characteristics of French, Spanish, Indian, and African influence. Usually, though, any dish that is labeled *Creole* (such as Shrimp Creole) is made with a rich sauce that contains tomatoes, red pepper, bell peppers, herbs, and spices and is served over steamed rice.

• **Crevettes:** This is the Cajun word for *shrimp*. But in New Orleans, hardly no one ever says it. Instead we say shramp, shrimps, swimp, swimps, and whatever other mispronunciation sounds good.

• **Croquettes:** Generally referred to as "cakes" or "patties" in New Orleans, these tasty entrees are made of some type of chopped meat (usually beef, chicken, veal, or turkey) that is held together by eggs, shaped, rolled in French bread or cracker crumbs, and deep fried.

• **Cube:** The technique of cutting foods into chunks of evenly sized pieces (usually used when preparing beef and cheese).

• **Daube:** Pronounced "dobe," this is traditionally a round roast—primarily beef—that is first seared and thoroughly browned, then braised in a high-seasoned stock with a myriad of fresh seasoning vegetables. Note, however, that in New Orleans some daube is served *au naturel* in its own gravy, while some is flavored with reduced tomato stock.

• **Daube Glace:** This is the *au naturel* version of daube that is either chopped or shredded after cooking, then simmered with a gelatinous mixture, cooled, and served as a jellied meat.

• **Dice:** This is the process of cutting foods into very small cubes; i.e. diced onions, diced carrots, diced tomatoes.

• **Drippings:** These are the pan liquids that render out of meat and seafood during the cooking process. They are generally concentrated in flavor and make up the base of a variety of popular New Orleans sauces. *Never throw pan drippings away!*

• **Ecrevisse:** Pronounced "a-cra-veese," this is the Cajun word for crawfish.

• **En Brochette:** The technique of cooking beef, chicken, shrimp, chicken livers, oysters, and other foods by broiling them on a skewer. Of course, in New Orleans cuisine these foods are always well-seasoned—and probably marinated—prior to broiling.

• **En Papillote:** Pronounced "n-poppy-ott," this is a French method of preparing food whereby it is first seasoned, then placed in a well-oiled paper bag (either brown Kraft or white parchment paper), and baked to perfection. The most popular en papillote dish in New Orleans is "Pompano en Papillote."

• **Etouffée:** Pronounced "a-two-faye," this is a Cajun word that simply means *smothered*. So essentially, you can take shrimp, crawfish, chicken, pork, or anything else that suits your taste, blend them with your favorite seasonings, put the lid on the pot and "smother" them . . . and you got etouffée.

• **Filé:** Pronounced "fee-lay," this is the finely powdered leaves of the sassafras tree and one of the most essential ingredients for making a good New Orleans gumbo. Basically, it is a thickening agent. But remember that filé should be used only sparingly and added only at the very end of the cooking process—*otherwise it will turn into nasty-tasting long stringy threads*.

• **Flambé:** This is a French word that means "to flame." You generally flambé foods to which you've added wine, spirits, or liqueurs to burn off the unwanted alcohol, leaving only the *essence* in the dish. I strongly recommend, however, that you don't flambé in *your* kitchen if you have a low overhead exhaust vent (especially one that's running!) . . . unless you have cooked enough for the entire fire department.

• **Florentine:** This is any dish (or anything) that you combine with *spinach* and cook. Except for oysters and spinach in New Orleans! We mix it with herbsaint and call it Rockefeller!

• **Fricassee:** Pronounced "free-ka-say," this is the Cajun word for "braised or stewed." For example, if you take a chicken, brown it all over, and cook it *covered* in just a little bit of liquid or sauce . . . you got yourself a pot of "Chicken Fricassee." In truth, you can fricassee almost anything.

• **Fritters:** New Orleanians will make anything into a *fritter!* It's a spicy, well-seasoned, heavy batter base into which meat, seafood (especially oysters and crawfish), vegetables, or fruit is blended, then dropped by tablespoons into hot oil and fried crisp. Apple and banana fritters are tremendously popular as after-dinner desserts.

• **Giblets:** This is the basis for many New Orleans dressings and stuffings and consists of the liver, heart, and gizzard of poultry. In Creole circles, giblets make up the flavoring base for cornbread and oyster dressing. Amongst the Cajuns, they are the essential key ingredients in "dirty rice."

• **Grillades:** Pronounced "gree-ards," this is a dish made with small pieces of beef or veal *round steak* that has been fried well-done in just a little bit of oil, then covered and slowly simmered until extremely tender in a browned tomato sauce. In New Orleans, grillades are traditionally served with grits . . . for breakfast.

• **Hollandaise:** This is a rich, golden-colored sauce made with egg yolks, butter, lemon juice, and other spices that New Orleanians just love to ladle over fried eggs and biscuits, sautéed trout, baked chicken, and broiled softshell crabs. Just remember, when you make hollandaise you must add the hot butter to the egg yolks, not the egg yolks to the hot butter!

• **Hush Puppies:** While southern Mississippi would consider it a mortal sin not to serve these little crispy cornmeal fritters with their fried catfish, most New Orleanians rarely cook up a batch of hush puppies. We'd rather have French fries with our seafood!

• **Julienne:** This is the process of cutting foods into very thin matchstick-like strips. Chicken breasts, pork fillets, roundsteak, veal cutlets, celery, carrots, zucchini, apples, and a variety of other meats, vegetables, and fruits can be julienned. The purpose of the technique is to allow the foods to cook quicker. It is especially useful in Oriental stir-frying.

• **Lyonnaise:** This is a method of cooking whereby onions are the major flavoring agent. For example, onions caramelized in butter or margarine and mixed into potatoes will give you a dish of "Lyonnaise Potatoes."

• **Marinate:** New Orleanians love to marinate their foods. By definition, *marination* is the precooked soaking of meat, seafood, or vegetables in a highly flavored mixture of oil, vinegar, herbs, and spices in order to enhance concentrated tastes. Depending upon the dish, champagne, liqueurs, wine, beer, apple juice, milk, and Italian salad dressing are also popular New Orleans marinades.

• **Mince:** The food preparation technique whereby seasonings are chopped into extremely fine particles, i.e. minced garlic.

• **Mirepoix:** This is a selected combination of freshly cut vegetables, primarily onions, celery, bell pepper, mushrooms, carrots, yellow squash, and zucchini. In its simplest form (onion, celery, and bell pepper), it is referred to as "The Holy Trinity," is sautéed, and is used as a flavoring base in just about every New Orleans recipe. In the full complement, it is also pan-sautéed in clarified butter, seasoned with a mixture of herbs and spices, and served as a vegetable dish.

- **Mirliton:** Pronounced "mel-a-tawn" by most New Orleanians, this highly popular vegetable is also known as mango squash, vegetable pear, or chayote. In the Crescent City, just about everybody grows them in their back yards and most of those folks prefer to stuff them with shrimp. But they can also be sliced, dipped in egg and bread crumbs, and fried . . . can be smothered with tomatoes and ham . . . can be baked into a rich casserole with Italian sausage . . . or can be simmered into a creamy spicy soup.

- **Mornay:** This is the old classic French sauce that consists of a good bechamel that is bound together with egg yolks, beaten with butter, and mixed with grated Parmesan and Swiss cheese. You talk about rich! But it's good!

- **Pain Perdu:** One of the most popular breakfast treats in the Crescent City, pain perdu is nothing more than French toast (also called "lost bread"). It is made by dipping either French or sliced bread into an egg and milk custard mixture and frying it on both sides in a heavy, sparsely oiled skillet until it browns slightly. Traditionally, it is served with either powdered sugar or molasses.

- **Piquant (or Piquante):** This is a French word that literally means "hot and tangy," and the dishes that come out this way (such as Rabbit Sauce Piquant or Crawfish Sauce Piquant) are generally made with lots of fresh seasoning vegetables, herbs, and spices that have been liberally enhanced with cayenne pepper. Make a note, however, that "picante" (like the sauce you buy in the bottle), while it's hot is not French or Cajun. It's Mexican! And they say you shouldn't buy the stuff made in New York City!

- **Refresh:** The technique whereby *hot* boiled, steamed, or microwaved vegetables are quickly dunked into *ice cold* water immediately after cooking to stop the cooking process and preserve the rich deep color.

- **Remoulade:** In New Orleans, this is a richly spiced mayonnaise-based sauce that is meant to be served ice cold and *used only* for dipping richly spiced boiled and peeled jumbo shrimp into! Of course, in other cities, remoulade is used as an accompaniment for poultry and meats . . . but not in New Orleans! Actually, there are so many different variations of remoulade hardly any two are the same.

- **Roux:** This is the basis for a wide range of Cajun and Creole dishes, and it is usually made by combining *equal parts* of all-purpose flour and a good grade of vegetable oil. But let me get specific for a moment—roux come in all varieties. There is the classic French butter-roux (flour and butter cooked together until smooth *but not browned*) for use in a white sauce . . . the Cajun roux (that starts white but changes color from beige to tan to brown to chocolate to black, depending upon how long you cook it) for use in gumbo, brown gravy, stews, and sauces . . . and the N'Awlins roux (the one that ends up being nothing more than burnt flour because you had the fire too high and you didn't watch the pot close enough). Throw the last one away!

• **Tender-Crisp:** The technique whereby fresh vegetables are cooked *only* until they are tender but still crisp (rather than soft and soggy). Preparing foods tender-crisp gives you perfection in taste and texture and preserves the rich color. But more importantly it retains most of the vitamins and nutrients found in the foods. *Don't overcook!*

• **Vinaigrette:** This is a basic marinade or salad dressing that is made very simply by combining oil, vinegar, pepper, herbs, salt, and spices. Of course, like mayonnaise, vinaigrette can be doctored up to produce a highly-flavored seasoning—i.e. by adding wine, lemon juice, applesauce, Dijon mustard, Worcestershire, soy sauce . . . the variations are endless. Generally, it is served chilled over salads, but I'd like you to try it over artichokes, on baked chicken, alongside fried or sautéed shrimp, and as a topping on softshell crabs.

Index